Praise for Souls of My Young Sisters

Souls of My Sisters let all women know it was okay to tell your story and now *Souls of My Young Sisters* helps young women struggling through life's challenges tell their stories and heal all of us. A must read for all women! —Kyla Pratt, Actress

Growing up is difficult and confusing at times. Young women may be looking for answers that are not readily available. *Souls of My Young Sisters* successfully helps you navigate through those growing pains.
—Melyssa Ford, Actress and Former BET Host

Souls of My Young Sisters helps with your struggle of self-acceptance and puts you on the road to a better relationship with God, yourself, and the beauty of sharing your experience with others. —Neffeteria "Neffe" Pugh

Souls of My Young Sisters is like having that sister who shares advice, tells you secrets, and helps you get a better understanding of who you are as an evolving young woman. —Tia Mowry, Actress

Also Available

Souls of My Sisters
Souls Revealed
It Happened in Church
He's Gone . . . You're Back
Tears to Triumph

Published by Kensington Publishing Corp.

Souls of My Young Sisters

Young Women Break Their Silence with Personal Stories That Will Change Your Life

Written and Edited by
DAWN MARIE DANIELS AND CANDACE SANDY

Foreword by
MADELINE N. SMALL and MARY J. BLIGE

SOULS OF MY SISTERS BOOKS
Kensington Publishing Corp.
www.kensingtonbooks.com

SOULS OF MY SISTERS books are published by

Kensington Publishing Corp. and Souls of My Sisters, Inc.
119 West 40th Street
New York, NY 10018

All Kensington titles, imprints, and distributed lines are available at special quantity discounts for bulk purchases for sales promotion, premiums, fund-raising, educational, or institutional use.

Special book excerpts or customized printings can also be created to fit specific needs. For details, write or phone the office of the Kensington Special Sales Manager: Kensington Publishing Corp., 119 West 40th Street, New York, NY 10018. Attn. Special Sales Department. Phone: 1-800-221-2647.

ISBN-13: 978-0-7582-3160-4
ISBN-10: 0-7582-3160-1

First Trade Paperback Printing: June 2010
10 9 8 7 6 5 4 3 2 1

Printed in the United States of America

Contents

Foreword

When You Honor Your Sister, You Honor Yourself!

By Mary J. Blige, Founder, and
Madeline Nelson-Small, Executive Director
FFAWN (Foundation for the Advancement of Women Now, Inc.)

God help you if you're a phoenix, who dares to rise up from the ashes.
—Ani DiFranco

We first met at a taping of *It's Showtime at the Apollo* and we barely said hello. We had traveled similar paths, through childhood. We both suffered mental and physical abuse at the hands of those closest to us from the time we were five years of age. We both grew up with family members and friends we trusted and loved telling us we would never amount to anything. We both had a strong need to fit in, which led us to feeling as if we should not strive for greatness. We both escaped our home lives in our late teens and we both entered the entertainment industry. And, though we had different roles in the world of music, we had very similar experiences. Most specifically, we were on a constant search for the love and acceptance we felt we had not received as children. Trying to find love in others inevitably led to very destructive and extremely painful relationships with men. Pain has a way of showing up in other ways: overindulgence, irresponsibility, and the lowest levels of self-esteem.

We never met as children, but as adults we realized we had lived parallel lives, nearly every step of the way. Like so many women, our childhood hopes and dreams, and the fire that burned inside each of us, were stomped out like the last bit of flames on a campfire. By the time we were young adults, all that was left inside of us—like an abandoned campfire—was the ash left from the embers. We had hope for the future of our careers, but neither of us had hope for ourselves as women. We knew how to survive, but we had no idea what it meant to actually live.

We met again, backstage at a concert, and we exchanged pleasantries, even shared a toast, but walked away with no inclination that we would meet again. We were two women on similar paths of self-destruction. Two women God saw fit to pull together for a greater purpose than either of us had ever imagined. On the many days we sat alone in our own personal prisons of shame, anger, and low self-value, we had no idea what was waiting around the bend for us. We did not know we would eventually come together for the purpose of empowering and inspiring hope in women all over the world.

As fate was determined to have it, our lives also changed for the better in the same way. We both knew something was wrong and we hit a brick wall. Each time, we found ourselves running away from people and situations and, most of all, we were running away from ourselves. Trying to escape from a problem instead of facing and claiming it. What we have found is that people are sent in your life to show you the way, open a door, or share with you a lesson. The question is, were we ready to recieve it?

We both met men who would force us to take a long, hard look in the mirror and face our fears, head-on. We each had met a man who loved us when we were stripped down to our bare souls and could not hide our fears and insecurities underneath the rock of our careers. These men were beautiful examples of the kind of people we are meant to have in our lives. With their help and with the help of women who held us up along the way, we each realized one day that what needed to change most was our attitude. Our journeys have proven that we can choose our attitudes in any given set of circumstances . . . simply by drawing strength from God and learning to control the only thing we CAN control—which is ourselves.

Anyone can overcome. Anyone can meet the challenge. Anyone can succeed. Anyone can choose to be better today than they were yesterday, until eventually, they are the best. We're not saying we're the best, but like Serena Williams at tennis, and Alicia Keys on her piano, we practice being better every single day because we want to be the best we can possibly be.

When we met again, it was to celebrate the birthday of a dear friend, Steve Stoute, who is the cofounder of our organization, Foundation for the Advancement of Women

Now (FFAWN), and even then, we had no idea that we were soon to join together to make a difference in the lives of millions of women. What we did know, on that day, was that we shared a moment that left each of us knowing that the other had something very special to give the world and it would have nothing to do with the talents that were defining our lives at that moment.

We have grown from abused children to career women to women on a mission, and with a very definite purpose. What has brought life to our purpose is a willingness to do whatever it takes to make sure that every one of you—your mothers, your sisters, your cousins, and your best friends—understands that you are a phenomenal woman. This is an attitude we all must develop in our hearts as we go out into the world.

Like us when we were young, you may not think you have the talent or ability to be thriving and successful young women with something of great significance to offer society, but because you are a woman and women are so very resilient, you can rise to every occasion.

We challenge you to rise up, like a phoenix, anytime anyone or anything tries to keep you down. We challenge you to be your sister's keeper. We challenge you to always like what you see when you're looking in the mirror.

Souls of My Young Sisters provides us with a truth we can hold on to . . . the truth that we are never alone. If we look out the window, around the corner, in the next room, or simply in the mirror . . . there is a sister there just waiting to walk us into the light.

Mary J. Blige

Mary J. Blige is an eight-time Grammy Award–winning singer-songwriter, producer, and actress who has sold more than 40 million albums worldwide since her career began in 1992.

Making an impact outside of the studio, Mary has been active with many community organizations and AIDS awareness programs such as Minority AIDS Project, and in 2001 was honored for community activism with Rock the Vote's Patrick Lippert Award.

Using her personal experience to further help her community, Mary, along with Steve Stoute, created and funded Foundation for the Advancement of Women Now, Inc. (FFAWN). Created in 2007, FFAWN is an organization dedicated to helping women overcome their personal difficulties and reach their full potential in life. FFAWN assists women through a range of programs that encourage women to realize their dreams and pursue their individual goals. Mary's hope is that FFAWN will provide women with the self-confidence, abilities, and resources they need to take the initiative to realize their full potential.

Madeline Nelson-Small

As the executive director of Foundation for the Advancement of Women Now, Inc. (FFAWN), founded by Grammy Award–winning singer-songwriter Mary J. Blige and marketing and branding executive Steve Stoute, music industry veteran Madeline Nelson-Small is on a mission. "My passion for what we're doing at FFAWN is limitless," Nelson-Small explains. "It was our goal from the beginning to make FFAWN a grassroots relationship between ourselves and the community of women we've vowed to help."

A Harlem native and City College graduate who strongly believes in the idea of "paying it forward," Madeline Nelson-Small arrived at FFAWN with a strong desire to help underserved women feel empowered to reach their full potential with scholarships, grants, and other supporting programs. "Having gone through years of mental and physical abuse when I was a child, I can understand all too well what happens when a woman feels she has no hope."

Acknowledgments

Laurie Parkin, we thank you for believing in us and the Souls of My Sisters imprint. Steven and Walter Zacharius, your support and guidance is just amazing. We have a talented young and brilliant staff without which we could not have made this possible: Donna Hill, for your tireless efforts. Kim Alvarez, Veneice McDermott, Bianca Payton, Cara Lawton. Thank you, Jessica McLean Ricketts, for your advice and kindness. Thank you to John Scognamiglio, Selena James, Karen Auerbach, Kate Duffy, David Lappin, Lesleigh Underwood, John Masiello, Valeece Smith, Adeola P. Saul, Mercedes Fernandez, Neven Gravett, and Daly Hernandez.

Special Thanks from Candace Sandy

To my parents, Patricia and Carlton Samuel, who love with grace and have instilled in me the need to make a difference. To my brothers, Sherwin Sandy and Sheldon Samuel; my nieces, Crystal and Taylor; and my nephew Ricardo, who has always been a constant source of love. To my aunts for their undying love, belief, guidance, and support. To Aunt Geraldine (Amu), Helen, Jennifer, Hemetta, Joanie,

Pat, and Joan Braithwaite. To my uncles, who are absolutely phenomenal: Uncle Vernell (Vush) and Trevor Hamlett. To my uncle Wendell Hamlett, who never stopped believing in us. To my cousins, whose love and support sustained me: Jackie, Ann, Paula, Torrie, Jodelle, Donica, Danica, and Natalie. To all of the boys I treasure: Kealon, Terrence, Mark, Trevon, Brent, Franklin, Elijah, Langston. To the Fraley family, my aunt and Uncle Frank, Lisa Fraley, Ollie Gables, and Grandmother Fraley. To my godmother, Cyrilla Laborde, and my extended family: Gary and Amy Krakow; Saundra Parks; and my godchildren, Mark, Martin, Chanel, Naomi, Eliana, and Alyssa. My sisters since I was nine years old, Cristina Colon and Maggie Goring, and their spouses, Jose Gerrero and James Goring. Al and Tiffany Ragin, who are simply irreplaceable.

To Congressman Gregory W. Meeks, his wife, Simone Marie Meeks, the Washington and the New York staff who have been encouraging and understanding during the development of the book. Special thanks to Dana, Tracie, and Teresa Frank, Steve Looney, Carl E. Simmons and Nadia Suliaman, and the Donna Karan family and Vera Gaskin.

Special Thanks from Dawn Marie Daniels

To my sons, Mark and Martin: You are my joy, and every day being your mom is a blessing. Your love and support, questions and answers, laughter and tears have been the best lessons I have learned in life. You are truly special sons.

I give sincere love and undying gratitude to my best friend and sister, Candace Sandy. Your unconditional love and support have sustained me for the last twenty-plus years of my life—you are truly my sister. Your love and compassion inspire me to be the best person I can be every day.

To some of my best friends—Antoinette Callistro, Tiffany Cordy, Maria Davis, Dana Gibbs, Joella Irving, Christine Saunders, and Seanette Vaughan—thank you for being my everyday sounding boards, cheering squad, and sisters. I appreciate your sisterly advice and love.

Mom, the love you have shown me and the lessons you taught me remain with me forever. I love you and pray for you every day! Only a really special dad would support his daughter's dream unquestioningly and unconditionally. Daddy, you are that special person and I cannot express in words how much I love you. Thank you.

Grandma, you are truly an angel. You are always there to support anything I do, and I am grateful for the love and joy you bring to my life.

Introduction

Young women encounter many daily struggles and obstacles similar to the women in our original book, *Souls of My Sisters*. Our next generation is filled with hopes and dreams, but they have extra baggage from dealing with many different issues, from drug-addicted parents to the pain of never knowing their fathers, to being stalked and subjugated on the Internet. Some of the women expressed fears that they wouldn't be able to attain their dreams, and others were concerned that the hue of their skin could get in the way of living a fulfilling life. As these brave women who are searching for self, exerting the power of choice, and dealing with the difficulties with the first woman in their lives—Mom—family, career, sexuality, intimate relationships, money, self-esteem, body- and self-image, friendships, faith, health, and death, through their struggles and pain, their perseverance shines through.

Young women are inundated with advice, some of which you know simply just does not make sense. We've all heard "a bird in the hand beats two in the bush" and "don't count your chickens until they are hatched." These are great phrases, but what can be even more valuable than old-time sayings are women telling you the truth, not worried about being judged, but giving you their honest perspective of their own life experiences.

When you are confronted with decisions that you know will change the course of your life, you are worried sick and you are constantly told to search inside yourself because the answer is within. It may be, but not today, and how can you search if you are not even certain of who you are?

We are all pieces of the love, pain, emotions, responsibilities, fears, scars, and lessons of those who did and did not raise us. Sometimes the pain was unbearable, and as a result you decided to raise yourself. Others found out terrible secrets. *My mother is really my aunt, I am adopted,* and *My father is not my father, who is my father? Your father was a one-night stand?* It's at the funerals that all the family drama unfolds—the new siblings that you never knew you had. The secrets that the family kept from you because of a desire to protect themselves have left you feeling betrayed.

Some of you were molested, beaten, or witnessed your mother being beaten, your sister being murdered, gun violence in the streets, family members succumbing to drugs, having a mother who is only fifteen years older than you and is hanging out at clubs with you, and the world still wants you to be happy.

Some of you succeeded regardless of the pressure to please your family. You stifled your dreams, pushed forward to be the very best woman you could be, and yet your family is never happy. You can do more. Why aren't you married? He's not good enough. Some of you pursued professional degrees, and after all that work, you were urged to hurry up and get married before you succeeded or else you would never find a husband. So you struggle through medical school, dental school, and law school hoping this brother will stick around when your practice takes off.

The whole thing can be a small mess—it's having the babies at a young age because you wanted someone to love, it is the tearing down of your friends because you were afraid they would succeed. It is the career situations where professional women were sabotaged. It is the sitting in a dark hole and asking, "How did I get here?"

Candace and I have endured a different set of questions and personal battles, and this is why we started the Souls of My Sisters series. In this volume, we go to the icons of Black America who have endured some of the same situations. What makes them different? Was there a special recipe that only they concocted for success? In these pages these icons of entertainment are asked, "If you knew then what you know now, would you have made different choices?" These women reflect and share their personal advice, personal stories, and challenges so that young women like yourselves can utilize the information as part of their personal journey.

Souls of My Young Sisters is a book that you can relate to, but also a book that can help your parents better understand the issues you may be dealing with in a day and age far different from the one they grew up in. It is our hope that *Souls of My Young Sisters* will be your quintessential guide to eliminating baggage before your life's journey truly begins.

Souls of My Young Sisters

I

Who Am I?

Yes, I am from the 'hood, but I'm a work in progress and I hope to continue to grow.
—Keyshia Cole

Young or old, who we are is an evolutionary process that can change from day to day. As a teenager you are often told, "You don't know what you're talking about." You also hear, "Wait until you get older, then you'll understand." You feel like you know what you're feeling is real and how dare older women like your mom, aunts, siblings, or at times strangers tell you what you know to be real and how you will feel about your decisions later. We honor your feelings and say it's okay to feel the way you feel, but we ask that in this moment you keep an open mind and ear to the lessons other women have for you.

When you get into your twentysomething years, it really seems like the reins have been loosened and it's your time to show and prove. You are given the freedom with what seems like less criticism, and you are ready to conquer the world. You may have some doubts and insecurities, but you're not letting anyone see you sweat. You may be more open to the advice of your fellow sisters during these years, but you are still firm in the belief that you and only you feel the way you feel. We just want to let you know we understand your feelings and would like to share ours with you.

As you are on the south side of your quarter life and fast approaching what you once thought of as old, you have been through a few things. You have gotten your feet wet—some of us have even been fully baptized in the water of life and think we know a thing or two. You definitely know something at this point in your journey, but there is still so much more to learn.

No matter where you are on your journey in life, getting to know yourself is in every step you take. Part of growing into the woman you will become is looking at other women as examples. The more open you are to hearing other women's life journey stories, the more opportunities you will create for yourself to understand who you are and where you would like to go as a woman. It is said that the true test of intelligence is not whether you can learn from your own mistakes, but whether you can learn from the mistakes of others. There are women who went before you who have paved the way for your success, whether they knew it or not—it's important that you know it. The journey to self-awareness, self-discovery, and self-esteem has been mapped out for you.

Whether you have been told you are a queen in the making or you've never been given words of support and encouragement, you have the power to shape the woman you want to become. If you are reading this book, the first thing you need to know is that you are making the choice to be aware of the experiences that women have had. The women who have chosen to share their experiences know that you are worthy and ready to receive the lessons that they want you to learn. Knowing who you are at all stages of your womanhood will determine the woman you will be tomorrow. Know that who we are is the essence of our beings, the truth of our intentions, and the substance of our souls, and enjoy the journey ahead of you.

Little Women

By Raegan L. Burden

My perception of physical beauty was formed by the visual landscape of women in my family. I suspect we all look to our mothers, aunts, and grandmothers as a reflection of ourselves. They validated that we, little black girls, are beautiful! Growing up, the Burden and Wilson women reflected the color spectrum—every shade of ebony God created, from café au lait to a smooth, dark chocolate. They were short and tall, with hair that was long or short, pressed, relaxed, or natural! Yet they had shapely, curvy bodies.

In fashion, their bodies would be described as hourglass, full-figured, top-heavy, pear-shaped, or plus-size. To me, that was Mama, Cousin Pearl, Great-aunt Queen, Aunt Edna, my second cousins Sparkle and Keisha, and my tall, statuesque aunt Ludia. Some of my fondest memories of my grandma Gladys are those reassuring hugs from her full, soft body. I would observe men eyeing them as they walked by. I couldn't *wait* to grow up! I was ready for my rite of passage!

By the time I turned sixteen, my reflection in the mirror horrified me. I had no problem being 5'2", but where were my mother's full, perky breasts (the ones that men would gawk at), or my sister's ample tush that could fill out any pair of jeans? Where was my body? Of course, my mother told me I was going to be a petite woman and that I resembled her (without the voluptuous boobs, of course). She'd even point out that I favored my great-aunt Margaret, who was 4'11". However, she was in her sixties, going through the shrinkage I thought all elderly women went through. I was completely devastated.

I believed God had given me the right mind and heart, but mistakenly put them in the wrong body.

Misconception of Being "Skinny"

Now, I'm sure a few of you are laughing at this scenario. How could I possibly have a problem with being a "skinny" girl? By and large, black America didn't buy into that Eurocentric philosophy of body image. Our community's picture of physical beauty has always been different from the mainstream. Oh, we might've killed ourselves at the gym, got on Slim-Fast, and cut back on the soul food, but even my friends will tell you, "I'll never be skinny, but I can be healthier." Our sheroes are Coretta Scott King, Dorothy Dandridge, Diahann Carroll, Tyra Banks, and Jill Scott. I didn't embrace the Twiggy standard of beauty. Why would I? That didn't reflect the women that I wanted to emulate.

I think self-acceptance would've come easier had the comments from black males been more welcoming. I distinctly remember several white boys thinking I had a nice shape, while I was ridiculed for my petite frame by the brothers. Maybe you, too, have heard some of these comments:

"You're cute and all, but brothers like some meat on their bones!"

"If you'd gain some weight, you'd get more play!"

"Are you sure you're a sister? I mean, you shaped like a white girl!"

"Black women have boobs, bootie, or both—how come you don't?"

Can you imagine hearing this, routinely, at fourteen, fifteen, sixteen, and seventeen from classmates? Those are the most formative years in your life as a young woman, and as a teenager your peers can have more of an effect on you than your parents. No matter how smart, sweet, or interesting I was, I simply felt I wasn't good enough. Maybe you've felt that way as well.

If you are "skinny" or know people that are, at least half of them have had this battle of the mind. We don't speak about it, many times out of fear. Can you imagine talking about this in the company of curvy or plus-size teens or women? The eye rolls would be endless.

The simplest way I can explain it is this: *Some black*

women think they're too big, and some little women think they're too small; we're all trying to get to the middle. Either way, it hurts. Personally, I never liked being called "skinny." It always sounded like a curse word, as though something were wrong with me. I was healthy, ate heartily, and loved being outside.

The Smart, Funny Girl

I inherited a boisterous sense of humor from my father, and I was an honor roll student. So I morphed into the "smart, funny girl." In fact, some of you were labeled the athlete, tomboy, or quiet one. Although I felt unattractive, I really wasn't. Though I had flattering features, it's amazing how I became so focused on what I didn't see. Many times, the negative comments drowned out the positive words and attention I got from brothers in middle and high school.

I've met girls who wore baggy clothes (to mask their petite frames), never wore shorts (to cover their small legs), padded certain areas of their bodies (to appear bigger), or would buy enhancement creams and pills from magazine ads. Even I, during my freshman year of college, overate as much as possible to try and gain weight. I had bad indigestion, high cholesterol, and excessive fatigue, and only five pounds later, I was still petite. I knew it was finally time to start the process of acceptance.

If wanting to fit in can lead you to mask your body type, I believe that lack of self-esteem can hamper your thought process. Maybe you'll start drinking with peers after school, skipping class, or engaging in sexual activities sooner than you're emotionally ready to handle. If you don't believe you fit in physically, you'll find a way to fit in behaviorally.

Thank God you don't have to continue viewing yourself in this distorted way! If I had known then what I know now, I would've been a lot happier with myself.

You're a Complete Package—Just as You Are

Having walked some of the same emotional roads, let me begin with one sentence: *You are attractive and good enough just as you are.* Of this I am certain! To get you started on the road to accepting what you see in the mirror, here are a few things I want you to start meditating on today (and yes, I've done every one and revisit this list when I need a reminder):

Memorize this scripture, and recite it when you get discouraged.

(Psalm 139:13b–14) "*. . . you knit me together in my mother's womb. I praise you because I am fearfully and wonderfully made; your works are wonderful. I know that full well.*" Since God spared no detail when he formed us, little women are just that—God's creation. You have a specially designed body made just for you!

You are more than body parts!

The size of your hips, breasts, and derrière doesn't define who you are, nor is it an indication of what you have to offer the world (much less a young man). Stop looking at those video girls, thinking they're somehow better than you! If we could put a microphone up to their thoughts, you'd be shocked and comforted to know that they struggle with the same insecurities. It takes more than a pretty face to capture a man's heart and respect. The beauty of black women is that our looks *are* so diverse. God hasn't made you unattractive to brothers. On the contrary, he's designed them with preferences as well. Believe me; I've met plenty of men who adore petite women.

Seek out peers whom you admire and respect that have the same body type as you.

No, I don't want you to exclude friends or loved ones if there's no physical similarity, but sometimes it's easier to receive praise and encouragement from people you can identify with. One of my former roommates and I used to discuss our body image, and I always felt better after confiding in her because we could relate. From a distance, I have long admired Jada Pinkett Smith. This sister is feisty and intelligent, a family-oriented woman, who just happens to be—petite! Even more, she's lauded as one of the world's most beautiful women and celebrated actresses.

Find the song "She's a Bad Mama Jama" by R&B singer Carl Carlton—dance to it at home!

I believe we always need a positive soundtrack playing in our heads to speak life into our issues. Since this song was released in 1981, it's "old school," but ask your parents or any of your aunts and uncles, and they'll know exactly what you're talking about. I want you to close your eyes and dance until you feel it—no, *really* feel it! I want you to hear this song and know that all your little curves are beautiful. Be confident, and walk in it!

Even as an adult, I still have those days where I feel self-conscious. That's just part of being a woman! I have embraced my petite frame and have grown quite fond of my appearance. I no longer want to change anything about my external physique. If anything, I'd rewind the clock to 1994 when I was sixteen years old. I'd close my bedroom door, turn on my CD player, and belt out the chorus to "She's a Bad Mama Jama"—while I point at myself in the mirror.

Raegan L. Burden is an Atlanta-based writer and managing partner of Raegan / Robertson Productions, a media development and TV production company. Her professional endeavors reflect her passion for exploring contemporary / pop culture, women's issues, politics, and religion. Raegan is an alumna of North Carolina A&T State University and holds a master's degree from the University of Georgia.

A Young Woman's Cry

By Niyah Moore

I developed low self-esteem when I was a teenager. By the time I reached high school, I managed to make more enemies than friends. With my snotty attitude, I hid behind my own insecurities of being overweight. Once I made the cheerleading squad, I bonded with other girls on the team. I was happy that I made the squad, but I became my own worst enemy behind closed doors because I was heavier than they were.

Everyone had a boyfriend except for me. I made it my mission to have one, too. The friendlier I became with my male peers, the more I discovered it didn't matter how pretty or how long my hair was. I was still a little thicker than they wanted me to be.

I pretended as if I wasn't sad at a size 13. An older basketball player noticed my low spirits and told me I was one of the prettiest girls and if I lost a little weight I could have any boy I wanted. He gave me a spark of hope and I ran with it, drinking water and taking vitamins. I starved myself, ignoring the hunger pains, and after a while the smell of food made me sick. With the rigorous training from cheerleading practice and camp, the fat melted off.

When I returned to school for my junior year, I was completely different, wearing a size 7. I wasn't the same chubby girl from the previous school year, and everyone noticed. I made out with more than a handful of popular cute jocks, but that sparked a new problem. I lost a lot of their attention almost as quickly as I gained it because they thought I was a tease.

The same boy who suggested I lose weight in the first place pursued me. He didn't want to be in a relationship, but he wanted to have sex with me. Instead of saying no, I gave in. For the rest of the school year, he ignored me, but would climb in my window any time he wanted to. After every visit, and with him ignoring me in front of his friends, my self-esteem was lowered once again.

My friends were in serious relationships, and just the sight of them with their boyfriends made me upset. I went through a few more short-lived sexual relationships until a starting player on the varsity basketball team revealed he had a crush on me. I didn't really like him at first because he wasn't attractive looking. Everyone in the school knew him for his bad attitude, but they respected him.

Our relationship blossomed and we became inseparable. Once I was in college, a few fraternity brothers pursued me. Because of the attention I got from the new guy, I didn't want to be with my boyfriend anymore. Every time I tried to break up with my boyfriend, he would verbally abuse me and blurt out he was cheating on me anyway. I think he knew I wanted to be with someone else. After hours of arguing, he would cry and beg me to stay. I would feel guilty, blaming his abuse on my own unstable feelings. I kept telling myself that he only wanted to love me and yet I wanted to be with another man.

After hearing the rumors about my boyfriend and other girls, I had enough. The final big fight left me with a concussion and a permanent thick scar on my upper lip where he busted it. We were officially over, but the ugly scar made me self-conscious, and it hurt to smile for a long time.

I confided in a male friend, vulnerable and in search of comfort. His kind words gave me the feeling that he could care for me in a way previous boys hadn't, so I gave myself to him sexually. The very first time we had unprotected intercourse, I got pregnant. Ashamed and afraid, I faced my responsibility, dropped out of college at nineteen years old, and moved in with my child's father. He was selfish and did very little to help me with the baby.

I slipped into a deep depression and had postpartum blues. My weight ballooned to the biggest I'd ever been, a size 18. We finally married and had a daughter after five years, but I couldn't change him or my unhappiness.

My friends gave words of encouragement, but nothing seemed to lift my self-esteem. I tried diet pills to lose the weight, but couldn't lose more than twenty pounds. I separated from my children's father on a mutual agreement and dedicated my life to the only higher power I could count on: God.

After a nasty divorce and custody battle with my kids' father, I could only make myself happy by doing what pleased me, and that was taking some time to find out what I liked and disliked without trying to impress others. I cut off all my old cheerleading friends and kept them at a distance because sometimes their words didn't help me much. I needed to find my own way without doing what they wanted me to do. I started getting my hair and nails done. I finished beauty school and began writing as an outlet. I even went to a psychologist to help find what my underlying problems were. With the kids gone with their father every weekend, I finally had time for myself. For the first time in my life, I realized I loved myself too much to give myself to a man who didn't care about me. There's no comfort in sex without true love. I'm still learning that waiting for the right man takes patience.

I love the way I feel inside, and my self-esteem is the highest it has ever been. I still have yet to meet my Prince Charming, but when I need comfort I turn to my faith in God. *Wait on the Lord: be of good courage, and he shall strengthen thine heart: wait, I say, on the Lord*—Psalm 27:14. *In all thy ways acknowledge him, and he shall direct thy paths.*—Proverbs 3:6.

Be encouraged and stay true to yourself. Do what makes you happy. As long as you try to please others before pleasing yourself, you will never be happy. Sometimes we as women lower our standards and open our hearts to the first man running, thinking we're in love. To build ourselves as strong women, we need to stop thinking as if our minds are weak. Confidence comes from within. No one can give that to you.

Niyah Moore was born in Sacramento, California, where she currently resides. She is a single mother of two. She's one of the contributors to the anthologies *Mocha Chocolate: Taste a Piece of Ecstasy* (March 2008), *Chocolat Historie D'Amour* (February 2009), and *Seduction*.

Self-Esteem and Identity

By Dee Vazquez

I grew up in New York City. Queens. In the *'hood.* When I was six, my parents divorced. I didn't see a lot of my dad after that. Due to his situation, it was best for us not to see him: He was addicted to drugs. We didn't understand why he left. Later we found out my mother didn't want us identifying with a father who was a drug addict.

When my parents divorced, there was a real major shift in lifestyle. Before, he made sure that we were cultured: He'd take us to the city, to shows, to parades. He made sure that we understood *life.* When he left, money got really tight. Dance school, all that stuff, all the extras, had to be cut, because we couldn't afford that dream. Everyone else had mothers and fathers. We just had our mother: single-parent household with five kids. We didn't have much, but what she gave us was aspiration and hard work. She told us, "Just because you're growing up in the projects doesn't mean that you are the projects."

Growing up, I never questioned anyone who was in any

position of authority. I think this comes from my mother's side. She's Dominican, and she experienced the backlash of having her parents grow up during the time of the dictatorship, under Rafael Trujillo. He was like a Dominican Hitler; it was crazy. It was dangerous for them to speak out. My mother grew up being very quiet; my aunts did too. So I was always very quiet, very timid. I learned, "You don't talk back to the people in school; you don't talk to the teacher," even if the teacher is wrong.

I remember when I was in the fourth grade and we moved to the projects, I was crying every day. The teacher said, "Would you shut up already?" I just looked up and said, "I have to get out of here." The teacher slammed the door on my hand and we got into a fistfight. I was like, "Oh, my God, I fought the teacher." My mother kept telling me, "You were wrong, you were wrong." But she didn't know the whole story. It was like, "Off with your head!"

I went to a Catholic high school, and it was more of the same. It was always "Bad, bad, don't be bad, be good." If you don't identify with what their definition of good is, you're bad. You were judged based on how short or long your skirt was, and how tight or baggy your pants were. You weren't supposed to talk or talk back. My sister got kicked out after her first year because they said she spoke out too much. She wasn't, as they said, "able to be disciplined." I never really understood why they kicked her out, because my sister wasn't bad; she just always spoke her mind.

From that, I understood that if you keep your mouth

shut and are able to be disciplined, then you are good. I was good in their eyes. If I got in trouble, I listened, instead of saying, "No, this isn't right." I swallowed my truth, absolutely. But I was confused, and I knew that I needed to find answers. I needed to find out my truth.

At the same time all of this was going on, I was dealing with something else. I grew up in a predominantly African American neighborhood and didn't really understand the Hispanic culture. I didn't speak Spanish until high school; my mother rarely spoke it at home because she wanted to practice her English. And there was a lot of tension between African Americans and Latinos at my school. It seemed very petty at the time. We listened to the same music, we all basically originated from Africa, but there was this cultural divide. We were like enemies. They'd say, "Oh, you're *Spanish,*" like it was a bad thing. You'd get cast aside: "You Spanish girls think this." It's almost like they were forcing an identity on me that I wasn't aware of. There's always so much drama going through a high school girl's life.

So I tried to fit into other people's world. If there was one way of being cool, I would do that. If that didn't work, maybe I'd drift a little bit over here. Maybe if I went with this clique, I'd find myself. I was really hopping from clique to clique, thinking, *Who am I? I am this clique.* They'd have the tough girls, so I got involved with a bad crowd for a while, and then I hung out with the nerds for a while.

I was attracted to the bad girls. They were talking about boys in their neighborhood and how they would hang out 'til all hours of the night. I thought that was the coolest thing ever. They had this "I don't care what you think" attitude. Before that, I never doubted my mother or any other authority figure. But now I saw that there were girls my own age that weren't listening to anyone and were doing their own thing. I was intrigued by their coolness. Then their coolness started getting me in trouble.

One day, one of my friends got into a disagreement with a girl. They started fighting. I found myself in the dead middle of this physical altercation, trying to stop it, and ended up getting beat up by one of the girls and her boyfriend. The cops even came, trying to break it up. It was insane. And I was the only person who got into trouble.

The dean of the school told me, "You know what, I see you flopping back and forth between all these people, all these girls, with different cliques. Just do your work and don't worry about this." She said, "It's time for you to open your eyes." At the time, I didn't want to listen to her. But eventually, I realized none of those cliques were me. The problem was, I didn't know who "me" was. Talk about confusion.

Bit by bit, I started figuring things out, by trial and error. I had this one teacher, Mr. Santana, who was Dominican. He asked me where I was from and wanted to know why I didn't speak Spanish. I said, "I don't need to know that." He said, "You need to know your culture." I guess he made me his project. He said, "You're going to learn it." I started reading up on it, what shaped the country and the culture. The more I learned about my culture, the more I understood what my foundation was.

But again, it was trial and error. I started getting back into religion. My religion teacher, Mr. Mittiga, really helped me identify as a Catholic. He helped me relate to the religion and the whole notion of penance and reconciliation. Before speaking to him, I had really been questioning the religion. He brought everything back on track.

And then he committed suicide, which is the biggest sin in the Catholic Church. If he was so religious, how could he kill himself? So much confusion set in for me then, but it also helped me to personally set out and find the truth, my truth. I couldn't get it from the dean at my school; she was too judgmental. I tried to follow the religion guy, but he committed suicide, and I knew that wasn't the way to go. I realized that no one was going to find the answer for me. So I said, "I'll have to find it on my own." That's when I created Dee-ism. It's all about everything that I am, everything that is true to me. That's how I got through those days, learning what is true to me, how I understand right and wrong. I really had to get in tune with who I was.

I'm still getting into my journey, my identity, establishing my own sense of integrity. This is so important. I learned this going out on auditions. If you show up with curly hair, they want it straight. It's really difficult when someone picks you apart in an audition situation. You just have to know who you are when someone tries to dissect your being. You can't let it get to you. You have to know yourself and be strong.

The biggest message is, know that no matter where you're from, no matter where you are at that particular moment in time, you have to second-guess authority and find your own truth. If they're keeping you down, question them. It's about thinking bigger, breaking down those boxes.

Dream big for yourself.

I learned from Nelson Mandela's example, to always have a bigger dream for myself, to carry myself with my culture on my back. If I can do it, so can you.

Dee Vazquez is creating a new standard for on-air personalities by captivating all audiences with her quick wit, sense of humor, and personable approach. As host of *No. 1 Countdown: Hip-Hop* on the Fuse Network, Dee brings the hottest videos and interviews from elite and groundbreaking hip-hop artists. Dee Vazquez is also an on-air personality with "The Drama King" DJ Kay Slay on HOT 97 and Sirius Satellite Radio.

Loving Me?

By Floree Williams

While recovering alcoholics fight an internal battle to put down the bottle, I fight with the Debbie Downer in me. We constantly wrestle as I try to uplift myself and justify why something I do or the way I look just isn't right. As I type this, I wrestle with the thought of whether or not this piece will actually be chosen, whether it's good enough.

When most people hear about a girl with self-esteem problems, they probably think, "Poor girl, she's a victim of the media's portrayal of the perfect woman." On the contrary, I kind of always knew that the women on TV and in magazines were not as they appeared. My problems stemmed from real people, the people that I interacted with every day. I can't pinpoint the exact age where it all started, perhaps sometime after I had begun to learn reason and logic but before I could figure out who I was. One day you go from thinking, "Hey, I am me and I am the best"—*Sesame Street* does that for you—to "Why is everything about me so flawed?" Slowly I went from the little engine that could to the little engine that is just going to pull back into the station and wait for the world to go away.

Sadly, it started at home, with family. It started with the comparisons. Being compared to others at a young age is not for the weak-minded child. If I came home with something less than an A+, I was reminded that at my age an older sibling brought home nothing less. This may seem like a small, silly reason to have low self-esteem, but when you honestly do try your hardest and your best isn't good enough, well, you start thinking, "Maybe I am not smart."

As an adolescent, my soft voice and standoffish personality never allowed me to be that bubbly, delightful child who lit up a room and held conversations with adults. Let's just say that I was no Shirley Temple. In fact, I'm sure some people wondered whether I was mute. I vaguely remember a specific incident that knocked yet another peg out of my self-esteem totem pole. Somewhere in my tween years, my parents had dragged me to some sort of social gathering held by their friends. I walked around with them and said my usual inaudible salutations and then retreated to a convenient seat next to the snack table where I could have my fill of cheese curls. Then a family friend who owned one of these "Shirley Temple" children walked in, and for most of the night I watched—between sips of soda—as she worked the room with personality, charm, and intelligence. I really could not have cared less, to tell the truth. I had nothing to say to these people. But as soon as we left and the car door closed, the comparisons started. By the time we arrived home, I was made to understand that being a "Shirley Temple" was the correct way to be. It's kind of hard to be told that you don't have the right type of personality.

Then came the high school years, God bless them, the ground zero of my mental destruction. By then the Puberty Fairy had waved her wand and given curvaceous blessings to most girls. She skipped over me. She forgot to give me another two cup sizes, some childbearing hips, and some "junk in the trunk." For goodness sakes, everyone had that one thing on their bodies that they absolutely loved. But to give me zero out of three was a pretty damaging move by that neglectful Puberty Fairy.

Appearance was one thing I never noticed or suffered a comparison from, so in a sense I never noticed my body. That is, until it was pointed out to me, jeered at, mocked, and trivialized in my teenage years. I will never forget overhearing a family friend make the comment: "She's never been Miss Body Beautiful." One can only assume that if you weren't Miss Body Beautiful, you must have been Miss Body Ugly. I could only build a thick enough skin to last me until the end of the day or until I got to the bathroom, where I could cry. Another comment I shall never forget came from a classmate who advised me to not go into sports because me in tights would only cause laughter. She didn't have to worry about that. I stayed far from sports after constantly being picked last to be on a team because I always contributed to losing points due to clumsiness and bad hand-eye coordination. I had already suffered enough embarrassment to last forever. Let's just say I still find excuses not to participate in friendly physical activity.

My lowest point came at around fifteen. I can clearly remember seeing my reflection in a tinted car window and absolutely hating, loathing, despising who I saw. So I went on a weight-gaining spree. I decided to gain weight until it went into the right places. Of course I was able to gain cushioning in some key areas and in other not-so-flattering ones. I can't say that this really solved my problems. I did feel less self-conscious until I gained too much and then became concerned about weight loss.

How far have I come since then? I won't lie and say that I am absolutely infatuated with myself. I have my on and off days. The older I get, the more on days I have. I have learned with maturity that there is nothing wrong with my personality. As for my body, well, does that feeling of inadequacy ever go away?

One day I hope to be blessed with a daughter, and I hope that the one thing I can pass on to her is to accept herself for who she is, and that as long as she tries her hardest, then her best is good enough.

As for me, I get by one day at a time, learning to love more of me slowly, but surely.

Floree Williams is a native of the small Caribbean island of Antigua. Floree has a published book of childhood short stories called *Pink Teacups and Blue Dresses,* which is available online. She has a novel on the way. She is a fairly recent graduate of the University of Toronto, where she majored in communications and professional writing.

If I Knew Then What I Know Now About Myself . . .

My philosophy is that not only are you responsible for your life, but doing the best at this moment puts you in the best place for the next moment.

—Oprah Winfrey

The evolution of self takes shape with time and experience. These women have shared with you a moment in their lives that is a part of who they will be forever. Yes, they will grow and change, but these precious moments they've decided to share are markers of who they were, and who they will be. Like Ms. Winfrey's philosophy, you must take those moments and learn from them to discover your best true self.

Your Soul's Sustenance

Women begin the pattern of envy when they are young with the simple wish that they could be someone else. That seed may be planted by magazines, television, family experiences, or peers, but regardless of where it began, setting on the path to being triumphant requires you to relinquish your feelings of envy. The everyday put-downs, dismissals, and negativity will hinder your ability to see things objectively, and losing focus on your blessings, plans, and implementation serve as a distraction. Distractions can cause us to stop what we are doing and sometimes get us so far off course that we can never get back on track.

Your Personal Book of Revelations

- *Describe who you are as a person.*
- *How did you get to where you are right now in your life?*
- *How do you feel about saying no to others?*
- *Do you just follow the crowd?*
- *Are you comfortable being alone?*
- *Who or what is the driving force in your life?*
- *Are you happy with your life?*
- *What are your next steps?*

II

Why Does It Hurt So Bad?

It's been quite a roller-coaster ride, but
I've grown and learned a lot about myself.
The greatest thing is being able to interact
with fans and touch people's lives . . . for
that I give thanks.
—Christina Aguilera

Oftentimes, we find ourselves in dark places in our life's journey. You may feel happy, successful, and accomplished one day and down in the dumps the next. Life is similar to a roller coaster. You wait in line with anticipation for the experience just as you wait to grow up. You get to the front of the line with butterflies fluttering in your stomach because you're next. That up-next anticipation is similar to the milestones we set in our lives, like what we'll do when we turn eighteen, twenty-five, or thirty.

Then finally it's your turn. You get in the car and buckle up. Just as in life, there are some things we need to brace ourselves for, so we, too, must buckle up. Then as the roller coaster slowly climbs to the summit, it feels almost like we know what's ahead, but this part is full of wonder and taking in the true depth of the climb. We, too, have those moments when things are moving steadily along in life where we can take in the experience and enjoy the view.

Then it happens, the plummet that takes our breath away! The wind and gravity blowing you back and feeling as if your stomach is in your throat—you think to yourself, *Why did I do this?* The fear and low points in our lives lead us to question the same thing—*Why did I do this? It was exciting, but it's scary and totally out of my control.* Once you get past the first descent, you may experience a few loops, twists, turns, and a couple of more drops. That's life. We get turned around sometimes, and twists and turns do arise.

Finally, you are back on the ground where you began, but in a different place. You exit on the opposite side and leave a little bit different for the experience. Life is much like this roller-coaster ride. You may go through the twists and turns of life, but you come out of these experiences different—new. Once you understand that the twists and turns in your life don't last forever, you are better prepared to take the risk to go through them. We all go through ups and downs, but how you look at the situation will determine how you get through it. If you never wanted to get on the roller coaster and you resist all the way, you will have a hard time and never want to get on it again. But if you look at the twists and turns of life as part of the ride, you will be able to move with them and know that you will leave on the other side a new person.

The women in this section of the book have had some mighty roller-coaster rides, but they have come out stronger, more confident, brand new, and able to tell you that you, too, can do the same. You may be saying that you don't even like roller-coaster rides, or you've never been on one, but we're here to tell you from experience, you have. You may not have gotten on an actual one, but you have experienced the ups and downs of life and you are different than you were before your experiences.

Know that if you anticipate the ride, you will be better prepared to be the new person after the ride. You may even want to dare to get on again and again. We want to see you enjoy the ride and become brand new.

I Am Free

By Sybil Clark Amuti

Be the change you wish to see in this world.
—Gandhi

I remember walking into the apartment on Forty-third and Eighth Avenue, in New York City, seeing this on the fridge door. The quote stood out in white text to a black background, amid other random, "not so memorable" magnets. I continued walking to the bedroom where Todd, the apartment owner, showed me the room for rent. We sat and talked about who I was, where I was from, and what brought me back to New York City after hating it so madly. We were total strangers, but quickly became fond of each other through hope and experience. I found myself speaking freely with this guy about things that very few people knew. He wanted to trust me to be a good, honest roommate, and I wanted that room with no holds barred. I didn't want the option of being imprisoned by my past anymore. I knew that freedom is an act of the heart that I should quickly adopt if I wanted to live at all.

"So tell me about yourself." . . . And there it began.

I took Todd into the story of my life: the youngest of five children, growing up in Memphis, Tennessee. Life was normal; we were a middle-income family, with two working parents that were totally devoted to our success. I left Memphis in 1996 to attend Dillard University in New Orleans, Louisiana. I majored in urban studies and public policy in school, and college life on the side. I spent a lot of time with my sister and friends, partying around New Orleans and experiencing life in a new way.

Along my journey were several influential people, one of them being the guy that raped me in 1997. He was an acquaintance of mine, someone I knew for months at that time. He came over one day in the summer of 1996 to see me before a road trip that I was taking to Houston, Texas. I will never forget: The car was packed, the snacks were prepped, the music was in the player, and we were almost ready to leave. I accepted the request to come by, as normal, because I trusted this guy and had no resistance to his company. I heard knocking on my bedroom door, and as I opened it he stood there with a warm greeting. We exchanged hugs, and he sat in the chair in the corner of my room. Within a matter of minutes and minimal conversation, I found myself fighting him off me and repeating "no." We tussled for minutes and I grew numb to the experience. The "no" began to fade and the moment was over. He left, I showered, and we headed to Houston.

Although I continued things as normal, I knew something was *wrong*. I knew that I said "no" and I knew that he heard me. I knew that I had been victimized because I felt hollow and pathetic inside. I felt ashamed and humiliated, and I felt vulnerable. I was confused about what to do; I always heard that rapists were strangers who broke into your house and took advantage of you. I then considered this foul play an act of immaturity and decided to go on as if nothing was wrong. Besides, this guy was a very well-known person—who would people believe?

I spent years erasing the moment from my mind and masking my emotional drought. *I never told a soul* and I pretended that I was normal. I focused on school by day and heavy partying by night, drinking excessively and hating myself nearly every moment. I wanted to kill myself, and wrote two suicide notes to my family and loved ones. I avoided mirrors and any reflection of myself; still, I dressed in fashionably chic clothing and stilettos to imagine that I felt as "fabulous" as I looked. I attempted to control any relationship with guys to protect myself from a repeat of that event. I worked twenty-four hours a day to shield my image from even the thought of brokenness. It was a total masquerade.

In 1999 I left New Orleans to move to New York for graduate school at Columbia University. I was only twenty-one years old and grad school was really tough, so I remained focused on school and moving away from the nightlife. In my last semester of school, my thesis writing grew extremely intense. It was proving to be the most stress I had ever encountered in my life. One particular night I was awakened by my own screaming and sweating. I was having a recurring dream about an incident that I put far behind me. I kept seeing the rape being replayed in my head, over and over again. I woke up, called my friend, and broke my silence. I told my dear friend about everything that happened in 1997.

I finally faced the fact that I had been raped, been depressed, been suicidal, and been in denial for about four years. I woke up to who I had become, and I began fighting back. I prayed daily for strength, understanding, and forgiveness. I called myself a survivor instead of a victim. I began to look in the mirror and see who I really was. I smiled at myself, and laughed aloud. I changed my perspective, and then changed my life.

I learned that living as a victim meant that I would always be on the downside of things, looking for the worst in every scenario and expecting people to support me out of pity. Being a victim meant I couldn't see the sun for all of the rain. I couldn't respect myself or other people. I was overly critical. I would disqualify myself from meaningful relationships. I feared life would get the best of me, and I had no inspiration for change.

I learned that living as a survivor meant that I was victorious. I could move forward from depression and live a joyous life. I didn't have to fear what people would think about me, or what I thought of myself. I could see potential for my future and work toward it. I could hope for God to shine His light in my life and make me whole again. And most importantly, I could be free. No more containment, because I was the winner. I held all of the power in my hands. I could control my destiny, and change became inevitable.

By the time I learned about the victorious person I was, I had been raped once again, by another male acquaintance, in 2001. Here again, there was another attempt to take my life, but it was unsuccessful. I fought back spiritually, mentally, and physically to ensure that my victory could be maintained.

I immediately prayed to the Lord for forgiveness in my heart over this incident, and the power to stand against the attempts of the enemy to destroy me. I meditated on scriptures daily that motivated me to keep living. I drew closer to God. *I broke my silence* and told friends about what was going on. I started reading about women who had conquered insurmountable circumstances in their lives. I started to exercise, eat differently, sit in the park and stare at the birds and the sky, and take deep breaths to keep my spirit calm. I learned what it means to survive, to overcome, to persevere, to achieve. My mind was transformed and so was my life.

No more living in a moment. I now live for my destiny.

After many nights of staying up late and exchanging life stories, Todd and I were no longer strangers. In fact, he introduced me to the man that is now my husband and father to our five-month-old son. Many times I asked myself why God allowed us to share so much with each other so fast, and I realize that God allowed Todd to be the bridge between my present and my future.

It's now over ten years later, and, though the circumstances remain the same, I am different. I am now a wife, a mother, and a friend to many. I am free from the life sentence that some call "depression." Free to live the life that God has intended, free to love people the way that God loves me, free to chart my path, free to dance and sing a new song.

I know that change is a choice. Change happens when we decide to be different than we were the second before. I chose to become the change that I wanted to see in my life. When I felt liberated in my heart, freedom rang forth from my being. I could no longer think or act the same because my spirit was renewed in Christ and my heart followed suit. I am free.

Sybil Clark Amuti works as a brand manager for myMuze Inc. in New York City. After many years as a GIS specialist, she has consulted with various companies and city organizations. She now lives in Harlem with her husband of three years, Kwaku, and their five-month-old son, Samuel.

Weathering the Storm

By Milani Rose

What I recall about my childhood is everything but hazy. I don't remember the sticky Popsicles, hopscotch. But I definitely remember those sandals that come in white with the pink flowers and my toes sticking out. I remember those frilly sundresses, the smell of Spanish rice and beans, lots of people, music, and everyone always seemed to be in a hurry.

Then it just stopped, at the age of two. There were strangers who arrived, packed up what I had in clear garbage bags, and that was it. No more family, just screams, and there I was in a foster home. This was in the eighties; the drug epidemic was in full swing and my parents were small-time drug dealers. They were looking for ways to put food on the table. I was really unaware of who my parents were, but everywhere I went, there was a letter that no one would let me see.

It hurt. All I knew was I missed my family, and all I

wanted to know was, where were they? There was no explanation, just the pain and tears streaming down my face, especially at night. I always wondered what would happen next. I became scared of the knock on the door or any loud noise, and I worried that I would be taken away again. The group home was filled with kids just like me, and I stayed to myself. I was tiny, with big brown eyes and pigtails.

I would not talk, and the other kids felt the best way to get back at me was to call me names: blackie and darkie. I did not even know what that meant, but I figured if I could put chalk on my face and body, maybe I could be lighter and they would stop. That was when my childhood stopped—not only did I have this pain, but I was engaged in a serious game of dodgeball, only there was no ball, and I was always it.

At the age of seven I was finally adopted, or so I thought. I knew that Mrs. Bell wanted the best for me, but after years of being in foster homes, you begin not wanting to be comfortable. I became more trouble than she expected. I had problems concentrating in school. The kids picked on me because I hit puberty early. I had a teenage shape and breasts at nine. To hide it I wore oversized clothes and hung out with the boys. My adopted mother worked for a homeless shelter—Providence House—so she would let me go shopping through the donated clothes and things. The girls in school were very cruel. They called me many names. One was "garden tool." I did not even know what that was; one of my classmates finally told me what it was—it's a "*hoe.*" How did I become a garden tool? When I told my mother, she said, "Stop hanging with those boys and they won't call you a hoe." What? I played baseball with them, and basketball, and they did not care how long my hair was, what I was wearing, or any of that stuff the other girls were almost relentless about.

My relationship with my adopted mom went from bad to worse, as she felt I was too much to handle and took out a PINS warrant on me at the age of ten. It got so bad that I ran away. I was sick and tired of hearing "get out if you don't like it," but I remembered the letter. I stuck it in my pocket and off I went. On the street I would meet guys and then stay with them. They would want me to have sex with them in exchange for shelter. I met a guy who was nineteen years old, and I stayed with him. Shortly thereafter I became pregnant and the father left.

I had a beautiful boy named Lamont. Lamont and I have been through a lot. A couple of days after I had my son, we moved into a mother-and-child foster home, where I continued to raise my baby. We lived in the first home for two years 'til we had to move suddenly. My second mother-and-child foster home was a lot different from the first one. My old foster mother was in her early thirties and had let me live a somewhat normal life. But my new foster mother was eighty years old. I couldn't go anywhere, she was so overprotective, which was good and bad.

I actually remember the double padlock on the door. She was the only one with the key to freedom. She locked me in the house a few times, but I quickly learned a way around that situation.

She was so old and paranoid that she had a padlock on the inside of the home.

A few times my child and I were locked in the house with no food, so I had to improvise, trying to find a way to get out. If I wanted to go out—even to the store—I would have to sneak out the window. She immediately requested that my child and I be removed from her home.

One of my last homes was in Jamaica Estates, where the foster family lived a very abundant lifestyle. They were extremely controlling and overprotective. I needed to be in the house by 6 P.M. each and every night, and the one time I stayed out late they asked that I get moved.

At the age of sixteen I left the foster care system with my little boy in hand. We stayed in an array of shelters. Covenant House was one of them. When I was seventeen and a half, my son and I went to stay with my adopted mother, who had adopted me when I was seven.

I was determined to finish high school and get my diploma. I went in and out of abusive relationships, hoping someone would love me enough to fill the hole I had inside me. One boyfriend beat me up so badly—once he hit me in the head with a dumbbell and I had to get staples in my head. Another time he almost broke my nose. Regardless, I kept going. I worked at a local pharmacy after school, and when I got older I just worked and worked. I became a barmaid at night at a local strip club. I was underage, but they still let me work. I was able to get the money necessary to take care of me and my son.

I was then introduced to escorting by one of the women

at the bar. It was simple, I thought: $1,000 an hour to date and sometimes sleep with men. I was able to move myself and my son out of a bad neighborhood. But I was paying a price, and I wanted to change my life. I moved for a fresh start.

That is when I met KK. A mutual friend introduced us, and ironically we had similar features. I had begun a modeling career; one of the men who was my former client helped me get photos, business cards, and set up my business. He knew I wanted out and was gracious enough to help. KK was doing the same, but I always felt like it was a competition with her. I just enjoyed this part of my life and was grateful for the opportunity to put my life behind me and start a career that I loved.

I decided to end our friendship, and that is when it all began. KK used the Internet to stalk me in an attempt to defame my name and ruin my reputation. I began to appear in an array of magazines, and as my modeling career started taking off, she became more angry and malicious with her attempts. I mean insanely angry—she used my success as a litmus test where she started a campaign to tear me down.

It started with e-mails, MySpace, Facebook, Twitter—and then she graduated to the ultimate: she put out a sex tape where she posed as me. First it was blurred, then I realized that she was able to get a tape from one of my former customers and had pretended she was me in order to get it. Her campaign was "Milan Rose is a porn star prostitute." This slogan was pasted all over the Internet, and it was viral. This was done out of nothing else but jealousy and envy.

KK had been using my pictures and setting up escort websites impersonating me and pretending to be me as an escort. Why would KK or any other crazy person do this? Was it to ruin my name or break my spirit?

It became so disturbing that I filed harassment charges with the police. I have had to involve attorneys and the FBI. We even had dueling radio appearances—I went on a show and then KK went on a rival's show. This was getting out of hand, and when no one else would book her on their show, KK started her own blog talk radio show. KK used my pictures and set up several escort websites impersonating and pretending to be me and providing services. She utilized my old escort name, "Milan," and current modeling photos.

KK was able to manipulate the men who had hired her for her escort services and my old clients to make them think it was the real me—Milani Rose—but instead it was KK the impostor. KK has had sex with countless men, leading them to believe that they were having sex with me. I had no idea there was a sex tape; one of my former customers filmed us having sex without my consent. KK then went out with this gentleman and convinced him to give her the tape. While checking my e-mail I received an evil alarming message from KK that read, "Your sex tape is going to be released in a few days and it is in distribution." Bitch! What sex tape? I could not believe it.

KK's main objective was to reduce my status as the model

everyone loves and is talking about and turn that around on me. It is so unfortunate that her need to get ahead involves defaming me. My life started feeling like the psychological thriller *Single White Female,* where the character Allie, played by Bridget Fonda, has it all: a great boyfriend, an amazing apartment, and a great career. Through the classified ads she seeks a roommate in order to keep her spacious digs. Hedra Carlson, played by Jennifer Jason Leigh, answers the advertisement. Hedra is seemingly timid and friendly and the unassumingly perfect roommate. Then Hedra begins emulating Allie and becomes obsessed with her to the point that things get ugly—even homicidal.

Cyberstalking is a serious form of abuse. It is more prevalent than we all think and can cause a tremendous amount of harm. All I can do is pray for KK and hope that the fame she is seeking comes her way and that she does not feel the need to destroy anyone else's life. My life story is really interesting. It's full of courage, pain, drama, inspiration, experiences, and triumph. I will weather this storm.

Milani Rose is an entrepreneur, actress, model, and celebrity blogger for Russell Simmons's Global Grind network. Rose is also a vocal advocate for change and is against cyberstalking.

DESPERATION

By Ebony Fletcher

Desperation: having lost all hope; reckless or violent because of despair; having undertaken a last resort, nearly hopeless; critical; extreme.

This is how Webster's dictionary defines desperation. I believe your life can go in two directions: you either become really successful or a menace to society.

My ex-boyfriend had nobody in his life to lean on. I was his everything, and he almost loved me to death!

Since I was five years old I knew I was someone special. Growing up in the projects wasn't easy. Peer pressure, drugs, sex, and violence was what I had to deal with. My great-grandmother raised me from birth. My mother was there, but she was off doing her own thing. My grandmother was a minister, so I've been going to church all my life. She sheltered me way too much from the outside world. I was dealing with college, family members dying, my horrible relationship with my mom, and bad choices in men. I felt that my life was spiraling downward. I got stuck spiritually. I felt God had forgotten about me and no longer wanted to talk to me, so I stopped talking to Him. I started doing things on my own.

We started dating in 2000. We were introduced by his sister-in-law. His sister-in-law took me and my friends to an event in Coney Island called Bro Day, which is a series of basketball games given in honor of a young man named Bro who was killed. Watching him play on that court was the most exciting moment. He was a ball player. He was a strategic ball player. The kids in the neighborhood were calling him "The Goat." I was so fascinated by his swift moves and jump shots that I couldn't take my eyes off him. I fell in love with the passion he had for the game. He put in his all and nothing less. His drive for basketball was a rush I couldn't resist. He was determined to be the best street ball player in Brooklyn, but I told him he would be the best in the NBA.

In 2001, we moved to the Bay View Projects. That's where his mother lived before she passed away. I'd seen the closeness that he and his mother had, but I also knew there was some anger on his end. He told me about his mother's drug addiction. I knew it was hard for him to talk about. I also knew he had an outlet, and that was basketball. He would play for hours. He would come home exhausted and dehydrated, but still feel a sense of release. When I first met his mother I thought she was cool. She had to be about four foot eleven and was tough as nails. She had four children, and three of them were boys. My ex-boyfriend was the baby boy, and she loved him the most.

We would talk about my ex's father and she would show me pictures of them together back in the day. The way they looked then was how her son and I looked at the time. He would always say to me, "You know, you look just like my mother." When I finally met her I saw the resemblance. We were both short, thick, with a big butt and a lot of attitude.

His mother had become very ill and needed to be hospitalized. I don't know why she was sick. It seems like it happened so fast. He would visit her all the time with his other brothers. One day he came home and told me his mother died. I was in total shock. I didn't know what to say or how to feel. I know I wanted to be strong for him. I had already known that his father died when he was younger. I didn't know how it felt to lose a parent, and he wasn't showing any emotion. He wouldn't cry, scream, curse, or anything. If he was playing basketball for five hours before, it just went up to ten.

In 2002, we moved to Unity Plaza. I thought everything was great at the time. He started working for a construction company and I was still working for the DOE. Our bills were paid. We had everything we needed. That was the year his grandmother passed away. She was a tough cookie and always got what she wanted. This was the grandmother that didn't use drugs; she sold them. When he told me his grandmother used to sell dope back in the day, I didn't believe him. I met her on Thanksgiving 2002. The whole family was there. They were all saying how good we looked together. I thought so, too, until everything started going really crazy. His basketball dreams weren't coming true. He was very depressed and was using drugs heavily. If he didn't get to smoke weed, all hell was going to break loose. He wouldn't talk to me. He wouldn't even sleep in the bed with me. I had to give him money to get weed first, and then we could start a conversation.

In 2003, he had become so consumed with doing nothing, he gave up on himself. I never gave up on him. I thought that if I loved him enough, things would be better. He would change sooner or later. In November he was incarcerated for eight months and sent to Rikers Island. He had a prior felony before we got together. I thought to myself, *What the hell is going on?* I couldn't be by myself. I had never been to a jail before in my life. I found out how to get there and I went. I went to see him on every visit. This is between working two jobs and going to school. I was taking care of him, myself, and a household. I thought I was big shit!

For the last four months of his imprisonment, he was sent to the Boat in the Bronx. I had to take two trains and a bus just to get to him. I went to see him in the rain, sleet, and snow. I wanted him to know that he had me above all else. He came home on June 21, 2004, and I thought things were going to change. I was exhausted from all the work I was doing on the outside while he was on the inside thinking I was sleeping with someone else.

When he came home it was good at first. The first couple of weeks were nice. We talked about life and how we wanted to make things better. And then the bullshit started!

I kept a bottle of Vicodin my doctor prescribed for my kidney stones in the medicine cabinet. It was prescribed for pain. I was in pain from all the pressure, working, and fatigue. He wanted to have sex all the time. I was scared from all the stories I'd heard about jail. I didn't want to sleep with him. I was just tired of the same old drama. I would pop one of my magic pills and everything would be numb. I didn't have to feel hurt. He didn't care after a while. He just felt as long as he was getting some, who cares. I would lie there and think to myself, *I wish he'd just hurry up, so he can get off of me.*

My life wasn't going well at all. I was physically, emotionally, mentally, and spiritually sick to my stomach. I had been with this man for four years and I was comfortable in an uncomfortable situation. It sounds crazy, but I understand it now. This man had never hit me. I didn't see a sign. He wouldn't even call me a bitch when we'd argue. He never raised his voice.

One day I popped out of bed and said to myself, "I can't do this anymore." I packed a bag and went to my aunt's house in Harlem. I'd finally had it. As much as we'd broken up and gotten back together, this wasn't one of those times. I had enough with taking care of a grown-ass man. He would call me on the phone to talk, and I didn't want to talk to him. He would ask to visit me, and I wouldn't let him in my house. I was done for the last time.

Two days later my ex-boyfriend came to my house to kill me. On that day, I agreed to talk to him. He was calm, sober, and he looked a little tired. We talked about getting back together, and that was a conversation that wasn't going so well. I repeated to him that we needed a break. At the time, I was going to school and working two jobs. I didn't have time for bullshit. He pulled the revolver out of his coat jacket. He said to me, "If I can't have you, nobody will." My first thought was, *I'm about to die!* I looked straight in his eyes and said, "We need to talk things over. Calm down and go take a walk."

I looked at him in total shock. I couldn't believe something like this was happening to me. I've read in the newspaper that this type of domestic violence happened a lot that year. There were plenty of women being killed by their boyfriends or husbands. We started to fight for the gun and he shot me in my leg. He sat on my back after I fell to the floor. He put the gun directly on the back of my head and pulled the trigger. When you hear people say their life flashed before their eyes, it's a true statement.

It was God that said to just lie there and don't move. After I closed my eyes, I never felt more assured in my life that God really had my back. I was rushed to the trauma unit at Brookdale Hospital and was asked all kinds of questions: Do you know where you are? How many fingers am I holding up? What's your name? The doctors and nurses were astonished. They were all wondering, if she got shot in her head, where's the blood?

My five-year journey after being shot wasn't easy. I went through horrifying nightmares. I used to wake up, screaming, in a cold sweat. I couldn't stop crying. I would think that if I fell asleep, I wouldn't wake up again. When I walked down the street I was so paranoid, thinking that someone was going to walk up behind me and shoot me in my head. I felt so numb; I couldn't talk half of the time. I had to walk around with a gash in my leg where I could stick two of my fingers inside. It was a time when I didn't want to look at my own leg.

My friends and family suggested that I go to counseling. They wanted me to talk to a stranger about what happened to me. I felt this was the most embarrassing thing in life. I'm a twenty-four-year-old female, and I wasn't a loose female. I graduated from high school and continued to college. My grandmother raised me in the church, and I was involved in every activity from the choir to the usher board. Why did this happen to me?

Being in a domestic violence incident had made me close off every part of my life. I isolated myself from everything and everybody. I was scared all the time. I didn't want to meet anybody new out of fear they might do the same thing. I needed something to keep me busy, so I enrolled in beauty school in 2005. Even though I'd been working for the Department of Education for seven years, I needed something else to do. I strived for the best grades in school. I graduated with a GPA of 98.7. I worked at the school in the mornings, went to school at night, and styled hair every day. I was angry, scared, frustrated, and sick about the whole situation.

I started thinking, *Maybe I can open my own hair salon.* I wanted to write an awesome business plan, so I got in front of the computer and started to type. I prayed and told God, "This is what I really want to do with my life, can you please help me?" It took two years to write my business plan, and I finally finished it in 2007. I wrote a sixty-five-page business plan out of sheer anger. At that point I didn't want to go to sleep. I guess God said, "If you're not sleeping anyway, let's put that to good use." After completing my business plan, I decided to get incorporated. My business is now called Ebbie's Hair and Nail Salon, Inc. I just love the Inc. at the end.

October 23, 2004, was the worst and best day of my life! It was the worst day because I never would have thought he could do something like that to me. It was the best day because my relationship with God became stronger. I was never one to take life for granted. I appreciated everything, especially life. I have so much planned for the future. I want to be married and have someone to share the rest of my life with. I just realized that I'm stronger than I think I am, and whatever life has to throw at me, I'm going to throw it right back. I have purpose and meaning in life. I'm here for a reason!

Everyone has a purpose in life—a unique gift or special talent to give to others and the world. And when we blend this unique talent with service to others, we experience the ecstasy and exultation of our own spirit, which is the ultimate goal of all goals!

Ebony Fletcher is the proud owner of Ebbie's Hair and Nail Salon, Inc., in Brooklyn, New York.

Fire and Water

By Ihotu Jennifer Ali

I love my parents. Truly I do. And I don't say that just because I should, or because I grew up believing that is what good children should do, or because television and music and pop culture taught me what I came to view as normalcy between a mother and father and their daughter. I actually love them. But love is complicated.

I was born into a family of great love, and in fact, "love" in my father's native tribal language was the name given to me: Ihotu. I was the eldest child, the pride and joy. And in the beginning, there was nothing but a love that was pure and simple. A love that drove my mother to follow my father from humble Minnesota to an equally humble Nigerian village where she endured lurking lizards and an unknown language and bathed her newborn child in public rivers. That love drove my father to also leave his family and return to the United States so that his children could experience the best education, one he had never known himself. That love also raised me to adore and mentor my two little sisters from the moment each was born. One, with mental and physical disabilities, I took under my four-year-old wing and loved her as if it were I, and not my mother, that had carried her for nine long months. An uncomplicated love compelled my mom to fight, even though she despised confrontation, for the ones she loved. She fought with immigration officials to allow my father back into the country; she fought with doctors for the best care for her daughter and her special needs. Despite humble beginnings, my family was rich in love.

But love, even in its richness, eventually becomes complicated. It began with my parents. My dad is a Nigerian. This would have been fine, except that not even twenty-five years in the United States, an American wife and in-laws, and American friends—not even years of marriage and family counseling—could teach him what it is to be an American husband, or father. I have brief, gasping memories of him carrying me on his shoulders or dancing to Okanga drums to the sounds of "Sweet Mother," and I admired his adventurous spirit and warm smile. Yet even I recognized a strained silence in the house. After years of abuse, neglect, and failed attempts at compromise, my mother finally ended it. She still loved him, even after he abandoned her and her children. My father became a distant memory, an occasional source of intense pain, and the impetus to my sister's nightmares and my emotional detachment.

I loved my mother and admired her strength. She fought for me to stay in a school district I knew, after multiple moves and new faces and so many changes I could barely keep up. We kept moving, and I never bothered to unpack, yet at least I could stay in the same classroom, if not on the same street. She and my sisters rooted me to reality; wherever we were was home, and anywhere without them would be foreign. It was a comfortable existence, insular and safe, and we were enmeshed in a tight love—too tight, perhaps.

Then she started to falter. As I grew older she seemed to grow smaller, less capable, less aware. Increasingly wrapped in her own world, occasional men wandered in and out of our lives, and I earned the nickname of "mom" among my sisters. I took over when she wasn't around, sleeping, unable to think clearly, or upset. In short, I took over. I love my mother, and I love my sisters, so I did what needed to be done for us. I was thirteen, and I began working, knowing that she would fall short for rent at the end of the month. And when she asked, apologizing and claiming each time would be the last time, I was neither surprised nor trusting. I knew we survived on the back of food stamps, community Christmas donations, and my hours on the clock or in the kitchen, rather than my hours in any classroom. When she took antidepressants for months, or spent weekends in the hospital, or threatened to commit suicide, I held her up and tried my best to show my sisters that nothing was wrong. I took over. I did this without regrets, because I loved them.

But over time, I realized the love they needed was more than just a shoulder to cry on, or a dependable hand that would prepare dinner or help with rent without complaint.

At a certain point, I realized that I had given up myself entirely, for them. I loved them so deeply that I would sacrifice it all—my happiness, my health, my ambitions for a future career and family of my own—for them, and yet we were still only barely surviving. I had fallen into a life of such dangerous love that I was little better off than my mother, and my volatile emotions had been so solidly suppressed that I could no longer feel. I cared for her in times of sickness with the same passion that I recoiled at her inability to raise her daughters. I felt she failed me as a mother by not teaching me to be strong, yet her absence forced me into a role that forever defined my inner resolve.

One day, I decided to leave. The guilt follows me to this day, but I promised myself that I would begin to love myself as deeply and with the same reckless abandon that I loved my family. I am not gone forever—I call, write, and visit, and am still very much a part of their lives. However, I am not so enmeshed in love that I cannot see the future, cannot understand and learn from the past, and cannot even discern the difference. I love my parents deeply, but I do not want them to need me. I may never have the parents I see on television: the mother who checks in to make sure I've eaten my breakfast or the father who congratulates me on my new promotion. I don't think I am abnormal; in fact, I'm sure many families are just like mine, when parents and children assume one another's roles. But now, I play carefully with love, since I know it is made of both water and fire.

Ihotu Jennifer Ali is currently attending Columbia University in New York City, working toward a master's degree in global public health with an emphasis on mental health and holistic healing methods. She has over four years of experience working with migrant and refugee women, communities of color, and community-based nonprofit organizations. She credits her faith, family, and love of words and music for her all her successes.

It's Not Over

By J. Nerissa Percival

I found my inner strength that night. I learned lessons about myself, the power of prayer, and about the cold-heartedness of men in just a few hours. Lessons that take most women a lifetime to learn, I experienced in one nocturnal episode, at the age of twenty-two.

I fell in love with Bobby when I was fifteen. He was eight years older. His grown-up persona and adult vocabulary, his charm, his smooth sexy voice, his sense of humor, and his constant attention and concern for me made me fall fast and hard for him. We became a couple. He told me that he loved me. I loved him, too.

We played the break up to make up game for seven and a half years. I went to Florida for college. He went to Canada for work. He visited me often in Florida and made arrangements for me to come to Canada to live with him. He even got me a job interview and rented us a beautiful apartment.

Something didn't feel right living with him. There was always something in my subconscious telling me that this wasn't where I was meant to be. He wasn't who I was supposed to be with. I left Canada and returned home. I got my own wonderful two-story apartment. I felt independent. I felt safe. Even though I missed him, I was happy.

A few months later he decided that he'd come back home to live with me. He didn't want to lose me, and if moving back home was what I wanted, then that's what he'd do. That pushed aside my doubts about us.

I had broken up with him, for good, the night before what I now refer to as "the incident." That "something is wrong" feeling returned when he did, and simply would not leave me alone. I was finishing up some laundry when he came home. Some chick had called for him earlier and I hung up on her for her lack of manners. She must have eventually gotten in touch with him, because apparently he was very upset about that. Little did I know that I was just the cook, cleaner, and caretaker of the three kids that weren't mine, while he had numerous other women for various activities—one back in Canada that he was actually planning to marry, and another that very recently had a son with him. The love of my life was a very busy man, with far too much love for just one woman.

He started talking to me, quite heatedly, about not interfering in his life and in his relationships. Not passing my place, and not being rude to his other women. Then he started conversing with his hands. He pounded them into my head, back, chest, and legs, leaving bright red marks on my skin that later turned deep purple.

He choked me. He watched life drain from my body,

than he released his grip and gleamed with power. He took away my cell phone, locked all the doors and windows, and refused to let me out of my own home. He told me that we weren't through. Our relationship would never be over until he said it was over, and he'd kill me before he ever said that. He told me that if I ever brought another man into *his* house, he'd kill us both.

I hadn't felt any fear until that moment, not until the word "kill" was introduced. Now I was terrified for my life. I tried to run from him and out of the apartment. I raced down the stairs and tried to unlock the living room door. He rushed behind me, practically flew down the thirteen stairs from my bedroom, and dragged me back up by my hair. I tried again, and this time he marched me back up the stairs with a pair of scissors piercing my back. He threatened to cut my hair off and teased me with them. Then he tied my hands behind my back and left me on the floor of my bathroom. This was reminiscent of scenes from the hundreds of Lifetime movies I watched every Sunday. I should have known a thousand ways to hinder him and get away, but my mind was void.

I soon realized that he didn't tie me tightly, so I knew it was just a demonstration of control. Eventually I slid my hands free, returned to the bedroom, and lay on the bed. Tears poured down my cheeks uncontrollably. He touched me as if to comfort me and I felt nauseous. I moved away from him, kept crying, closed my eyes tightly, and started to pray. Almost instantly I felt a remarkable sense of tranquility. I was no longer afraid or timid, and I now had a plan.

I washed my face, then continued to put away the laundry as if nothing had happened. I started down the stairs. He sprang to his feet and ran behind me, ready to stop my escape. I ignored him, began to pack away dishes, and prepared to cook dinner. He watched me for a while, then gradually went back upstairs and turned on the television. I continued to clean pots, pans, and cupboard doors so that he'd think I was busy in the kitchen. He came down to check on me a second time; still, I ignored him. A minute later, the phone rang upstairs. I listened for him to get settled into his discussion, opened and closed a few more cupboards while I slowly opened the kitchen door, and snuck out. I crept over to my neighbor's apartment. I began to get edgy as I knocked on her door. I envisioned him pulling me back into the apartment by my hair and stabbing me to death.

Finally she answered, slowly opened her kitchen door, and locked it after I entered. Tears fell from my eyes as I walked toward her telephone. I was safe.

J. Nerissa Percival was born and resides on the beautiful Caribbean island of Antigua. Traveling, reading, and writing are her favorite diversions. Nerissa completed a bachelor's degree in computer science in 2001. In 2006, at the age of twenty-four, she published *Butterfly in the Moonlight* and *Butterfly in the Sunlight*.

If I Knew Then What I Know Now About Depression . . .

Dust does rise, doesn't it? And so can I.
—Dionne Warwick

Depression is an insidious disease that has left many women ashamed of feeling the way they feel about themselves and about their lives. The one thing that is certain about going through situations that may leave you feeling depressed is that you are changed by those situations. No matter how low you get, you too can rise from the state you're in or above the situation that got you there. It is often better to speak about your feelings to friends and family members. Sometimes, if the depression is severe or debilitating, you may need to speak with a professional.

Your Soul's Sustenance

To sustain your soul, you must maintain a positive attitude. No matter what situation comes your way, look for the positive in it. You may not be able to relate to positivity during a time of despair, so in those cases concentrate on the lesson. What can I learn? How can I be a better person through this experience? When you are looking at the benefits of a situation that may seem hopeless, it helps to distract yourself from "Why me?"; "I can't do this anymore!"; and "Things will never change." Change your perspective to "Why not me?"; "Yes I can!"; and "This is a temporary situation that I can grow from."

Your Personal Book of Revelations

- *What pain have you experienced in your life?*
- *Do you feel like a victim?*
- *Do you feel like you don't know when your happiness will return?*
- *Do you ever feel like your situation isn't normal?*
- *What responsibility do you take for your current situation?*

III

Fear Is a Four-Letter Word

You can't make decisions based on fear and
the possibility of what might happen.
We just weren't raised that way.
—First Lady Michelle Obama

Fear is a strong emotion. How you deal with your fears can be a powerful tool. As we are on life's journey, many of us fear change. Going from the care of your parents to being on your own to becoming a parent are common fearful milestones in a young woman's life. Due to our varied experiences as women, fear can come much earlier in life or much later, but how we learn to deal with our fears is one of the greatest lessons we will learn in life.

Learning to face your fears is something that we learn as women through trial and error. Sometimes we are forced to face our fears. Whether it's the loss of our innocence or the fear of the unfamiliar, we are forced by the evolutionary power of change to face our fears. We're not talking about phobias, but everyday fears that are a part of life. What comes to mind is an anxiety disorder related to fear known as agoraphobia. People with agoraphobia fear being in places they cannot easily get out of, causing panic attacks. Agoraphobics are depicted in the media as people who don't leave their homes due to fear of the outside world. While this is a clinically diagnosed disorder, we think of this fear as paralyzing, crippling, and limiting for the person, a total disconnect from the outside world due to a fear beyond their control. If you think about this in a rational manner, you may not be able to understand the fear that an agoraphobe bears. You may be thinking of all they are missing: the sunshine on their face, the smell of fresh-cut grass, the bustling pulse of a big city, the joy in meeting new people in person, and the list goes on and on. You have a point, but let's understand that their fear is beyond their control and the person with agoraphobia has to learn to cope with their fears with the help of a trained professional or suffer alone in silence.

Our fears may not be as extensive as that of an agoraphobe, but they can be just as limiting. As we have traveled the world speaking to women, we have discovered that fear has been a crippling factor in why many haven't pursued their dreams. We also found that tied to fear was low self-esteem due to many young women being told they weren't good enough. So instead of proving the naysayers wrong, they were too scared to find out the truth for themselves. They just believed the negative words they heard. Not that different from the agoraphobe.

The old saying "Nothing beats a failure but a try" comes to mind for us when we think of fear. The basis for fear is the failure to cope with the unexpected. To be able to not only cope, but to succeed in dealing with the unknown is the triumphant moment that we participate in every day. By recognizing those triumphant moments and feeling a sense of joy in the little things we conquer on a daily basis, we are able to face and cope with the larger fears. As women of color, we need to know that anything is possible for us as long as we believe in ourselves. The following women are here to let you know that they have faced some of their fears and have come out stronger and more capable of dealing with any other challenges that may come their way. Read, take notes, and know you are not alone.

I Am Bigger than My Fears

By Quintrecia Lane

From childhood to late adolescence, I would often experience emotional highs and lows that would put me in a dark and gloomy place. Although I did not have the words or the awareness to articulate or understand what was happening to me at that time, I now realize that I was having depressive episodes and that I was prone to slipping into these states without reason or explanation. These episodes of depression were overwhelming to both me and my family. They would heighten negative emotions and insecurities that I had within me and they shaped my perception of myself. I preferred not to be seen or heard. I was also embarrassed about who I was.

A lot of my fears and insecurities stemmed from me judging and comparing myself to others who I felt were better than me. I constantly thought I couldn't possibly be as brilliant, beautiful, and talented as they were. I was so used to functioning in my dysfunctions that I didn't know any other way of being. My dysfunctions became the closest things to me, so much so that the pain I felt and my sense of being were inseparable. I moved through life like a lifeless being, always looking for an escape. I found these escapes by removing myself from settings where I would have to interact or compete with others my age. This happened in school and other social settings.

Trying to cope with the many highs and lows of my depression was a task I never thought I could handle. I didn't want to live in reality because I didn't feel strong enough to deal with what I was truly feeling. Emotionally, I felt out of control and like a burden to those I loved. I hated feeling like the negative one and would often end up feeling guilty for not being what I considered "good enough." I was ashamed of who I was becoming and I desperately wanted to feel normal. Sometimes I would wish to be someone else, someone I considered to be better than myself. I allowed depression to take over my life, and this led to stagnation, procrastination, and sickness in every aspect of my existence.

It wasn't until I told myself "I am bigger than my depression!" that I finally saw who I was. I remember the day I decided to free myself from the person I didn't want to be anymore. I drew a picture of the "me" I didn't want to see anymore. After I drew the picture of her, I cried for her and told her that she could transform. Within a moment in time, I saw someone beautiful and enlightened and no longer felt the burdens of the old person I was. For once I didn't fear being seen or heard, and I could relax and enjoy life. Every moment after that became a moment to celebrate who I was. Spirituality, ritual, and prayer became the foundation of my life. Every day I would affirm my greatness. I began putting myself back together piece by piece and started educating myself about the power of feminine divinity. I taught myself how to love myself and studied the ways of powerful goddesses from around the world. I learned how to embrace my flaws and share who I was with others.

The journey toward self-preservation was one that took time, patience, and willpower. In the midst of my confusion, I didn't know how I would end my despair. I couldn't see the brighter side to life, but I was determined to find it. Now that I am free from the turmoil of my earlier years, I know that anything is possible and that it's never too late to transform. I am able to see the beauty in life and myself, and that is the greatest thing I've gained from my experience. The greatest thing that I have gained from this experience is that now I am able to see the beauty of life and the greatness that lies within me. I am glad to relay this message of hope to other young ladies like me. You can overcome anything.

Quintrecia Lane is a twenty-one-year-old Brooklyn resident who is a singer, belly dancer, performance artist, and aspiring writer. She shares her gift of artistry with the community by performing at various venues across the New York City greater metropolitan area.

My Father's Absence

By Crissinda Ponder

Nearly eight years had passed by since the last time I saw him, and now I was on the way to see the man who *still* manages to call himself my father. He continuously failed to realize that being a father entails being more than a sperm donor. Despite his fear of my mother obtaining his personal information, he finally decided to disclose his place of residence to me when I called his cell one random day and declared that I was coming over.

Sharing his childhood with both parents and five siblings, he did not experience the effects of a broken home. He met my mother at age twenty-one. Although the two were unwed and unstable, I came along one pregnancy term later. Within the first year of my life, he left, never to return.

On that late December evening that I drove up the interstate to his apartment, a combination of thoughts raced through my mind, and all at once, I felt every emotion possible. There were so many things that I wanted to say to him, but I could never build up the courage to open my mouth. Although I did not see him regularly, I was still intimidated by his indifference and angered by his inconsideration.

I never understood why he did not want to be in my life or what I could have possibly done to make him run away. Though he was never there when I needed him in the past, now that I was a young adult, I had a glimpse of hope that persuaded me that things were going to be different. As I was approaching his residence, I was a bit excited about the reunion, but all the past emotional and mental wounds that he left behind were beginning to resurface.

Every time he tries to come back into my life, he always ends up neglecting me. I keep setting myself up to get hurt, I thought, while recalling all of the hurtful experiences. But I knew that since I now had a vehicle and could locate him on my own, I needed to take a chance.

I immediately felt out of place once I arrived at his apartment. I wanted to turn around and head for home, but my little sisters were with me (products of his former marriage to my stepmother). Though mindful of their presence, I could not help but feel alone.

My father married my stepmother when I was six years old, and she birthed my sisters, who are twins, the following year. My sisters had something that I never had the chance to experience: a complete institution of family that includes both mom *and* dad. Even though my father and stepmother were no longer together, I still experienced a sense of jealousy that sometimes prevented me from being the big sister that I have always wanted to be.

I was brought up by both my mother and grandmother, and I was always provided for in spite of a struggle. There was always something missing, however. The absence of my father often sparked anger, which influenced me to be bitter and mean to my loved ones. I would blame myself for him not being a part of my life, and label myself a bad child while my grades and performance in school reflected otherwise.

Walking through the threshold of his place seemed odd. No furniture. No decorations. An empty unit, representing the void he failed to fill in my life. While my sisters and I stood around and talked among ourselves, I saw him come out of his bedroom with a small box.

"Happy birthday and merry Christmas," he said. "I was going to send it to you, but you're here."

Oh, whatever, I thought as I was handed the box.

The picture on the front of the box displayed an MP3 player, and as I opened the box to see the device, I was hoping a portion of the back child support he owed would be a part of the package.

"Um, thanks," I said.

Apparently, my father was under the impression that an MP3 player would make up for several years of abandonment and heartbreak. I felt that he insulted my intelligence by giving me a "toy" to occupy my time with, so that I would suppress my resentment toward him.

Finding out that I had another younger sibling, age eight, further upset me. I was shocked to hear that when one of my sisters blurted it out on the trip over to my father's place. When I brought the issue up while we were face-to-face, he could barely look me in the eye, while his facial expression conveyed that he had only the least amount of concern for her, the same amount he clearly had for me over the years.

However, when I left his home, I perceived that our relationship would take a turn for the better. Unfortunately, things became worse. I finally opened up and did something I never thought of doing—asking him for help. He had helped me purchase one of the *many* textbooks I needed for my courses, so I figured that since I was now a college student he would not mind helping me with my expenses periodically. That was not his intention. He never attempted to support me financially, and I was foolish to think that he would willingly change.

Coming out of my shell to face rejection was the hardest thing to deal with. I grew up refusing to pick up the phone and ask him for anything, and when I finally decided to let my guard down, he disappointed me as he had regularly done in the past. I regretted my decision for the longest time, and I concluded that I would be better off if he stayed out of my life completely.

I still feel remnants of pain occasionally while I try to create the "what-if" scenarios in my mind. A part of me will always long to be that naïve child who would hang on to my father's every promise over the phone, but I understand that in order for me to move away from the hurt, I must mature in that sense.

Accepting the fact that some individuals are only meant to be in my life for a season, I have come to realize that I never needed my father to be a part of my life, I just wanted him there. The challenges that have been placed in my life during this struggle within our broken relationship have motivated me to strive for the best in the most difficult of times.

Looking back, I recognize that I have never allowed the unresolved problems I have with my father to interfere with my academics. I received my high school diploma without him, and I *will* receive my bachelor's degree without him. In fact, his lack of participation in my life has pushed me to work harder and want more for myself.

I might not have a clearly defined relationship with my father, but the family I do have has remained constant in my life since the very beginning. Knowing that I have their approval is all the encouragement that I need to continue to move forward and strive for the best.

Crissinda Ponder is a writer for the *Red and Black* at the University of Georgia, where she is currently pursuing a bachelor of arts degree in journalism. Her work has also appeared in *VOX*, an Atlanta-based teen newspaper. She can be contacted by e-mail at crissponder@gmail.com.

MARKED

By Jasmine Nicole Gibson

When we wake up each morning and move through our day, there are things that we expect to experience and others that we would never dream would occur. Some of these so-called random occurrences impact us greatly and create feelings of joy and powerful memories, while others taint our views and perceptions of both people and the world. I have learned over the course of my life that even the seemingly mundane situations can quickly transform into devastating life events that can change your entire world view.

Who would have thought that a church BBQ, answering the front door, and riding the train would have outcomes so devastating that my beliefs, interactions, and discernment about the opposite sex would be permanently altered? I am a nineteen-year-old female living in New York City. Since I was younger, I have continuously found myself in uncomfortable, sometimes traumatic, situations with men. I started doubting myself, asking, "Why me? What is it about me that these things started happening?" These events were not physical in nature, but their impact has scarred me emotionally and caused me to question and blame myself. Over and over again, I have encountered perverted men, strangers who have appeared in both public and private places and done unspeakable things. From about the age of fourteen, I have experienced multiple situations where these men have exposed themselves to me, have made lewd comments, or have made me feel afraid for my life. Most of the time these incidents have occurred in places where I normally felt safe and secure.

The first time I recall it happening was during a church BBQ in upstate New York. I would have never expected that something like that would happen at such a gathering. My best friend and I were taking a stroll down a path in a wooded area close to where everyone was eating and relaxing. A lot of people from the church had walked the path and come back, so we decided to go also. We enjoyed it so much that we went more than one time with different people. The first time we went it was with a group of girls, and while we were walking we heard a man's voice call something out to us; however, none of us paid attention to what he said. The second time we saw a man and a woman making out in the woods, and we were all shocked because this was a "church" gathering. The third time we went, it was just my best friend and I. We were coming up the path, and we hadn't gotten very far when a man approached us and said, "I really have to use the bathroom. All of the porta-potties are full. Can you two look out for me and make sure that no one comes while I use the bathroom?" Now, we were a bit shocked and we didn't know what to say or do. It seemed like it could have been an innocent request, but it still felt weird. After all, we didn't know this man. So I thought to myself, *I will be the lookout and then I'm going to leave as quickly as possible.* I turned around for a quick moment to look to see if anyone was coming, and when I turned back around my best friend had disappeared. In that quick moment she had left me behind. I didn't know what to do. I was panicking. Then I heard him say, "Do you think my penis is big?" Before what was happening could fully register in my mind, I looked down and was horrified to see this man standing there with his penis exposed. I remember thinking, *Should I run? Is he going to chase me if I do?* At that very moment, I was so blessed by the appearance of an older couple who came walking down the path. When the man saw them, he quickly ran off. I also ran, but in the opposite direction.

When I arrived back at the gathering, I immediately told my friend what happened. We decided to tell her parents, since I had come to the event with them and not with my own family. As soon as I shared the story, all of the men from the church started to search the area for the man. They soon found him and he was confronted by my pastor and the rest of the men. When they questioned him, he denied what he had done, but they still ordered him off the campground and told him to find his way home on his own. When my friends and I talked about the incident again, we quickly realized that the man who called out to us in the woods, the man who we saw making out with the woman, and the man I had encountered were all the same person. This frightened me even more.

In that particular experience I was blessed to be surrounded by loving and protective people who could help handle the situation, but I wasn't always this lucky. On another occasion, while on the number 3 train en route to Brooklyn, I got another reminder about how vulnerable I could be. When I first got on the train, I was surrounded by people. However, I fell asleep during the ride, and when I awoke the train was empty except for one man who was sitting across from me. By the time I came out of my sleep state and my eyes began to focus, I realized that the man was masturbating. My heart almost jumped from my chest. I immediately got up from my seat to move to the next car and realized that it, too, was empty. Since the next stop was mine, I remained in the car, but I stood by the door and watched his reflection through the glass to make sure he didn't come near me. I could see him looking at me and I felt disgusted. One stop between stations never lasted so long. When the train finally pulled into the station, I hurriedly got off that train. I tried to look to see if I saw a conductor somewhere, but I didn't see one. I was hoping to tell someone so that this man would be caught and the same thing wouldn't happen to another innocent woman or girl. Unfortunately my plan did not come to pass because the doors closed and the train pulled off. As the train pulled out of the station, I could see the man walking through the cars, probably looking for his next victim. I remember my feeling of disgust and my stomach aching at the thought.

The last experience that I will share happened in a place where I felt the most secure: at my own house. Home alone, minding my business, and enjoying a Ring Pop. I was expecting my stepfather to come to the house, so when the doorbell rang I thought it was him. At that time we had this really old door, and when you looked through the peephole you couldn't see people clearly. I couldn't make out the face, but I thought that it was him so I opened the door. Once the door was open, I discovered a man whom I had never seen before. He began speaking to me with a heavy accent, asking if we were planning on selling the house. He asked if he could speak to my parents and I told him they were on their way home, but wouldn't be interested in selling the house. As we were speaking, I was standing in the doorway innocently licking my Ring Pop when he asked, "Do you have a boyfriend?" I was shocked and tried to ignore his question. Then he looked at the Ring Pop, smiled, and said, "You suck good." At that point, I was shocked and scared, so I slammed the door in his face and ran upstairs. I was really nervous and wondered if he was still at the door. I decided to call my stepfather to see how close he was and to tell him what happened. When he heard the story he was furious! He drove to my house in what seemed like four minutes flat. He told me to get in the car so we could drive around the neighborhood to see if we could find the man. Sure enough, we found him within a block of my house. When I pointed him out, my stepfather pulled up next to him and called him over to the car, but I guess he recognized me, so instead of coming over, he jumped into a car with another man and pulled off. We gave chase and sped after them, beeping the horn to get their attention. I was scared because at one point I thought this was going to turn into a high-speed chase and eventually a physical altercation. Finally they stopped and my stepfather got out and told the story to the other guy that was in their car. This man explained that the violator was his brother and that he didn't speak English well. My stepfather did not accept this excuse and the police were called but no charges were filed because of the nature of the issue. Once again I was violated by a man, and, although I was defended, the degrading nature of the offense stayed in my spirit.

This happened to me so many times that I started to question and blame myself. I started expecting to be violated, and each time I walked past one man or a group of them, I would get nervous. I wondered what it was about me and my energy that attracted these perverts and brought them into my reality. I wondered if I had an invisible stamp on my forehead that said, "I am a victim. Come harass me." As I got older and began to study and understand the law of attraction, I recognized that my thoughts and fears about men and their motives had manifested into dangerous situations. I have learned that when I think negative things, I can create that reality, so I've worked hard to change my beliefs about all men trying to harm me. I also acknowledge that there are sick people in the world who get pleasure from inflicting pain. Women can take back their power by refusing to stay silent. We must speak out so that things like this don't continue to happen. I didn't always speak up; however, I have found my voice and reclaimed my power. I realize now that since I have been working on changing my thoughts, my experiences with people have been very different. I also know that it is a constant reminder for me to use my voice and believe that I do have the power to effect change and make a difference.

I thought it was important to share this story because I know that women experience men following them, touching them, or saying degrading things to them on a daily basis. This creates fear and a sense of helplessness. I want women and girls out there to know that we are not marked as victims, but we are marked as beautiful, powerful survivors of all circumstances.

Jasmine Nicole Gibson is a nineteen-year-old sophomore, majoring in fine arts at Adelphi University. She is a writer, singer, lyricist, and actress and a founding member and mentor for a rites of passage program called Spirit of a Woman (S.O.W.) Leadership Development Institute. Jasmine is an aspiring business owner.

If I Knew Then What I Know Now About Fear . . .

I have learned over the years that when one's mind is made up, this diminishes fear; knowing what must be done does away with fear.
—Rosa Parks

We all know how crippling fear can be to our lives, but have you ever thought how your fears can hold not just you back, but others around you? Rosa Parks is a good example of facing your fears and how your courage can propel you and those around you to create positive change. The simple act of refusing to sit in the back of the bus, which she had done so many times before, changed her life and the lives of black people forever. We're sure she was afraid, but her frustration at segregation and the conditions she was faced with propelled her to say, "No more!" Ms. Parks has often said that it wasn't her choice to be the face and catalyst for a movement, but her action is a part of her legacy.

Fear Is Not Knowing What Your Calling Is in Life

By Tweetie

Fear can hold you back; it is the reason why people don't move forward. They're scared, so they settle. I can relate to that so much, because I let fear hold me back, big-time. Dance has been my passion since I was a little girl. I graduated from LaGuardia High School of Performing Arts, the *Fame* high school. I'd been dancing professionally since I was seventeen. I was on the road, performing, while I was in high school and performed with some of the top artists in the country. I also started teaching hip-hop classes. I believed in the mantra *practice and more practice*. It paid off. I was bold, and in between gigs I would get a temp job to get by. One day I decided that my life is dance and stepped out on faith and was fearless. I left my temp gigs behind. My career flourished and I was excited.

Yet fear can still creep in and stop you in your tracks. I remember a specific audition, and I will never forget this. It was a Madonna audition a few years back for her world tour, and a really big deal if I landed it. The choreographer told me that he'd heard of me, that people had said really good things about my work. That was good on my end.

The audition was in New York, and it was *huge*. It was an open call and my audition number was 800. The place was filled with dancers, both male and female. First, they had you come in and freestyle. If they liked your look and freestyle, you could stay. I made it through the first round.

Then there was choreography. For some reason, the choreography would not stick. My body went into a panic mode: I couldn't breathe; I couldn't think; I couldn't feel. I was shaking. I wanted out, so I went to the choreographer and told him, "I can't do this." I was so disappointed in myself that I began to cry. Everyone was staring at me. He said, "I've heard about you. I'd like you to learn this choreography. Finish this. Do the best you can do."

I pushed my way through it, and I was sure this would be my last round. But he gave me an opportunity to stay. The whole room clapped. I could not believe it. Then we had to go into the next part of the audition, which was learning a partnering routine, either salsa or tango. I had no idea how to do that genre of dance. Here we go again: I can't dance; I can't move. And we're doing all this choreography. I'm thinking, *You're sure I'm supposed to be here? I can't learn this stuff.* I am sweating, I'm choking, I'm crying. I went to the choreographer—again—and he said, "No, go back."

Another dancer helped me to calm down. Because he was so familiar to me, he understood my style of dancing. We spoke the same language, not only verbally but through dance. He helped to calm me down. But it wasn't enough, because as soon as I got back in that room, I was a wreck. But he tried. He said, "Bird, are you okay? Tweetie, calm down." He gave me a hug.

It was just his energy that helped me to calm down. He would hold my shoulders and my face. He said, "Look, you can do this, there's no reason you can't do this. You're one of the best dancers out there. Are you kidding me? There's no reason you should be second-guessing yourself."

But I couldn't stop second-guessing myself. There were so many people in the audition room and it was overwhelming. You have all these dancers—trained dancers, street dancers—and it's just little old you. You're thinking, "Do I have what it takes? It should be me that you pick. It should be me that you want to pick." And girls go through image stuff: Am I tall enough, am I pretty enough, do I have the body type—it's all of those things. And then you always have a new batch of dancers that come in, the next generation of dancers, and they're younger and you're older. It really messed with my head.

I had three panic attacks that day. Three. And I just couldn't pull it off. I was paralyzed, paralyzed by fear. I went back to the choreographer the third time. He could see my face, and he said, "I am going to have to let you go." I went home and I cried.

As a dancer, a person in the arts, that is the worst thing you can go through. At the time I was hosting a group of dancers at my home who were teenagers and less experienced than I was. I encouraged them to go to the audition with me. One ended up going on tour with Madonna. I was happy for them, but I was upset because I felt I couldn't be strong enough for them or myself. I came home. I didn't want to see anyone. At that point, I felt like, "I am done. There is no point of doing anything with dance again."

What was wrong with me? It wasn't like I was new to the business. I felt like a failure, I felt like everyone who saw me at the audition saw me at my weakest point. That's it, I quit.

Then I did a workshop, Ladies of Hip-hop, with the Montage Performing Arts Company. I really didn't know what I was going to teach. I had cried all night, it was the first time I had danced since that audition. I was so uninspired. I listened to this song by N.E.R.D., "She Wants to Move." I also listened to Sheila E's "The Glamorous Life," psyching myself up. So I ended up teaching the routine to the N.E.R.D. song. I made it up as I was on my way to class. I pretty much freestyled the whole class. It was one of the best routines I could have done. I was at such a low point, and creatively I couldn't think. But somehow, everyone in the class really related to it. In the middle of the class, I ended up crying and telling them about my failed audition.

They motivated me to start dancing again. There were about fifty or sixty women. Some of them were trained, some of them were not, all different levels dancing together in one room. From the weakest dancer to the strongest, everyone was learning at one level.

The audition created an atmosphere of *I am better than you*. But in that class, the atmosphere was one of mutual respect and admiration. Dance is supposed to inspire you. It's supposed to be fun, without the cockiness behind you. And that's what it was for them in that workshop. At that moment, I broke down and I cried. They helped me to remember why I started teaching, why I loved dancing so much, why I went from having a temp job to just saying, "I want to transition to dance full-time."

But still, something was holding me back. I would get to a certain point and I would still have this fear, even after that workshop. I didn't know what my calling was. I wasn't getting certain jobs I was supposed to get when I went out on auditions. But I was having success, teaching in different countries. I taught in Japan, Switzerland, Korea, China, and Saudi Arabia. And yet, even when I was teaching, I still felt there was something holding me back. What's holding me back? I realized that the only time I feel like I have no fear is when I'm performing, or dancing by myself. I love to teach, how it makes people feel. It's my expression, how I'm telling my story as to why I even do what I do. But I still didn't know if I was supposed to dance, to perform.

Fear still had a hold of me.

One thing I did learn was to meditate, to chant. I am not a Buddhist but I was with somebody who was a Buddhist, and he was like, "Hey, this can work for you." And it did. He taught me to chant, "Nam-myoho-renge-kyo." It took my focus off fear. I would chant, and I would pray. And that helped a lot. My mom and dad always said to make sure you say your prayers at night, so I incorporated my chanting with my daily prayers. Bit by bit, I got more grounded. I got some clarity. I realized that fear, for me, was not knowing what my calling in life was at the time.

You have needs and you have wants. Many times your needs and your wants become the same thing. Some people mix them up. What I wanted to do—perform—wasn't necessarily something that I needed to do. It wasn't what I'm supposed to do. I wanted to be dancing with all these great choreographers and these great artists on tour. That's every dancer's dream. If you don't get to do those things, does it mean you're a failure? No. I've done those things, maybe not to the level I wanted to do. That might not have been my path.

Teaching is definitely my path, on many different levels. That is something that I have accepted. It's not closing the door to performing with artists. But I've been able to travel the world, teaching. I can be in China, and people there appreciate what I'm teaching. And I get to tour the country and climb the Great Wall of China. And I get to do it on my terms, not dancing behind some famous artist onstage. I'm still performing, but in a different way. I make my own schedule; I make my own plans. I make my own rules, and I'm still able to do what I love and travel and share that with people.

I still come across fear every day. It's just how you deal with it that will determine if it takes over your life. Are you going to let it stop you or are you going to move forward? You always have fear. Some people don't allow the fear to keep them from moving forward. You can get nervous, you can get upset, some people even cry. Do what you've got to do to release the fear. And then when it's time for you to make that move, don't allow fear to keep you from making the move you are meant to make. I teach a beginner's hip-hop class at the Alvin Ailey American Dance Center. I say two things to my class: "Don't be lazy" and "Don't mentally shut down because of fear." People will tell themselves no, and your body will react to what your mind tells you. People are lazy. You don't know what you can accomplish until you push yourself. You've got to put your all into it, all the time. If you're trying anything, *try it*! Give it all that you possibly can. So many times, I have shut myself down, from fear of not being accepted.

It should really be about having fun.

In my classes, I tell my students, "If you mess up, I'm going to laugh. If I mess up, you laugh." You're learning something brand new, you shouldn't be afraid.

It's the mess-ups and the mistakes that are going to help you be better. You're not going to get it on the first try. You've got to work out the kinks first. It's the pressure that gets to you; that's the pressure that I don't have in my class, it's the pressure that I no longer put on myself. In my class, we have a block party, a house party; we're at a club. It's fun. There's no room for fear.

One day, Gayle King, Oprah Winfrey's friend, came and took my class. Afterward, she told me, "I'm really interested in you and your class." It went from getting an interview in *O* magazine to, "Hey, why don't we film your class?" It's like I woke up from this long period of time when I'm chanting and praying and not knowing what I want in my life to suddenly I'm on *Oprah,* literally because someone came to my class and had fun.

I'm learning every day. I'm learning how to teach different people every day. Now I have a television show on MTV. I still continue to audition. I still continue to teach. And I am blessed.

Tweetie hosts her own show, *Dances from tha Hood,* on MTV and is the host of MTV's *Dances from tha Hood* Mobile Phone Series, available on Sprint, Verizon, Cingular, Amp'd, and Helio phones.

Your Soul's Sustenance

Fear is in total opposition to the care of your soul. Fear doesn't allow your soul to soar and become a true reflection of your God-given abilities and talents. Everyone has a talent, and if you are afraid, you will not be able to express that talent and bless others with your gift. Know that fear is a barrier between you and the greatness you deserve. Be brave and look at the fears you may have as the finish line of a race. You must cross the line to receive your trophy. Don't be afraid to receive the things you have worked hard for, because you are truly a winner!

Your Personal Book of Revelations

- *What are you most afraid of now?*
- *Have you faced your fears and come through unscathed?*
- *Are you afraid of success and what that brings?*
- *Are you afraid of failure and what that brings?*
- *What does fear feel like for you?*

IV

Am I My Mother?

I blame my mother for nothing,
but forgive her for everything.
—Mary J. Blige

As we get older and look back on our relationships with our mothers, they are vastly different from when we were teenagers and in our twenties. Some of us had great relationships with our mothers, while others had tumultuous and chaotic relationships. What we've learned is that our mothers did the best they could with the information they had.

In our travels, we've met so many young women whose mothers were addicted to drugs or were young when they had them. These young ladies would tell stories of how their mothers cared more about getting high or partying than they did about being a mother. Many of them still carry the hurt and rage at their mothers for these situations. When we speak to them, we hear the disappointment in their voices. The most important thing that we stress to these young women is that they learn to forgive their mothers, because they too did the best they could with what they had. You may say, "How can a mother who abandoned her child for drugs or left her child home alone to party have done the best she could?" There is no manual that tells you how to be a mother; no test to take, no course to pass, just the examples of other women that have come before you or who are mothers around you. This isn't an excuse, but more an observation. As young women grow into motherhood, they begin to reflect and understand the roles their own mothers had to play. Whether it was peacemaker, homemaker, breadwinner, teacher, preacher, or sinner, it is who she was and is as a woman. By forgiving and understanding the roles and the situations our mothers were in, we can be better equipped to be mothers. Whether you had the best mom or the worst mom, there is always something to be learned.

You may admire your mother and desire to be just like her or you may think you had the mother from another planet. Whoever your mother is or was, the most important thing is to learn from her example, be it good or bad. Learn to be like your mother if there are things that you truly admire in her or learn to change the negative examples she gave you and make them positive ones in your life. We believe it's important for you to get to know your mother as a woman, not just as your mother. You may just be surprised at the woman you meet.

Left Behind

By Shampale Williams

Twenty-one years ago on a cold Christmas morning in Tulsa, Oklahoma, a fifteen-year-old teenager lay in a hospital bed with contractions that pierced like a needle and pain that felt unbearable. While the average teenager was opening gifts on what is probably the most celebrated day in the United States, my mother was giving birth to a child who was destined for greatness.

Five years after my mother gave birth to me, she was incarcerated in prison for five years for possession of drugs. In a conversation that my mother and I shared, she told me that she was hanging with the wrong crowd; she was dating a young man who was involved with selling drugs. As a child I did not quite understand what was going on and how her actions would change my life forever. When she was sent to prison in the state of Texas, my grandmother took full responsibility of raising my brother and me.

I still vividly remember traveling from Oklahoma to Texas

to visit my mother. It did not seem like she was sad to be in such a horrible place. I later realized that sometimes God will put us in places to make us better people. Everyone's test is different; my mother's test was being in prison.

As the years passed and I saw my mother less and less, I began to call my grandmother mom. She was all that I knew. I did not question why I had two moms and neither did I search for an answer. It became hard to explain to people where my mother was and why I was living with my grandmother.

People began to tease me. I remember holding in tears until I was alone and knew no one could see me cry. It was not my fault that my mother was not at home, though I know in the depth of my heart that she wanted to be with me, her daughter.

I recall sitting on the sofa in my grandmother's living room staring at the photograph of a young and beautiful woman. Her hair was down, she wore gloves, and snow was in the background. I believe the snow in the picture represented how cold life must have been for her not being able to be with me on my birthdays and see me cheer at football games on Saturdays.

The lady in the picture had a smile that could light up the sky, eyes that shined like diamonds, and the face of a model. The lady in the picture was my mother, and I felt like the luckiest girl in the world to have such a beautiful mother.

As I grew older I would constantly hear people say, "Girl,

you look just like your mommy!" I had also learned that she was extremely photogenic and enjoyed modeling and taking pictures, something that I loved to do.

The summer of 1998 is one that I will always remember. I did not get a new bike and neither did I attend camp. It was a memorable summer because I received a phone call that would change my life forever. I had just finished playing with some of my neighborhood friends when I walked into the house and my grandmother told me my mom had just called. "Okay," I said nonchalantly.

Tears raced down my cheek when my grandma told me my mother was coming to get me and my brother. She had been out of prison a little over a year, was married, and had relocated to Orlando, Florida.

This should have been the happiest day of my life, right? I had been waiting on this moment, a million nights of lying in bed dreaming of having a relationship with my mother. Two days after the "phone call," my mother's red Pathfinder pulled up into the driveway. The sound of music blasted from the speakers and poured out of the tinted windows. The rims shined and protruded from the tires like the cars I had seen in music videos.

When the door opened, there was a tall beautiful woman who gracefully stepped out of the car. Her figure resembled Tyra Banks—she was attractive, confident, and stylish, and she was my mother!

As I hugged my grandmother I had mixed emotions. I loved my grandmother dearly and I did not want to leave her. At the age of ten I knew that our time was up and that her raising me for that period of time was a part of God's plan and her purpose in life.

I jumped into the backseat, filled with excitement, fear, and anxiety. As my mother put the car in reverse, I knew my life was about to be in drive; I could only go forward at this point. Tears fell from my eyes like rain from the clouds because I knew that in order for a new chapter to begin in my book of life, one had to end.

I was living in a new state with no friends and a new family. Society has a way of belittling people who work at fast food restaurants, but my mother was the hardest-working woman that I had met. She was the manager at Burger King as well as a student in cosmetology school.

Within a year of me moving in with my mother, she had received her cosmetologist license and had saved enough money to open her own hair salon. Three years after that she was in school again. This time she would receive her license for child care. Before I knew it, she was opening up her own child-care center. Here was a woman who had just got out of prison proving to the world that she would be successful.

In the beginning my mother and I did not have much of a relationship. Though she was my mother, we were like strangers to each other. We had to get to know each other. We were starting from scratch. She learned that like her, I was creative, had a passion for fashion and expressing myself creatively.

On Saturdays I would help out at the salon, wash clients' hair, sweep the floor, and clean the bathroom. The salon played a major role in my mother and I establishing a good relationship. It was at the salon that I learned how to clean up, how to take care of my hair, and of course how to be a lady so that I was never the topic at the salon on Saturday mornings.

When her salon first opened, there were days when no one came in and she had no clients, but she was there every day because she was dedicated and knew that her work would soon pay off. Some days we would just sit and talk about life, love, and challenges that made her stronger.

As we conversed more, we developed a bond. It was through our conversations that I discovered people who are in prison are human, too. The only difference between those who are in prison and the individuals who are living in society is that they chose a different path, yet all roads have a way to connect so that the final destination is the same.

In high school, my mother consistently pushed me to excel in and out of the classroom. She told me that just because she did not go to college did not mean that I would not. My mother ensured that my head was in the books, not in boys, fitting in, or being popular.

When I walked across the stage and proudly received my high school diploma, it was Mother's Day for my mom. No words can express the joy she felt to know that I was going on to college with an academic scholarship and athletic grant as well. My mother was proud of me, and she will be even more proud when I walk across the stage to receive my bachelor's degree.

She is always motivating me to stay focused and determined. People wonder how a black woman who no one believed in managed to bounce back like superwoman, put two children in college, be an entrepreneur, and just recently finish real estate school.

There are girls who take their mothers for granted; I appreciate every moment that I spend with my mom. I know what it is like to look at pictures and yearn to have your mother read to you at night, tuck you in, and be there when you fall off of the bike for the first time and get a scar on your knee.

My mother and I have come a long way. Family members talk about her and constantly throw her past up in her face. They remind her that she had me at the age of fifteen, and are even more eager to tell me every chance they get that she was in prison. It amazes me how when someone is doing badly, everyone is okay with it, but as soon as God begins to pour blessings into their lives, it becomes a problem. At first, I admit I did not come to my mother's defense when I heard the negative comments about her. I was always taught to stay in a child's place, so I sat there, forced to listen to the belittling comments. Later on, as I grew stronger, I simply reminded them that nothing they say can break our bond, and I am my mother.

It is said that blood is thicker than water. I learned that is not always the case. A few members of our family felt like my mom thought she was better than them when she was just simply turning her life around so that I would have better opportunities. In reality, they were the ones who were afraid of being left behind.

Shampale Williams is a senior at Voorhees College where she reigns as Miss Voorhees College for the 2009–2010 academic school year. Last year she was Miss Black Journalist, voted the most talented and unique student at Voorhees College, and first place winner of the United Negro College Fund (U.N.C.F.) Pre-Alumni Talent Show. She is a member of the Voorhees College women's basketball team, VC Poetic, and the Mass Communications Club. Her career goals are to be a journalist, write for a magazine, publish her poetry, own her own publishing company, write plays, be a songwriter, model, motivational speaker, and become a college professor.

Time to Tell

By Charon Acevedo

"Hello."

"Hi, Mom! Can I speak to Jazzy?"

Two seconds later a little voice comes on the phone, saying in such an excited way, "Hi, Charon!"

"Hey, Jazzy! How are you?"

"I'm good . . . just watching TV."

"Great! How is school?"

"School's good. I got my report card!"

"Really? How'd you do?"

"It's good. I have good grades."

"That's great! So . . . how is everything at home?"

"Good."

This is the beginning of a normal conversation between my sister and me. I realize that I ask her a lot of questions. I just want to make sure that she is safe. Then and only then will I allow myself to rest at night.

Overall, I was raised by my paternal aunt. I would spend weekends and holidays at my mom's house. I looked forward to visiting my mom on the weekends, but sometimes, the experience left me feeling sad, alone, and afraid.

It all started when I was five years old. I spent the weekend at my mom's house. Her male friend slept over, too. Mom had other company, so she allowed him to sleep in my room. In the middle of the night, mom's friend took me off my bunk bed and laid me in the bed that he was sleeping in. He began to touch me. I woke up because his hands were cold. As I opened my eyes, I looked around and noticed I wasn't in my bed. He was still touching me! Each time I allow myself to remember, I experience the moment as if it were happening again.

I start to cry. I want him to stop, but he doesn't. Instead, he turns me on my back. He takes off my pajamas and then holds my hands. He then inserts himself into me. Pain . . . *so much pain. I start to scream but no one comes. I yell for my mother,* Mom-may!!!!! *Tears begin to run down my face quickly and uncontrollably. I am screaming so loud, but still—*No one is coming. *He covers my mouth and tells me to shut up. I am so scared, but I keep screaming. Still—no one comes. It feels like the pain will last forever. Then he gets up and I run to the bathroom to pee. All of a sudden, I notice red stuff coming out of my vagina. Ouch! My poo-poo hurts.*

I'm still crying. Mom finally comes to see **why I'm** *crying. Before I can tell her how he hurt me, the man comes to the bathroom door and tells mom that my sister peed in the bed. I can't talk. My eyes plead out for me, "Mommy?" But before I know it, Mom says, "Okay," and walks away.*

Tears still rolling, vagina still sore, I keep my head down. He's still standing there. Before he walks away, he tells me I better not say anything. I look up at him and notice his eyes. . . .

All I remember was the scary look in his eyes after he made that statement.

From that day on, my relationship with my mom was never the same. I kept the secret. I didn't tell anyone for eight years. From my experience that night, I lost trust in men and women. I always stayed to myself. My aunt would often wonder why I didn't care whether I went to my mom's house on weekends, but I never told. By the age of seven, I moved back in with the lady I called my mom. She said she wanted to start over. She regained custody of both me and my sister. We moved to Pennsylvania. While I was out there, I missed my aunt, my granny, and my baby cousin the most. I wanted things to be great. I wanted to start over with Mom and forget about the past. It seemed like things were getting better.

After about a year living in Pennsylvania with my mom and sister, things began to change again. My mom wasn't acting the same. I didn't know what was wrong with her. Mom took me to day care in the mornings before she went to work. One day on the way to day care, Mom dropped me off at the corner where the bus stopped and told me not to move. I watched her as she walked up the hill. I was scared. I turned to see my surroundings, but when I turned back around, she was gone.

I was lucky to see my mom's friend coming down the

hill with his kids. He asked me where my mom was, but all I could reply was, "She left." He then took me to day care. Later that day the police came to my day care. I was so afraid. They took me home. They told me that I would be staying with my mother's neighbor. They said my sister was already there. I asked them where my mother was, but they didn't answer me. While at the neighbor's house I asked about my mom. She told me that my mom was in the hospital and that she was very sick. I began to cry. I didn't want to hear that my mom was sick. That night we were taken to my aunt's house to spend the night. We were able to call my mom the next day at the hospital.

"Hello."

"Hi, Mommy!"

"Hi, Neicy!"

"This isn't Neicy. This is Charon." I wondered why she would call me by my sister's name.

"Who is Charon?" she asked very seriously.

"Your daughter." Why was she acting like she didn't know who I was?

"I only have one daughter."

"No! You have two daughters, Mom."

"No, I have one child."

I started to cry when I realized that she was serious about not knowing who I was. All I could think was, *How can my mom* really *not know who I am?*

We later learned that my mom had lesions on her brain and had experienced a stroke. My aunt in Pennsylvania allowed me to reach out to my paternal aunt. I cried to her.

I felt sad. My father and my aunt drove to Pennsylvania to pick me up and I moved back with my aunt.

Although I felt safer and to some extent, more secure, I was still upset because my aunt was taking care of me instead of my parents. It was painful to see my friends with their mothers. Over the years and even now, I acknowledge that I have built up anger in me. In the past, I didn't know how to release it, so I did things with hopes that I wouldn't feel anything like hurt, anger, or rage.

By the age of ten, my baby sister Jasmine (Jazzy) was born. She looks just like me. My aunt had legal custody of me, and my middle sister moved in with her father and grandmother, but Mom vowed that no one would take Jazzy away from her. Memories from my past kept haunting me. To numb myself to the feelings, I began to cut myself. My little cousin wouldn't tell my aunt. Instead, she would hide and / or throw all of the knives away. I resented my little cousin. I was mad because she had her mom. I regret being mean to her. I regret many of the choices that I've made. As the years went by, life seemed harder to appreciate. I was separated from my mom, and my middle sister lived with her father and grandmother. Mom recovered. She moved back to New York and I resumed visiting her on weekends and holidays.

At the age of fourteen, I felt the need to "protect" Jazzy. After much hesitation, my aunt allowed me the opportunity to move back with Mom for the second time. I pleaded with her that I was old enough to understand everything that went on. I wanted to be with my sister. At first everything was fine and I thought I'd be happy to be with my mom and my sister. All that was missing was my middle sister. I thought maybe we could finally be a family. However, those thoughts never became a reality. See, the truth is that my middle sister never really did live with us in Brooklyn. The truth is that my mom and I *never* got along, not even for a second.

That house was a hellhole for the both of us. We threw out words to each other like there was no tomorrow. While I was living there, I performed horribly in school because I stayed home a lot. I chose to stay home because my mom had a boyfriend that I was not too fond of and I didn't trust him alone around my baby sister while Mom went to work. I used to close the door, lock it, and then push the bed in front of the door so he couldn't get in. In my mind, I'd never let him do anything to my baby sister. Mom broke up with him a couple of months later.

Living in the house with my mom became overwhelming for me because I couldn't deal with her. It seemed like we fought over everything. I felt like I was living with my worst enemy. My aunt and I continued to attend the same church. She would often say that she wouldn't butt in because things needed to take their course. It was too much to bear. I finally decided it was time to tell. One night after attending church, as I was ready to take the train from East New York to Greenpoint, my friend's mom offered to drive me home. Before we got to my house, I blurted out every detail of my story. I told her why I didn't want to go home. I told her why I was afraid for my sister. I told her I wanted to go back to the only true home I really knew, with my aunt and cousin. My eight-year secret was out, and she encouraged me to tell my aunt and let her know I wanted to come home.

I moved back in with my aunt in the middle of the school year. I was sad because I was leaving my sister, but I knew I couldn't help her if I wasn't happy. When I moved back with my aunt, I started going to school. Picking my grades up was a struggle, but I tried. Three years later I graduated from high school. My relationship with my mom got much better because I learned to accept that she did the best she could do. I learned about my mother's childhood and understood why things were the way they were. I learned that hurt people, hurt people. My mom experienced the same things I did in her younger years.

I am still overprotective of my sister. I still remember *that day* as if it were happening right now, but I am inspired to *tell*—for Jazzy's sake. It's getting better. I still wonder how and why my mom could forget her oldest child. However, I am learning the *power* of forgiveness. I learned that I don't have to live with my sister to nurture her. I am still learning how to forgive my mom. I am not fully ready to accept my mom as my mother, but I love her and I can finally call her my friend.

Charon Acevedo is nineteen years old and resides in Brooklyn, New York, with her aunt and her cousin. She continues to search for answers as she participates with women's growth groups and other community activities to help others build connections and transform their lives.

Motherless Child

By Barbara L. Jackson

I recently wept for my mother because I could no longer let her weep alone in the face of being a motherless child. As each year passes, the well of her tears runs dryer as Leola Cooper remains a present memory.

I had a front-row seat for years as she spent Mother's Day after Mother's Day silently questioning why her own mother died when she was a child, just a few days after what would be her last Mother's Day.

Growing up, I had always noticed her somber air and tear-stained cheeks every May, but it wasn't until recently that I deeply contemplated what life could be like for a girl growing up without a mother. One night as I lay in bed alone with nothing but my thoughts, I wept uncontrollably at just the notion of growing up without a mother. Then I began to consider the even more compelling thought of how a woman with no mother could become an example of the perfect mother.

January 26, 1967, was the day the Cooper family welcomed Trina Marsha into the world at St. Margaret's Hospital in Montgomery, Alabama. With two sisters and four brothers preceding her, she was the seventh of what would be eight children. Just four months after her second birthday and seven months after the welcoming of the last addition to the family, she witnessed the death and burial of her mother—an event she was too young to understand. She and her younger sister were not able to attend the funeral, so her years of mourning can be attributed to her inability to mourn as a child.

In spite of the major absence, she grew up in a home that was grounded in family and God. With a father who was a pastor and a responsible older sister, she was well taken care of. Two months after the death of her mother, Trina's father remarried. Although she was given a new stepmother who would be the only mother she would ever know, a concrete relationship never solidified between them. She was her father's wife.

At eighteen, the circumstance of her teenage pregnancy caused her to look for housing outside of her home. She found herself on Oak Street under the roof of her future husband's childhood home. There his mother became a supreme mother figure to her, providing food, clothing, advice, and shelter so she could complete her high school education and make a life for herself and her child.

March 7, 1986—nineteen years after her birth and seventeen years after the death of her own mother, Trina became a mother, to me, the first of her three children. After getting on her feet and finally accepting my father's request of her hand in marriage (on his third attempt), she began her journey as a military spouse. With my father out to sea months at a time, it was just she and I for a while. I don't remember much about those years aside from what can be seen in a scarce collection of old photos, but from those I can tell that we had an undeniable connection. I do remember, however, at the age of thirteen, when that connection was threatened by the force that was my teenage years.

I remember the day I told my mother that I hated her as though it was yesterday. We had been butting heads for a while because she was trying to raise me to be something that I just wasn't ready to be: a productive young woman. One afternoon, months of contention came to a head, propelling me to say the very thing I had sworn I would never say to her. Filled with confusion, anger, and under the umbrella of adolescence, I felt the regret circulating in my heart just as the words rolled off my tongue, but a deep pride wouldn't let me trap the words before they escaped. This was what I felt, or at least thought I felt at the time, so I had to say it. I remember the look on her face as she received these words while sitting in the study of our cramped apartment. No doubt the space, which was too small for us, could not fit the girth of the word that I had put in the atmosphere, but it was there along with my mother's tears and heartache. And it was quickly joined by her words: "I am not perfect, but you treat me like I'm a villain. I only want what's best for you and wish I had a mother to teach me the things I try to instill in you."

I never knew the weight the latter part of her statement bore on all of our lives, nor how much her words would later haunt me, but they did one night while I lay in the bed of my whitewashed Syracuse apartment. Looking up at the ceiling, hoping to see a glimpse of God, I wondered how I had gotten to this place. How at age twenty-three I would soon hold the title as a master's graduate, how I had a strong sense of God, how I hadn't repeated the family cycle of becoming a teenage mother, and how I had a strong will to never give up. The sum of this equation was and is my mom.

Her strength and desire to see a life for her children that she herself never had lifted me to a plateau of success. Although she has not yet had the opportunity to go to college, she was the reason I was able to make it to grad school. When I left undergrad she said to me, "Okay, we got you through college, now you have to get yourself through grad school." I was prepared to do that, but when I arrived in Syracuse I had signed up for a little more than I could handle—living expenses, food, bills. My heart was heavy and my head was about to explode. Lo and behold, my mother sacrificed a large portion of her monthly checks to make sure I had a place to live, food, and a few luxuries, even though allowing me that caused her to go without.

She was always a strong motivating force in every area of my life. Her keen sense of spirit has loomed over me and no doubt protected me from many situations. Like the old song says, "My mother prayed for me, had me on her mind." When I was younger I never understood that she was overprotective because she wanted to be ever-present in my life, as she didn't have a mother in hers. All I could comprehend was that she didn't want me to stay the night at my friend's house. I was oblivious to the fact that the reason she kept her face in the Bible and eyes stayed on *Him* was in part because she was searching for instructions on how to be a good mother because she had no example of her own. I thought that she was seeking God wanting me to behave, and not on my behalf. I only wish I understood then what I understand now, that by the grace of God a motherless child can be an effective presence in the lives of her children. Although it took some time for me to fully see my mom's point of view, I now see it and I praise, adore, and above all honor her for who she is in my life. And I praise God that I am not a motherless child.

Barbara L. Jackson received her undergraduate degree in English from Mary Baldwin College and her master's degree in magazine, newspaper, and online journalism from Syracuse University. She is a poet, singer, and creative writer who enjoys capturing the lives and stories of others. Her future plans include traveling the world as well as reporting an extensive piece on the African American experience from plantations to present.

Orphan on the Block

By Denika Donahue

Surrounded by over eight hundred other college students, sitting in anticipation as the loudspeaker echoed one of the guest speakers' voices, I started to reminisce. I was my mother's first child, born on the Fourth of July in Chicago, Illinois. There were four of us, and as my mother's drug addiction increased, we were removed from her legal care and released to my grandmother's custody. We were happy; our grandma was everything to us.

Until the summer of 1993. It was my seventh birthday, and I had a party complete with BBQ and fireworks. My mom came to the party, which was such a treat. It was getting dark, and my little sister Miata saw my mom walking away and ran after her. My mother was not allowed by court order to take us anywhere. Miata was told several times no, and eventually my mom allowed her to go. A few minutes later we heard screams and my sister's cries. My sister had been struck with a firecracker rocket that landed directly in her left eye.

Every adult rushed out of the house. It was then, in that moment, I knew something had gone terribly wrong. Before you knew it, my baby sister was pronounced dead. Within an instant, my siblings and I were removed from my grandmother's home and placed in the custody of the Illinois Department of Children and Family Services (DCFS). It was difficult being separated from the family that I grew up with and loved. It was even harder to be separated from my sisters. I barely had a chance to mourn.

There was a series of shelters and foster homes. Since I was the new foster child, everyone picked on me. I became depressed and would keep to myself. There was one foster parent who starved us and slapped us for no apparent reason. There were people who left us locked up in a room for hours or days, and foster parents who mentally abused me and the other foster children. I did not get it—they were supposed to be nurturing, but instead they were brutal.

I was constantly reminded that I would be like my mom: a drug addict. There were others who said I was never going to amount to anything, that I was ugly, stupid, or dumb. I was finally placed in a stable foster home. My tears, fears, and lots of strangers kept me scared and feeling alone. I remember praying every night to God to be back with my sisters, the only family I knew, trusted, and loved. I remember also screaming to God, asking, "Why did this happen to me?" Praying was something my grandmother taught me how to do when I was a toddler that stuck with me my whole life.

My way back down memory lane was interrupted by the claps and screams of joy and happiness as the dean asked the crowd to give applause of appreciation to the speaker who just finished her sermon. As the dean announced one of the professors who would be reading off the names of the graduates in the field of arts and sciences, I drifted back into time. Once placed into my stable foster home, I stayed to myself. I wouldn't speak to the other children or my foster mom. At school I would stay to myself, afraid to let anyone in. I needed to repeat the second grade, but I was slowly beginning to open up to my new family.

By the third year with my foster mom, I was beginning to trust and develop love for her and her family. But I always felt unhappy because I couldn't be with my biological family, and I had not seen my siblings in almost four years. I began to have visitations with my younger siblings in 1997, which made me happy.

After about two years the visitations stopped and I began to feel angry at everyone and everything. My sisters were abused by their foster parents and there was nothing I could do. I hated my birth mom for years because she was not able to control her addiction. At times my foster mom tried to comfort me, to make me feel like I was a part of her family, and so did her kids. When the neighborhood children learned I was a foster child, they treated me differently. They would whisper about me, then point and giggle. They talked about my clothes and how I had a mom who was on crack. They picked fights with me and deemed me the "orphan on the block."

It was seventh grade when I met a teacher who seemed to understand me, who seemed to understand what I was going through, who helped uplift me and connected with me. It was then I declared I had the ability to choose the outcome of my life. As I got older, my foster mom became even more frustrated, and it turned to mental abuse. I decided that I was going to love myself and become a strong person! I transformed from that scared, crying little girl into a teenager who set out to accomplish goals. Once I got to high school, I made the choice not to be sexually active because I didn't want to catch a disease or become pregnant. Since I was a victim of drug abuse without ever taking drugs myself, I made a decision that I would never consume any drugs. I made the choice that I would not be like my mother!

By the time I was a sophomore in high school, my foster mom was under a tremendous amount of pressure, and although she was a caring person, it just did not work out well. Her sons treated me like I was their biological sister. Her youngest son always looked out for me; he talked to me about guys, life, and peer pressure.

To avoid any issues, I decided if I stayed busy at school, when I came home it would be time to eat and go to bed. I got on spirit club, yearbook, newspaper, played softball and basketball. I felt incomplete, unhappy, and empty at times, but I was determined to achieve my goal and set an example for my younger foster sisters and for my biological siblings.

I reconnected with my biological family, and after the

threats of my foster mom saying she was going to give me back to the shelter, I had my caseworker push for me to return to my grandmother. I left a safer South Side environment to the West Side of Chicago, which some would say is "the ghetto."

One thing that I have learned is that when you move around, you never really feel like you fit in. I had to adjust all over again to people I hadn't seen in years. I continued to attend the same high school, and when senior year came I was an honor student and I started receiving scholarship offers from various colleges. My first goal was accomplished! I graduated from high school on the honor roll and had no children! I was determined not to be another statistic!

In my freshman year I made the mistake of going out to parties, then coming back to the dorms and trying to study for exams at the last minute, and the outcome was AP (academic probation). Once I saw this, during the second semester of my freshman year I knew I had to get focused. I realized my dreams and goals had to be reinforced because I never wanted to be a failure to myself.

By sophomore year I was off AP. I had tutors to help me study for exams. I stopped hanging with associates who didn't care about their grades and focused on hanging with people who were positive and had a similar goal of achieving their dreams. These three people became my friends / family, as we used to say. I was a part of Poetry Pioneer, NAACP, and found a part-time job. I struggled financially in college. I remember when $20 lasted me for a month.

I didn't have a mom or father to send any money like many of the students. There were times I wanted to quit. Things became tough; there was rent, car note and insurance, groceries, etc. But those were the choices I made, and I struggled, but I learned to manage money to make things work. When my grandmother got very sick and had surgery, she went into a coma for two months. I was scared and couldn't focus on my schoolwork. Then there were the relationship problems with my boyfriend. But in order for me to stay on the right track, I had to stay focused and know God was my rock!

I often thought about my siblings, wondering how were they doing, did they even remember me, did they even have the same thoughts I had. I made the decision and choice that I would try to get in touch with them. One summer I came to visit my family and I was able to go back to work as the assistant coordinator for the Teen Scholar program. I told my GAL as well as my caseworker of my determination to find my siblings, and with their help I located several of them. Some were adopted, and the adopted parents wanted no contact with their real family. But I found out about my two sisters, the ones I've always thought about since we were seven. One was adopted and the other had a legal guardian. I obtained their foster parents' contact numbers and called them, hoping they would allow me to meet with them and show them the positive, smart, loving, strong young lady I had become and they would allow me to visit with my sisters. We stayed in touch from that point on. I have overcome obstacles that I can't even seem to put into words, yet I continue to get on my knees and thank God for the blessing and positive people he put in my life!

"Denika Donahue," I heard over the loudspeaker, bringing me back in tune with the reality of this very moment. With tears slowly emerging from my eyes onto my cheeks, I stood up and walked to the stage, shaking the professor's and then the dean's hand while I received my degree cover. As I looked out to the many families and friends and fellow classmates, I smiled with amazing belief. Though many people face adversity, obstacles, and different struggles each day that may be considered worse than mine, if someone lived in my shoes up until now, they would understand those tears of happiness, joy, confidence, and maturity! Making it back to my seat while the other graduates' names were being called, I drifted back into my thoughts.

I was able to emancipate out of the DCFS system, and I worked on the relationship with my mom. I stopped blaming her for the past and realized that I had control all along on the outcome of my life because I stopped and made the choices necessary to get me where I am today. It was not easy, but I made it.

I felt a finger tapping me on my shoulders, summoning my attention to one of my classmates yelling with excitement, "Denika, girl, snap out of it. Looks like you was in a daze or daydreaming." I smiled, thinking, *If she only knew*. Then over the loudspeakers and on the different TV monitors the dean said, "Will the graduate class of '09 stand, take your tassels, and place them to the left." Then he presented us: "Congratulations, graduates of 2009!" Cameras flashing, lots of people screaming and yelling with joy, tears flowing down some of my fellow classmates' cheeks, hugs being passed from every direction, caps being thrown in the air, excitement all around. The power of choices many of my fellow classmates made to experience the same feeling on this day—May 10, 2009—to succeed no matter the obstacle faced! Not bad for the orphan of the block.

Denika Donahue is a caring, dependable, and loving individual who's very ambitious and smart! Denika Donahue is a strong-minded, self-determined young woman who challenges obstacles and roadblocks and overcomes them! She loves to help others and is inspired every day to stay focused and positive in life!

Mothers Are Wise

By Tinisha Nicole Johnson

I have many fond memories of this woman, now in her late fifties. Mrs. Eula, as some called her. She's old school and walked the same streets as did Dr. Martin Luther King Jr., telling her stories to me about the struggles and the mayhem in the Deep South. This woman is known for her kind heart and giving nature. I have learned a lot from her, and who wouldn't? She has many stories to tell. Coming from a family of eleven siblings, she was the second oldest, so taking care of people was a trait that she knew very well. Her deep southern Memphis accent is abrupt, yet welcoming and loving. I went over to her house the other day, my normal routine.

"Is that you?" she asked as I came through the back door.

"Yes, it is, ma'am," I called back in a muffled voice. I had a white small prescription bag for her high blood pressure and arthritis stuffed between my lips, while trying to juggle two bags of groceries, a bag of ice, my keys and purse.

She sat in her favorite brown leather chair as usual when I arrived. She began humming a song from Stevie Wonder called "I Just Called to Say I Love You." It was a hot summer day, late August, and the trees stood still in the dry heat and the birds played and chirped their own melodies in the top branches of the trees. Across the way, kids raced against each other in the yard, but not before they changed into their play clothes, jumping through sprinklers, and playing Slip 'n Slide. Watching them, I remembered back to my childhood and a smile presented itself on my face.

I walked back over to Mrs. Eula and picked up a hair comb from the side table. She looked back at me with her big dark brown eyes, which had a long history in them. She grinned from ear to ear and I could see the gap between her teeth. She turned back around and handed me some green hair grease. I began parting her hair into sections with the comb as she continued to hum, moving on to a song I've heard before by Smokey Robinson.

I tuned in to the song while I applied a thin layer of green grease, which was nothing more than a mixture of petroleum, aloe vera, vitamins, and castor oil, onto her scalp. Her hair was thick, pepper-colored, and coarse. I combed through from the root to the ends. Afterward, I pulled her hair up with a scarf and noticed she'd fallen asleep. I grabbed a bottle of lotion and rubbed a little on her dark, swollen legs. I knew elevation would help the circulation, so I propped them up on a leg rest nearby.

We have always had a close relationship. She is an outgoing woman. She tells it like it is, bold as she may be with her words sometimes, but her point is understood and heard loud and clear. Her kindness is noticed, and people from her church love to visit us on Sunday afternoons for a meal that completely satisfies an empty stomach.

As a young woman, I needed that. I wanted the wisdom from someone older, so I could maybe learn a thing or two and apply it in my life without having to learn by failing so many times. We didn't always agree on everything, but to know she cared and would run to my rescue was reassuring.

I looked in the refrigerator to get some sugar for my tea, because I knew that's where she kept it. She refrigerated everything from bread to cereal, even peanut butter. I scooped two spoonfuls in my cup and turned around to go back into the living room where she was.

I walked around the living room, looking at the many pictures she had placed across the shelves above the fireplace. You can't help but think of your childhood. It's what contributes to who you are. I can't always say I had a close relationship with my father, although he was in my life, but I did have a close relationship with Mrs. Eula. The type of relationship I think every young woman should experience. She was dear to my heart and taught me many lessons—like not to settle, and how to cook, how to think for myself, and not to open my legs to every man who charmed me—simple lessons, but ones that can be overlooked when you're young and naïve and living in a world with so many opportunities and tests.

I sipped on my steamy hot tea—now, why I was drinking hot tea on a hot day was beyond me, but it felt soothing going down my throat as I continued to walk down memory lane, wondering how I became the person I am. I looked back over at her as she lay peacefully with prescription bottles scattered on the coffee table. I knew her weight was the cause of her health problems. Exercise was not a part of her life. Instead, foods like fried catfish, fried chicken, collard greens with salty neck bones, ham hocks in the green beans, and candied yams drenched in brown sugar and syrup made up her diet. And let's not get on all the soda cans that filled her cabinets. She was the best cook I knew, besides my grandmother, but I also knew if anything, it was not healthy her five-foot-three, 290-pound frame.

I sat down on the couch next to her and rubbed my hand gently up her arm. I continued to sip on my tea, reminiscing. It truly dawned on me that I had such a wonderful mother and best friend. I love Mrs. Eula, and so do the many people whose lives she has touched.

I know many women have stories relating to their mother in the past and present tense, childhood memories especially. Even to this day, I am still very close to my mother, Mrs. Eula, and I learned so much from her. Everyone can learn something from their mother. She has knowledge and experience that should not be taken lightly.

If I learned anything, it's to always listen to your mother sincerely. You may not agree with her words or even follow her directions, but at least listen intently and understand where she's coming from.

I now know why Mother's Day is so important and so celebrated—in recognition of the wealth of generational lessons learned from wise mothers everywhere.

Tinisha Nicole Johnson is an author, poet, entrepreneur, and cofounder of Authors Supporting Authors (ASA), an organization that promotes avid reading and provides support and resources to authors. Her work has been featured in *Chicken Soup for the African American Soul, Chicken Soup for the Soul: Moms & Sons, Step Up to the Mic: A Poetic Explosion,* and the *Denver Examiner,* and she is a columnist for Sisters Space—Empowering Women of Color. Tinisha is a mother of two and currently resides in Denver, Colorado.

If I Knew Then What I Know Now About Motherhood . . .

Lately, I've been going to all these high schools talking to the students, answering their questions, listening to what they have to say. It has been an incredible journey to be around them and try to give them what my mother gave me.
—Jill Scott

The African proverb "It takes a village to raise a child" makes us all mothers. We as women are responsible to mother those who come up around us. We need to take responsibility as mothers, sisters, aunties, grandmas, and nanas. We need to stand side by side in the nurturing of all women. We are called to be those mothers who pick up the slack and give the best they have to offer to the daughters who don't have the information they need to become the next generation of mothers.

The Window Within

By Latonya P. Story

I never want to pass judgment or blame when it comes to my childhood struggles. At the age of twenty-one, which seemed so young, I felt as if I had been through more than a sixty-year-old. You name it, I experienced it in my childhood: humiliation, abuse, desertion, pregnancy, poverty, loneliness, and pain. My mother was on drugs.

My mother was on anything she could get her hands on. She would disappear for days at a time and still somehow seemed like a fit mother to friends, family, and the community. We were whipped into not saying anything to anybody about our home. When I spoke out at school and told a teacher that my mother was on drugs, she showed up and adamantly denied it, calling me a liar, and when I got home I was whipped so bad that I fell asleep from the exhaustion. But my younger brother and I knew better. As I saw it, for my mother to turn to drugs was a strong indication of something vital lacking in her life. Was she not happy with my brother, my sister, and me? Was she unhappy with her husband, my stepfather?

As I knelt at the foot of my bed each night, I would pray that things would change. Was it too much to ask to grow up in a normal family? My dream of normal was a supportive mother at home with dinner ready, a loving father going out to make a living, and a little white picket fence. Who's to say that this was the norm?

I did, and it was what I longed for. I longed for the life we had when the house smelled of a combination of Pine-Sol and Clorox. The kitchen was filled with the aroma of mackerel cakes, fried potatoes and onions, and spinach. My mother had dark, beautiful skin. She was short in stature with strands of hair under her chin that you could see as she leaned over the kitchen sink with sweat dripping from her nose, saying, "Hello, baby." The windows were open and the sunlight filled the rooms.

She would be singing Shirley Caesar songs and other gospel classics. When I was a child, I hated for my mother to sing because she would always sing so loud and had such a strong gospel voice. She was not one who could sing R&B; she would turn everything into a gospel hit! I can't imagine what was going on in her mind to make her want to give this up.

The strict disciplinarian, yet loving mother, changed into an entirely different person. It was the day she had my stepfather arrested for molesting me. He had done it for years, and I suffered in silence until I could not take it anymore. Maybe she blamed herself, but after he was arrested and sentenced, she never returned to herself.

It was as if she gave up on us and herself. I received social security checks, and our cable and light bills were behind. We did not have any clothes and we were hungry. When the check arrived, I cashed it and paid all of our bills and bought my brother some new clothes. When my mother got home, the rage in her eyes was incredible when she recognized that the check was gone. She terrified me. She beat me so badly and said she was returning my brother's clothes for cheaper ones. She returned a week later without the clothes.

I escaped at sixteen and had a baby, hoping to be loved. My relationship with my children's father was a cry for love, attention, and acceptance. Every relationship since has been an unsuccessful attempt at searching for the love I was denied in my youth. Now I see it was parental love that I longed for. This love I've since found in God. Parental love is unconditional, encouraging, rewarding, and stable. All my stability was snatched from me because my mother needed to find her own.

In high school, I was in almost every activity I could get in. I was in honors and Advanced Placement courses. I stayed busy. I would catch the late, late bus home from school activities to avoid going home. I was happy on the outside, but no one knew the pain inside. School was an escape for me, to put up a façade on a crumbling life at home.

Getting off the bus and approaching my house was a

gamble. If the shades were open and the door was ajar, it usually meant my mom was sober and happy. If the shades were closed and it looked dark, it was a strong indication that she was high and ready to explode. At times, I would have to hold her when she was crying, defend myself when she wanted to fight, or call an ambulance when she had an overdose. She was once a heavy, big-boned woman, but began to dwindle in size to look like my equal. I've witnessed my mother being punched in the face by a drug dealer and losing her front tooth. I've witnessed every single piece of furniture in our house sold in order for her to buy drugs.

I had to shelter my younger brother and pretend everything was all right. He was young, but so smart. He found traces of cocaine on the dresser, but I told him it was baking soda. He found syringes in the clothes dryer in her failed attempt to hide them. I would be up all night waiting for her to come home. Sometimes she would stay away for days at a time. I would get up early to get my brother ready for school, then go to school myself. Two kids, left alone to fend for themselves. My teachers never knew, my classmates never knew, nor our extended family. There is too much to tell, too much to relive, but I do not hate her. In her, I see myself. In her, I see what I do not want to become. I see similarities, but I am taking steps to resolve them. She tried through drugs and men to find happiness.

On July 7, 2003, my mother died in federal custody. She had been sentenced to prison on a felony charge. I hadn't spoken to my mother for two years prior to her death. My brother and I had decided to set a date to visit and reach out to her, but that date never came. For the past five years, I've had to deal with the guilt of her not knowing how much we loved and cared for her and, most importantly, that we forgave her. We are adults now and are responsible for our own actions and mistakes. When I'm alone, I often cry, thinking back on what could've been had she not begun using drugs. There are other dark pockets that I wish to not let the light expose, but even in those secrets, there is forgiveness. Upon burying my mother, I received a call from the prison chaplain, who shared with me that my mother had given her life to Christ before her death and was heavily involved in prison ministry. I received a bundle of letters from other inmates who described a woman who was foreign to me, a woman who read a Bible daily, ministered to other women, and was kind and generous.

As for me, I am now living my dream. I am CEO / founder of LPS Consulting PR, which represents athletes and celebrities. My children, two of whom are now adults—my oldest son is twenty years old, my daughter is eighteen, and my youngest is thirteen. I located my biological father. He is more than I could have ever imagined in a dad. Although I wish I would've known him when I was younger (my mother's pregnancy was kept from him, so he was unaware of my birth), I met him when I was supposed to. He traveled with me to West Virginia to bury her along with my wonderful stepmother and newfound brother and sister.

I miss that short, black woman singing her songs. I miss the smell of mackerel cakes and potatoes. I miss her warm, cuddly hugs. I miss her discipline. I miss her. Not to understand what caused her pain would be a tragedy. Not to forgive her, not to love her would be cruel.

She wanted the approval of others so much, just as I do at times. Maybe I should have complimented her magnificent voice. I know now it is not my fault. I have to keep living. And God, He finally gave my mother a new life.

IN HIS ARMS

In His Arms I place my trust
In Him I place my all

The cares and temptations that held me down
I now place upon His Throne

In His Arms I place new Faith
I'm armed with the Word of God

For no weapon formed against me shall prosper
For He leads me beside the still waters

In His Arms I place my son
God, keep him safe from harm

Let him know I'm in a better place
And that I believe he will go far

In His Arms I place my daughters
God, show them who they are in You

Virtuous women, destined to be great
Living examples and overcomers in Truth

In His Arms I now rest my head
My course, this race is now complete

My struggles, my addictions I've overcome
Rest assured, take comfort, I made it over to ETERNITY.

Read at Homegoing Service of Margaret L. Loving. The window within is where I found peace and where you can find a new beginning. . . .

Latonya P. Story is the CEO of LPS Consulting, a premier public relations firm that represents several players in the National Football League. LaTonya serves on the board and is director of special events for the National Football League Fathers Association.

Your Soul's Sustenance

Find the mother in you. Physically giving birth isn't what makes you a mother, but nurturing our young women and being a positive example to them make you a mother. Know that you have a great influence over young women just by the example you are to them. Don't judge them, but lead them. Meet young women where they're at and listen intently to what they're saying, even if it doesn't make sense to you. Be that quiet compass to lead them on the path to the greatness that they have the potential to achieve. Go ahead, mama, and show them how it's done!

Personal Book of Revelations

- *Do you have a mother figure in your life besides your biological mother?*
- *How would you be different from your mom?*
- *What are the qualities that your mother possesses that you admire and want to emulate?*
- *Is it okay to dislike your mother?*
- *Do you know your mother as a woman?*
- *What are the sacrifices your mother has made in your life?*

V

Is This Love, a Relationship, Marriage, or Just Hooking Up?

There's definitely a dangerous feeling when you're in love—it's giving your heart to someone else and knowing that they have control over your feelings. I know for me, who always tries to be so tough, that's the dangerous thing.
—Beyoncé Knowles

Love has the power to both nourish and feed the soul. It can be the most amazing experience to have someone that you love, trust, and respect and to have these feelings mutually returned. It is almost a breath of fresh air to have a partner that you can share your hopes and dreams with, exchange ideas; together you can do almost anything.

Times have certainly changed, and now young women are settling more and more often to just "hook up" for a physical relationship with no strings attached. We see more instances of "sexting" and meeting in chat rooms to hook up for sex. There is a huge disconnect between what we were taught and the evolution of what has become of dating in America. But didn't we see this coming? With the advent of the video age and the introduction of the Internet, we see more girls succumbing to the sexual images instead of believing in having a solid relationship with a respectable young man.

While many young women have revealed to us that they desire a stable, loving relationship, they just aren't sure if it exists. Once you begin to doubt your true desires for a mutually respectable relationship, you are susceptible to giving in to the desire to just have a man in your life. We can't tell you how many women we've met that just wanted a man and got just what they asked for. For the sake of saying they had a man in their lives, many women were left miserable, never feeling loved or fulfilled. Some were mentally and physically abused, while others believed the lies they were told that they would never be able to find another man.

The only thing you can control in a relationship is how you will accept being treated. If you accept mediocrity, you will get mediocrity. If you accept meaningless, emotionless sex, that is exactly what you will get. You can only be treated in a relationship in the manner in which you allow someone to treat you. Know that you deserve the best a man has to offer. If you know this, there is nothing less you will accept in your life. In this chapter, women share their joy and heartbreak in hopes of healing their hearts and opening up yours.

"I Love You. Do You Love Me? Can We Be Friends?"

By Syreta J. Oglesby

Love can often deal you an interesting hand in the game of life. Sometimes, it works out, and other times, things fall apart. This story is one that is not unusual. Breakups, be they good or bad, can be heard as a subject on television talk shows, in books and magazines, and among groups of men and women everywhere. Yet everyone can agree breakups are difficult.

Victor and I appeared to be on the road leading to marriage. He and I met through a mutual friend during my senior year of college. What was just a friendship soon developed into a deep love and admiration for one another. He and I would bond and support one another through everything, despite me having to move back home to New Jersey after graduation. Many of my peers and family members thought that I ought not continue to date him due to our distance. However, Victor and I were determined to make it work. Therefore, we relied on constant contact with one another, and on monthly visits. He and I both knew that eventually we would have to unite in one place. As that discussion became more relevant, the concept of marriage became more real to both of us after two years of being together.

Marriage is an interesting dynamic, because while it unites two people as one, it also has the ability to cause a rift between two people. Though I had my reservations about marriage, I had convinced myself that it was not a bad idea. Victor had received a lucrative offer to move to a new job in Seattle, Washington. While I had been working and sacrificing so much to achieve my dream of becoming a success story in the entertainment industry, I contemplated giving it up for the sake of love and happiness. This was a life-altering decision, but I would make it with no hesitation because success without anyone to share it with sounded like misery to me. Just as I was drafting up my resignation to submit to my corporate employer, pack up my life, and move, Victor informed me that he no longer wanted a relationship.

I could not believe that a week before our three-year anniversary, the man I came to love and adore could say that he did not feel the same way about me. After all, I was supportive, loyal, faithful, honest, sincere, considerate, and unconditional. I could not understand what was so hard about loving me back when I tried and gave my all to make it work. I was never much for crying over relationships, but when I thought of my investment of time, energy, and emotions, I could do nothing but cry. I could only compare this experience to the grief of losing a loved one. My grieving was not only of sadness, but one of anger and rage that had me wanting to be vengeful toward the man who had once put a move on my heart.

"I love you. Do you love me? Can we be friends?" are the words that were texted to me on what would have been our three-year anniversary. When I read those words, so many things ran through my mind. Though I had been deleting all of his prior attempts through e-mails, text messages, and voice messages to apologize for hurting me, this text message had me feeling that my heart was going to burst. Though I was extremely saddened, I could not deny that part of me that still was in love with him. I decided to acknowledge his message by calling him back. I wanted to hear what he had to say.

Our conversation began as a general one, with little to no mention of the breakup. It quickly turned into one filled with me expressing the feeling of deep confusion of how conditional and selfish I thought he was for acting as if my emotions were objects that could be as mechanical as an on-and-off switch. While I did all I could to contain my emotions, the fact remained that I was still hurt. There was no apology that could change the feeling of betrayal I felt toward Victor.

My breakup had me at my breaking point as a woman. I kept thinking, *How am I to pick up the pieces to my life, especially since I made plans and included Victor in every one of them?* It was then that I received a reality check like no other. There was nothing more to say. There was nothing more for either one of us to do. Our relationship had run its course. I have no regrets, because what Victor and I was, was beautiful when we were in love. Yet the fact remained that I had to move on with my life. I would rather not let another person destroy my spirit, my need to love and be loved, and ultimately determine my desire to be happy.

My breakup in many ways made me a stronger individual. Being in a relationship can oftentimes make a person lose sight of self. The separation made me see things through a much clearer set of eyes. It allowed me to understand that I am never to make others a priority when they make me an option. It made me understand that it was okay to have high expectations for a mate, so that I wouldn't settle just to be with someone who did not understand or appreciate me. It gave me the courage to shed my corporate shackles to pursue my dream of being a success story in the entertainment industry. More importantly, it made me understand that there is a reason for everything. I may or may never get married. I may or may never experience love again, but I am grateful all the more for having the chance to love. However, for this moment and until I meet the one who I am to share my life with, I shall remain in love with Syreta.

Syreta J. Oglesby, twenty-eight, is a lifelong native of Jersey City, New Jersey. She is a proud graduate of Spelman

College, where she completed her B.A. in English in 2003. Syreta serves as the group director of the Purple Agency and serves as a lifestyle PR and marketing consultant to Universal Motown Records, and is a member of Delta Sigma Theta Sorority, Inc., Northern New Jersey Chapter of National Alumnae Association of Spelman College, and Women in Entertainment Empowerment Network (WEEN).

Big Country

By Kristen Rogers

I was running late for my hair appointment at one of New York's most trendy salons in Brooklyn. Fifteen minutes late, to be exact. My list of things to do was getting longer as I prepared to fly to Detroit the next day to attend an international conference for entrepreneurs. It is rare that I venture outside of Manhattan since I moved here several years ago, but I was working on becoming more open in my endeavors to explore the unknown. Since this was only my second time visiting this hair salon, I exited the subway station at the wrong intersection. When I reached the street corner, everything looked unfamiliar, and in my haste I headed farther away from the hair salon.

As I walked by one of the outdoor cafés, I caught a glimpse of him. It seems like every woman has one. The man that built you up to break your heart. His back was toward me but after eight years, I knew it was him. Big Country was from St. Louis, and with eight million people I could still pick out that head and those shoulders anywhere. He was seated with a woman, and my first thought after initially passing them was that I should keep going and not acknowledge him. I got halfway down the street, paused after the shock subsided, and after my heart went back to its normal rhythm, I gathered myself and thought, *No—I am stronger now.* I doubled back to where they were sitting—it was part curiosity, but more of *you're over him.* I tapped him gently on the shoulder.

Big Country spun around to meet my eyes and the look on his face said, "I just saw a ghost." He stood silent for a moment and then gushed, "I didn't expect to see you here!" I responded, "I know, me, in Brooklyn, in the middle of the day . . ." Immediately, in my politically correct way, I extended my hand to the young lady seated across from him and introduced myself. "Hi, I'm Kristen." She smiled and reciprocated the gesture. His lunch companion was lovely, had innocent eyes, and was well put together—not a hair out of place. Still in shock, Big Country asked me what I was doing in this part of town. I answered, and without my having to ask, he explained his reason for being in New York on a random Friday afternoon. To my knowledge he had not traveled to New York City in four years, since we stopped dating and officially stopped consistent communication.

Big Country and I met in college. I was young and naïve, and he was preying on my type. Meticulous about most things, including his women, he expressed his interest in me for an entire year. Four years older, former college football jock, more life experience and certainly more street-wise, he finally won my affection. We began dating my junior year in college. At first we were inseparable. He cooked me breakfast and dinner, took me to the library on weekends, attended church religiously on Sunday, gave me life advice, and made me feel safe at night. You could say that he picked up where my dad left off once my parents sent me to school. Big Country had the father-figure demeanor. He always warned me of the sour intentions of others, even those close to me. In my naïveté, I never backed down without a fight, arguing that he was wrong for always looking at the faults of others instead of the good. Truthfully, most times, he was right. Some friends turned out to be counterfeits and some guys were trying to hit on me while posing as "just friends." A couple of years into our relationship, I stopped fighting him and began loving him. I listened and took his counsel with an open ear and an open heart. Little did I know that this cautionary counsel would one day apply to my relationship with him.

Our relationship was not an easy road. Big Country saw things one way and I saw things another. We came from two different worlds. His was more like *Good Times* and mine was similar to *The Cosby Show*. But somehow we made it work. With every disagreement, there was an equal make-up session. When his mom died, I flew from school to St. Louis and spent a week with him and his family to show my support. After the dust cleared on this unfortunate event, we came to a crossroad. Discussions began brewing about him moving back to St. Louis to help settle his mother's estate and be there for his family. Three months later, he was gone. We made the decision to continue our relationship long-distance, but that didn't last long. I had been there before and although he had not, we both knew the outcome. I decided to end our relationship; however, that, too, was short-lived. We continued in an on-and-off status for another year. Afterward we returned to friends, but it was never "just friends." There was always a romantic air between us, one that for me became unhealthy and unrealistic. Shortly after I finished college in Hampton, Virginia, I moved to New York, and the divide really began. I started a new life and he was still stuck in his St. Louis way of thinking. I took on the big-city life and big-city dreams, and he settled for being a big fish in a small pond. We were again unequally yoked.

Looking back, opposites certainly attracted. I remember wanting to take him home to meet my parents. It took me almost two years into our relationship to invite him to Florida to meet Mr. and Mrs. Rogers. I grew up in the south suburbs of Chicago. My parents sacrificed for me to go to the best schools in the best district, and later, to a private high school. The Rogerses were an institution, a privilege to grow up in this household. You knew that since you were a Rogers kid, you not only were afforded the best, but the best was expected of you. Sometimes I missed the mark, but most times I made my parents proud.

When I moved to New York, I had one thing on my mind: to *take over*. New York is the place for big dreamers, and I inhaled that as soon as I stepped on New York City streets in 2003 to do an internship for *Savoy* magazine. I fit here.

I could be a struggling artist, and it was accepted here. No one would look down on me or expect me to be conventional in my approach for success. I could spread my wings and fly and not be contained by the thoughts of others less ambitious. I set out to make a name for myself. Big Country always understood my big dreams, but we never came back together on our plans for life and the future. He was in his world and I was in mine, and they never met in the middle again.

When I decided once and for all that we would finally go our separate ways, I have to admit I had my second thoughts. He had been a fixture in my life for nearly the last eight years. I prayed, "God, did I do the right thing? Is it over for good?" I quickly got my answer. Fifteen minutes late and a wrong turn from the subway station gave me all the confirmation I needed. It was over, but it wasn't a total loss. He taught me how to love with my heart and not just my head; how to believe what people do and not just what they say; how to protect myself from those people who had bad intentions and didn't care about my wellbeing. He taught me how to stand on my own two feet and fight back. He also taught me how to make a decision and stick with it—walk away when it was over and never look back.

All of a sudden the tables had turned. This once dominant, strong, confident, and assured man was now stumbling over his words and struggling in his speech. Big Country thought he could quietly come to New York with another young lady and I wouldn't find out. God had a plan bigger than his. It was time to move on—for good. No more questioning myself and no more looking back. Off to bigger and better things, and to continue the path that I set out for myself: to take over.

"What are you doing later?" he managed to say under his breath.

"Packing. I'm flying to Detroit tomorrow for an entrepreneurs conference. Take care, you guys." No time for small talk. Good-bye, Big Country. Big things await me, and New York City demands my attention right now.

Kristen Rogers is the founder of a nonprofit empowerment organization called the King's Daughters, Inc., based in New York City. The organization helps young ladies discover their purpose in life and remain abstinent before marriage. Kristen is also pursuing a career in media as an on-air personality.

YOUR MOM'S IN MY BUSINESS

By Shalena Broaster

I hope I'm not dating myself by plucking my title from an early 1990s rap song by K-Solo in which he complains about his girlfriend's mother's involvement in their relationship. However, this song captures the very essence of what I'd like to share with you regarding maintaining healthy relationships with your lover, family, and friends.

This past summer, I went through a trying time with my fiancé, and I didn't think our relationship would survive. I panicked because I really love him and I wanted our relationship to work. I went to people whom I loved and trusted and I cried upon their shoulders, seeking out their advice. My mother and father said one thing, my sister said something else, my one girlfriend said this, my other homegirl said something completely different, etc. After all the crying and confiding, I had so many conflicting opinions about what I should do. I was so confused. I didn't know what to do. I was a hot mess.

Finally, one night I recalled Proverbs 3:5–6, which encourages us to seek the Lord in all our ways and He'll make our paths straight. Well, I got on my knees and prayed for guidance. Unlike the noisy advice and opinions I heard from my family and friends, my answer in prayer was quite simple. I was led to quiet the chatter in my mind. You see, it's hard to make wise decisions when your mind is cluttered like an old attic. I cleared the chatter in my mind by hanging up the telephone and not seeking out so much "advice." Basically, I stopped telling everyone all of my business. This was hard because I had to distance myself for a few weeks from people whom I loved and respected dearly. I realized that I was a grown woman and that I could think for myself. I also realized the power of prayer and how it changes things. Once my mind was clear, my relationship improved. Both my fiancé and I were able to see the roles we played in our relationship's turmoil, and we focused on becoming better lovers to each other.

The interesting thing about quieting the chatter in your mind is that this process weeds out the people who are truly for you and those who may be envious of you and not have your best interest at heart. My mother, father, sister, and homegirl understood what I was going through and gave me some space. But I found that my relationship with one friend was never the same. We don't talk much anymore.

The lesson learned: You can't involve everyone in your business. Here's why. When you tell your business to family and close friends, you invite them and their opinions into your life. When my fiancé and I went to pre-marriage counseling, the counselor told me that I shouldn't tell everyone my business, especially family members and close friends. "Always remember," he said, looking me deep in the eyes, "your family loves you. But your fiancé, well . . . in their eyes, he's simply all right because he's with you." He further explained that because our family and close friends love us, they tend to be partial and takes sides in matters. Like clockwork, you run to them crying about your problems, complaining about your significant other, and they listen. When the dust settles and you and your boo are back together again, smiling and basking in your undying love, those same people who you aired your dirty laundry with are still upset with your lover and feel some kind of way. You see, when your family and friends were listening to you complain and cry about your relationship problems, they were also registering and harboring all of those things against your mate. Put simply: They don't forget. If they are like most people, they will dislike anyone who they think is hurting you in any way, no matter who it is. Don't be surprised when there is tension at the next family function. Don't be surprised when you find out that your family member or friend dislikes your lover. Don't be surprised when your family or friend reaches a point where they don't want to hear anything about your honey because they can't stand him or her—based upon the things you shared with them.

The unfortunate reality of involving so many people in your relationship is that it can ruin many other relationships. Let's face it, we want everyone to like and respect our significant other, but we make it harder when we put our business out there. In my case, some of my people still don't like my fiancé and vice versa. It's a reality I have to deal with because I helped to create it. But I know that with prayer and time, things will improve.

In closing, I'd like to offer you some practical advice in balancing your relationship with lover, family, and friends. Promise me that before you air your dirty laundry, you'll pray about a situation and seek out God's counsel. God may give you the answer, help you to think your way through your problems, or lead you to someone who has been through what you're going through and can offer wise and impartial advice and not hold things against you or your lover. Finally, use some common sense. There will be times when you should confide in a family member or close friend because the situation calls for it. In cases of domestic violence or any other kind of abuse, you should get people involved and get out of that hostile situation. But not every relationship problem calls for such drastic measures. Be discriminate and use good judgment. In most cases, you already have the answers you seek. You just have to quiet the chatter in your mind and look within yourself.

Shalena Broaster grew up in a drug-and-violence-plagued neighborhood in South Philadelphia. She was determined to overcome these obstacles and follow her dreams of attending college. Upon earning her bachelor of arts degree in political science from Duke University in 2001, Shalena returned to Philadelphia to work in corporate America for several years before she left her secure job in March of 2006 to put more of her energy into freelance writing. She is actively involved in her community as a board member for Positive Praise, a nonprofit organization whose mission is to enrich the lives of young people infected with HIV, in memory of her father.

Too Good to Be True

By Dr. Ravaughn Williams

On June 10, 2006, my dreams started to come true. It took eight long years, but I was finally fulfilling one of my dreams—the dream of becoming a doctor. It was a victorious day for me, my family members, and my loved ones. All the people that were near to my heart were there to witness this milestone in my life, including the man that I hoped to marry some day.

After the graduation ceremony, the celebration continued at a Jamaican restaurant. On the way there, I jokingly asked my boyfriend of two years, Monty, if he was going to propose to me that night. We had been talking about marriage soon after we met. There was one issue, though: He was still married to his ex-wife, although he claimed that though they were not legally divorced, he had already divorced from her spiritually and emotionally. Back then, I was so wrapped up in love and being in love that anything Monty said, I believed, and though I would sometimes disagree with what he was saying, I somehow always became influenced by what he had to say and I would start believing him. As someone once said, Monty could talk a snail out of his shell. You see, if you met Monty, you would believe anything that he said as well. He is very confident when he speaks, very charming, loving, thoughtful, and nothing like any of the other men I dated, and I just knew that he was the one for me.

The graduation celebration took off in full swing. I was so joyful that I could not even sit long enough to finish my meal. Then Monty convinced me to sit and eat. As I was wolfing down my food so that I could get up and dance again, the room lights got dim, the band stopped playing, and the song "All My Life" by K-Ci and JoJo started to play in the background. It was all happening so fast. And before I knew it, Monty was on bended knee holding out a beautiful solitaire diamond ring with small diamonds along the sides as he asked, "Will you marry me?" I went into shock. I could see all the people around me jumping and shouting, though I could not hear them. I was shaken out of my sense of shock when I heard my sister say, "Say yes." Then, somehow, I got the words out. "Yes! Yes!" I opened up my arms to Monty and embraced him, wishing that I did not have to ever let him go. Well, the graduation celebration turned into an engagement party. Everyone was so happy for us, including my close girlfriends, Indira, Khyla, and Nyasha. I did find out later that night that his ex-wife had signed the papers and they were proceeding with the divorce.

Our life was off to a great start as we moved to Houston to begin our lives together. Everything was coming together perfectly. I was starting my optometry residency at the University of Houston and he would be doing one at a prestigious eye center in Houston. Monty and I had so much in common, it seemed. We were both eye doctors, after all; he told people that he was the one who taught me everything I knew, as he was two years ahead of me in optometry school. We were both originally from different countries, and our core values on family and everything else that mattered in life seemed to be the same. And of course, we were both Christian. We had all that we needed to have a great marriage and to do great things together.

I will never forget Easter Sunday of 2007. If I might say so myself, it was the best wedding I had ever been to. I might be a little biased, as I am talking about my wedding, but everyone else was saying the same thing. The wedding was held on a golf course in Trinidad, the country of my origin. The ceremony was outdoors, and though it could get steamy in the islands, the midafternoon sun had dissipated with a cooling and calming breeze. As my parents walked me down the aisle to meet my groom and as the saxophonist played Luther Vandross's song "Here and Now," I thought, *I can't believe this day finally arrived.* The man that I was going to spend the rest of my life with seemed to be eagerly waiting for me to be by his side. The wedding ceremony was representative of both Monty and me. The pastor gave us wonderful words of advice and wisdom, topped off with humor. The hour-long ceremony seemed to go by so quickly, as it was filled with musical renditions, heartfelt vows, and of course the universal wedding Bible reading, 1 Corinthians 13.

The saxophonist continued to serenade the guests during the awesome dinner, and after dinner, the local music of Trinidad filled the air as one of the nationally acclaimed bands played. This was truly a dream come true. I had a $100,000 wedding but only paid $50,000 for it because of the kind contributions of friends and family and, frankly, the goodness of God, who blessed me despite the fact that I was embarking on a journey that He allowed, but if I had bothered to ask Him, He might have told me not to do it. But surely, with as blessed a wedding as we had, I just knew that the Lord meant for Monty and me to be together. The wedding reception turned into a big island party that went on into the wee hours of the morning.

People say mother knows best, and I have lived to learn that is true. Two months after our wedding, a very dear friend of ours, Indira, came to live with us for what I thought was going to be a short period. Indira was as close as my own sister. She was dealing with so many issues—she was getting acclimated to a foreign county, and my heart went out to her.

When I first migrated to the United States, I too had no family or friends, just like Indira. So it was so easy for me to befriend her. Monty also befriended her, yet I was feeling hesitant. The day before Indira was to move in with us, I called my mother and I explained my anxiety about the move. Mom said, "Trust your intuition, don't do it."

Indira's apartment in Columbus was already rented out,

the ticket was already bought, and she was so excited to be able to see Monty and me after a year. I expressed the same anxiety to Monty and he simply put me on a guilt trip. So I ignored my feelings and I proceeded with the plan.

The day after she arrived in Houston, I found myself asking my husband the same question I had been asking from the day that Indira entered our lives: "Why are you so close to Indira?" The response I would get was, "She's like a little sister" or "She's a friend."

When Monty and I were dating, I used to ask him this question every week, and his responses never comforted me, but heightened my suspicions. Upon Indira's arrival in Houston, I told both her and Monty about how uncomfortable their relationship made me feel. Well, my words seemed to go in one ear and go out the next, because they continued being "close friends."

My husband and I were newlyweds of two months, and the tension between us was already very thick. I still gave Indira a chance as a friend, but my relationship with her became strained as well. However, the relationship between Monty and Indira just did not seem to change. The dream that had seemed to come true was slowly becoming a nightmare. Monty could not understand why I did not support his relationship with Indira, and I could not just settle with the response, "She is just a friend." I became very uncomfortable in my own house, and there seemed to be nothing I could do about it. I had absolutely no support and understanding from Monty; instead, I was accused of being insecure. But my instinct continued to lead me to believe that something just was not right. I did not quite know what, but I knew that what was in the dark would come to the light.

I prayed and prayed that God would move Indira from our lives, since she refused to leave during my many attempts to get her out. I got resistance from her and Monty. I was told, "There is nowhere for her to go . . . she has no family in the United States . . . we are her only family." Then one day, after a big fight between Monty and me she finally left, but she was not out of our lives. Monty arranged for her to live with one of his good friends, Jimmy.

Indira became sexually involved with Jimmy, and he became her third sex partner since she moved in with us. During that time, although she did not physically live with us, she was still very much present in our lives. She did not have a job, so Monty insisted that we meet her financial needs; she could not drive, so it became our responsibility to make sure she learned how to drive. While she was staying with Jimmy in Dallas, we would leave Fort Worth and drive about an hour to go to Jimmy's house so we could have a meeting about Indira's life. My whole life was about this woman. I was still "friends" with her, but I started to become very resentful toward her and my husband, and very unhappy in my marriage. And of course, the response to the question remained the same.

Later that year, Indira left for South Carolina to go to a college friend's house. I made it clear that I wanted her out of my house, against her and Monty's will. While she was in South Carolina, I distanced myself from her, but of course, Monty stayed in very close contact with her, and supposedly, he was the one that stopped her from committing suicide one day. While she was gone, there was a sense of relief and I thought that surely Monty and I would start having a normal life once again. Our life still seemed to be about Indira and the fact that she had no job and no this and no that.

The following year Indira moved back to Fort Worth in order to find a job. And, you guessed it, she wanted to stay with us. I let her stay for a couple nights while she looked for somewhere else to live. She did get an apartment—which we had to pay for, of course—and she got a job at the company I worked at. As a newly married woman, your desire is to please your husband as best as you can, and that is what I was trying to do, so I did many things that I was not comfortable with. I learned, though, to trust my instincts and to hold my stance.

When Indira stepped back on the scene, my marriage went downhill. My feeling of frustration toward Monty's relationship with Indira intensified. I became very angry and resentful, but my husband still had me on a string and I would do things for Indira because of the manipulative things he had told me about my duty as a Christian to help the woman who was destroying my marriage.

I prayed and prayed but yet, there was no relief. I had many discussions with Monty about his relationship with Indira and for the most part, they were the same, but now, the conversations were taking on a new direction, as he would hint at the fact that his relationships with Indira and me were both important to him and were on the same level. That just did not resonate with me, and that is when it was confirmed in my mind that his relationship was far beyond friendship. One night Monty and I were arguing as usual, and at about 3:00 that morning, he announced to me that the Lord had revealed to him that Indira was going to be his next wife.

As you could imagine, when he told me that, it felt as though a ton of bricks fell down on me. I asked him if Indira believed the same thing, and he said that I should call and ask her. So I picked up the phone and called her, and she said that God told her the same thing and that I should ask Him, too. By this time, I was convinced that I had died and gone to hell.

After that day, I lived to make sure that I did not lose my mind. My close family and friends prayed with me and supported me. I had no idea how I functioned on my job. Well, I do know. It is called God's grace and mercy. In the midst of God's provision in the situation, I still felt like I was either going to die or that I was going to lose my mind. One of God's ways of providing for me in this situation came in the form of two ladies at my job. They became my counselors, encouragers, and prayer partners.

While I tried to restore myself after that blow, I insisted that Monty cut Indira out of his life. Well, he did—reluctantly, I know, but he did it. He did not stop believing that God gave him a vision to practice polygamy and to have two wives. Now that she was out of our lives—or so I thought—I thought God was giving us a chance to work on our marriage.

I was willing to work on the marriage, and apparently so was Monty. And I thought God was big enough to remove Indira from our lives. As we were working on our marriage, all our conversations always digressed to an argument about whether polygamy was right or wrong, so in essence we were not working on our marriage. Now Monty was focused on the conversation on whether polygamy was right or wrong. We would go to counseling and the session would become a debate between Monty and the counselor, someone who was a pastor. Everyone who counseled us took the stance that polygamy was wrong, and Monty tried to convince them that it was right and God approved it.

He had done extensive research on the history of marriage and polygamy, both biblically and otherwise, so he presented a very strong argument, complete with all the biblical examples of polygamy. I would leave counseling in even more despair than when I went in.

My heart has always been to be a woman of God, so though my marriage was in trouble, my response was not to run out but to have faith, pray, and surely God would work it out. But at the same time, Monty's belief in polygamy and his vision became just as strong. There were nights and days that I would just cry out to God to help me and to remove that woman from our lives.

I was convinced that God brought us together and He was going to keep us together, but Indira's presence could not seem to depart from our lives. Though I would have nothing to do with her, Monty continued on his relationship with her, mostly in private, but his deceitful actions were always brought to the light. When I would confront him and her about it, they would make no excuses for their behavior but would simply say that they needed to learn to be more open to me about their relationship. And they would both reassure me how much they loved me and needed me. I could not believe they would say that they loved me, given what they were doing. They disguised everthing they did with Christianity.

The more insistent I became that Indira had to be out of our lives, the more she and Monty held on to the relationship. Monty insisted that he had to follow God's direction for his life, and God was directing him to polygamy. I grew stronger in my stance against their relationship, and the conflict in our marriage increased. I started to detach myself emotionally and spiritually from my husband as I started to seek God's face for the will for my life. By that time it was exactly a year since Indira had returned to Fort Worth, and I knew that the life I was living was not what God wanted for me.

As I sought God's will for me, I still continued to pray for my marriage and I tried to talk and reason with Monty. I was even willing to compromise, but the one thing I could not compromise was my stance on polygamy and his relationship with Indira.

One day, I was driving to the airport to go on a business trip. That morning I was feeling very discouraged. God felt so far away from me, and I really needed some assurance from my Heavenly Father.

As I was driving to the airport, I remembered having a conversation with myself about where I should park. Typically, I would park at the terminal for a one-day trip, but that particular day, I decided I was going to park remotely and take the shuttle, as it was cheaper. When I arrived at the parking lot, the parking attendant presented a very enticing offer for me to park at the terminal at a discounted price. For a brief moment, I considered the offer, but then I decided against it because I was running late. I got my parking assignment and I proceeded to the spot. As I pulled into the parking spot, there was a shoe sitting on a ledge as though it was being displayed in the window of a store. I looked closely, and it was a shoe of mine that had gone missing about two weeks ago. I jumped out my car, grabbed the shoe, and cried. I was not crying because I had found the lost shoe, but I was crying because I knew that God was showing me that He was near. About two weeks earlier, Monty had parked in that very same parking lot, and obviously in the same parking spot. He flew to California to join me for our second-anniversary celebration trip. When he took his suitcases out of the trunk of the car, the shoe must have fallen out, and somehow, it ended up on this ledge in just as good shape as it was when it was lost. That day, I knew that God was communicating to me how much He loved me and that He was going to order my steps through this situation so that joy, peace, and happiness could be restored to me.

That was the beginning of something new that God was doing in my life. My situation in my marriage was not improving, and though I never stopped believing that God could fix my marriage, my prayer now became: Whatever Your will, Lord, let it be done. Monty held on to his belief, reassured me that he still wanted to be married to me and that he knew that one day, he would also marry Indira and practice polygamy. And I knew that was not God's will for me. So I took the steps to initiate divorce proceedings. I sought legal counsel, and each step along the way I would talk to Monty and let him know what I was doing. He seemed to maintain a sense of denial about me divorcing him, and he refused to change his belief and he refused to relinquish his relationship with Indira. Indira was holding on just as tightly to her belief that my husband was also hers.

Well, I took the step, as painful as it was, to have Monty served with divorce papers. Each step of the way, I sought God's face because I wanted to make sure I was doing what He wanted me to. I made many calls to the lawyer putting off the serving of the papers, but I eventually did it with a sense of peace in my spirit. As of today, we are awaiting our court hearing and Monty has finally moved out, though he threatened many times that he was not going to. I guess the restraining order made up his mind for him.

Monty was married before, and I had a chance to speak with his wife for the first time a few days ago. She told me that as I was telling her my story, she was experiencing déjà vu. Apparently, when Monty decided he wanted to divorce his ex-wife, he told her that God wanted him to marry me and he had to do God's will for his life. Our experiences with him were very similar. So, though we both thought the problem was us, we learned that it was actually Monty who had the issues, but he is too prideful and in spiritual bondage to realize that. But that is no longer my problem. It is now the problem of his next wife, Indira.

I am about to be thirty years old, and I can say that this experience has been the most painful one that I have ever been through. During the last two years of my life, my emotional, mental, spiritual, and physical health has deteriorated. At times I even questioned if God existed and why He was allowing this to happen to me. But I learned that God allows situations that the devil uses for evil for our good, and while we are going through them, He makes provision for us. It is because of God's grace and mercy that I am alive today in my right mind. It is also because of the prayers and support of family and friends. I thank God for my mother, who is a spiritual powerhouse and has helped me get out of this situation. And though my marriage failed, I felt like I did all I could do and now I am relieved, yet there is a sense of loss because a person who was so connected to me is now out of my life. **But I** believe my latter days will be greater than my former days, and I am hopeful that I will find the man for me according to God's time. In fact, let me rephrase my last statement. The right man will find me, because the Bible says, "He who finds a wife finds a good thing," and that I am.

Dr. Ravaughn Williams is a native of the Caribbean island of Trinidad. She has been in the United States for almost eleven years. After completing optometry school in 2006, she moved to Texas, where she works for a leading pharmaceutical company in Fort Worth as a research optometrist.

80s Baby

By Star Toile Murrell

I always had some shame when it came to revealing my story. My story seemed so far-fetched, but as I sat down in a room full of women with completely different backgrounds, I realized we all want the same things. We all want to be in love and be loved. The kind that stands the test of time—you laugh at his jokes when no one else thinks it's funny, and his face lights up when you walk into the room.

I witnessed that love between my mom and dad. I was an eighties baby. In between Puma sneakers, boom boxes, Gloria Vanderbilt jeans, Run-D.M.C., and the emergence of rap music in New York City, my mother fell in love with my dad. They met in high school, the typical girl-meets-boy story. It was the sweet kind of love filled with Juicy Fruit kisses and waiting outside my mother's window to get a good look at her before she went to bed at night. They were married and worshiped each other. It was like a secret oath between them: I ride for you and you ride for me and no one shall come between. This is what I saw, and I couldn't wait to have someone ride for me.

I was my parents' only girl. Although they were young, they worked hard to provide for me and my brothers. My dad made sure that I had a strong sense of self. My mom taught us that your family was all you had, and my dad was my best friend and my biggest fan. In his eyes I did no wrong, and the sun didn't shine if his baby girl wasn't happy.

My parents made serious sacrifices for our family, and it took a toll. As I got older, we went through a lot. I remember my mom saying Daddy had to go away to school. I finally figured out that my dad had gone to prison. I didn't want to ruffle her feathers and have her worry any more than she already had to. So I just grew up overnight and helped my mother with my younger brother.

To keep things light, I would perform for my family. I would move the furniture around in the living room when my mom wasn't home and put on my records. Then I would dance my heart out. My mom and dad made sure to put me in every dance class, talent show, and school recital there was just so I could do what I loved. As I got older I got better, and by the age of fifteen I started dancing professionally.

I began touring with really big-name artists and living the life, but there was always something missing. I wanted to be loved like my dad loved my mom. Even through a few failed relationships I never gave up on love, but in hindsight I started to settle for what I could get, hoping that I would be able to turn it into true love.

I was dating rappers and music-industry types. I thought since I was in the industry, it would be good if we had a common interest. Then I met the person I thought I would spend the rest of my life with. He always made me feel special, and we quickly became best friends. After several years of dating, we both knew that this was it, and the next step was marriage.

My dad had just passed away from liver disease, and I believed that this would make me feel whole again. So I integrated him into my family and allowed our relationship to develop. I thought I could make him be the man I wanted. He proposed and it took my breath away. We decided to move into a beautiful house in New Jersey. His mother assisted in purchasing the house to help us start our life together.

My career had taken off and I was now appearing in music videos as both a dancer and a model and was considered one of the top video vixens. He encouraged me to slow down because I was going to be his wife. I agreed and started nesting. I cooked, cleaned, and paid the mortgage, bills, and everything in between. I wanted this to be an equal partnership. After a few months, all of his stuff was not completely moved in, and I would ask him what was up. He said it was a time issue.

Some days he would not come home. He had an attitude and seemed distant overall. I thought it was the distance in the drive from his job. Sometimes he would spend his nights at his mother's house. On a warm June morning, I was awakened by a phone call from a male friend.

He started to ramble about my "man" not being who I assumed he was. My friend gave me a telephone number and urged me to call. It took a few hours for me to have the nerve, but eventually my curiosity got the best of me.

Instead of calling, I chose to send a text message. Sometimes a text is the best way to communicate, and I needed to get straight to the point. I went on to text once, no response; twice, no response. After the second try I gave up! Later that evening I received a response, but only after I checked my phone a hundred times prior.

"Who is this?" I then returned the same response in addition to a short message: "I just wanted to know who you are. I see my fiancé speaks with you quite a bit." The immediate response was "Who's your fiancé?"

I then went on to tell her and added that she must know, as they spoke and texted quite a few times a day. She then responded with, "Oh, that's my fiancé!" If you could imagine my dismay, that would still be an understatement. I was speechless. We both called each other and she told it all—this woman was with my fiancé for six years. He also failed to tell me—ready for this, ladies?—they had an eight-month-old daughter! I didn't want her to hear the pain in my voice, so I thanked her for the information and quickly hung up. As I sat there, a cry came so deep from my chest. How could he? When did he?

All these questions just ran through my mind. It was then in those few short moments that I let a man determine my worth as a woman. I beat myself up, thinking this would have never happened if I hadn't gained weight or stopped dressing a certain way, or maybe if I did things differently he wouldn't have done this. I punished myself by not eating and I began to stay in the house all the time. I felt like everybody could see that I was broken in some way, and I didn't want to be the butt of everyone's jokes. I cut off my friends and even my family members—I just wanted to die. I guess I just wanted someone to love me the way my dad loved my mom. But I didn't understand that the love they shared was more than love, it was a friendship. It was a special bond that only true friends and lovers could share. But I still wanted that no matter what. I was going to find someone like that one day!

I struggled for a few months after I confronted my "fiancé." He turned into someone I've never known. He said things that I can't even repeat. I was no longer the special person he made me think I was. Now I was the side chick! He then told me to leave. What? I paid the bills in that house and my name was on the deed. Or so I thought. Guess what? My name was nowhere to be found on any document.

He had told his mom that we broke up and the house was vacant. Shocked to know I was still living there, she pushed for me to leave although I was paying most of the bills. I stayed there in that house for two months. I had nowhere to go, no money, and no job because that's how he wanted it! I felt lower than low. It was a far cry from the way I felt onstage or on a video set. I was the sexy dancer, the video vixen who's in all the magazines, and any man who laid eyes on me lusted for me. How could I be all these things and yet hate myself? I was sitting in the hell house trying to figure out my next step. By this time my family was getting worried. My aunt called and said she was fed up and sent my uncle in a van all the way from Brooklyn to come and get me! My uncle arrived forty minutes later with a van, as promised.

We packed up the house and all my belongings in fifteen minutes. Before I knew it, I was on my way back to Brooklyn with a van full of my belongings and the *hell* house in the rearview mirror. At that moment I felt like myself again, finally free of the boulders that lay on my shoulders. But also a feeling of uncertainty came across me. How could I do this alone? Could I even *try*?

My family helped me to see my worth—something that I had lost long before I knew I misplaced it. I started to rebuild myself from that day, and even until the present moment I'm still rebuilding, always striving to make myself better, never to let anyone put me in a dark place and never to settle for less. I'm now independent and stronger. I realize that a man or a relationship can never make me feel complete. The eighties love my mom and dad had is out there somewhere, and I will let God choose him.

Star Toile Murrell is a former model and video vixen who works in fashion in New York City.

If I Knew Then What I Know Now About Love . . .

What he showed me was not what I had to get, but what I already have. I am just myself, and who I am is a lot.
—Phylicia Rashad

The best thing we learn about the relationships we have in our young lives leading into adulthood is the information we learn about ourselves as women. We learn what we are willing to tolerate and what we're worth. In any relationship, but romantic relationships in particular, if we're open, we can learn so much about who we are just by how we interact with our mates. What's important is that you maintain the best of who you are and learn from the bad habits you may have created for yourself.

Your Soul's Sustenance

Regardless of the circumstance, one of the most important factors for a healthy relationship is listening to the backstory. Everyone has one, including you. The backstory comes not just from your partner but from his family. Is his family life similar to yours? What are his views on home, family, money, friends, work, future, religion, self-esteem, personal space, commitment, trust, and sex? You must have these questions answered before you can have a mutually healthy relationship. You may think, well, if I get all in his business, then he'll think I'm nosey and move on to the next woman that doesn't ask too much of him. Well, if that's the case, then he isn't for you. Tough questions are answered by people who value your concern, because you, too, will be answering these critical questions. You bring value to a relationship and you deserve to be valued.

Your Personal Book of Revelations

- *Are your parents still together? Were they together when you were being raised?*
- *Describe the worst relationship you engaged in.*
- *What did you learn from that relationship?*
- *What is your definition of a successful relationship?*
- *What is it that you desire and need from a relationship?*

VI

Overcoming Life's Challenges

I'm not used to crying. It's a little difficult. All my life I've had to fight. It's just another fight I'm going to have to learn how to win, that's all. I'm just going to have to keep smiling.
—Serena Williams

Who hasn't faced a challenge? Challenges help us grow, learn, and develop our womanhood. Some of us have greater challenges than others. Others make their challenges look easy while some only bemoan the depth of their obstacles. Challenges are our blessings. Yes, that's right, our blessings. We may not feel that way when we are faced with a challenge or come across an obstacle in our lives, but there's a reason we are being challenged.

Life has its trials and we are oftentimes put to the test, but isn't it our best selves that rise to the occasion? Challenges come our way to help test our mental, spiritual, emotional, and sometimes physical muscles. Think about it. If children aren't challenged mentally, they act out. What would you do if you didn't face some mental challenges? Become lazy or complacent, perhaps, or would you act out, too? Mental challenges keep us on our toes and let us put on our thinking and problem-solving caps.

Many of us are faced with spiritual challenges—questions of faith that confound us and leave us asking why. In the case of our spiritual challenges, we get to exercise our faith and in turn grow stronger in our beliefs. Emotional challenges can be exhausting because they involve how we feel. When we are connected to a situation emotionally, it is sometimes hard to discern between what is right and how we feel. Emotional challenges allow us to get in tune with how we feel and meter out our feelings appropriately once we become in tune with them.

Finally, our physical challenges can become connected with the mental, spiritual, and emotional. Physical challenges bring the fragility of our humanness to light. We realize that we are not immortal and will not live forever. Our physical challenges bring us closer to our humanity. Many people speak about how their physical challenges make them more compassionate toward others, or how they deepened their faith.

Regardless of the type of challenge you face, there are choices to be made. Are you going to give in to the challenge, or face it and grow from it? How you meet your challenges determines exactly how long they will be challenges. If you look at your challenges as catalysts to learning and growing, then chances are they won't be challenges for long. You will be able to find the lesson in the experience quicker than if you cried, shouted, screamed, complained, or shut down. We're not saying you can't have your panic moment, or a moment of denial, even a good cry, but remember it's just meant to be a moment. Welcome your challenges. As the women in this section have learned from their challenges, you will, too.

I Am Blessed

By Jennifer Lewis

1995 was the year that changed the course of my life. I was a senior in high school. These were supposed to be the best years of my life. I should have been excited about college, graduation, and my upcoming prom. Instead I was a senior in high school, pregnant, and I'd never felt more alone. I managed to hide my pregnancy for nearly six months. I couldn't find the strength to tell my family that I was pregnant. Saying I was in denial is an understatement. This sort of thing happened to other people, not me, not my family . . . yet here I was. I was young, uninformed, and thought I was in love. Looking back, I was more in love with the thought of being in love.

I managed to keep my pregnancy a secret as long as it was physically possible. I never had a chance to enjoy my pregnancy and celebrate the life I would soon bring into the world. Instead, I was making future plans with someone who did not intend for us to be a part of their future. I went through my entire pregnancy alone, without support or assistance from the person I thought was "the one." This was my first error in judgment. Instead of making someone else "the one," I should have focused on making myself the priority. The birth of my daughter was the hardest sixteen hours of my life. Nothing could have prepared me more for what I was getting ready to experience. I never felt pain in my life like the pain of childbirth. I had no clue what I was doing. I labored for sixteen hours without the assistance of medication, listening to the advice of my mother, sister, and nurse in the labor and delivery room. With each contraction and each push I became in tune with my body and with what I had to do in order to bring this life into the world. At that very moment, my life and purpose for living had changed forever. I became a mother.

The months leading up to my daughter's birth were full of emotions. I began my freshman year at a local community college instead of attending one of the large universities I was accepted to. My relationship with my daughter's father was nonexistent—it didn't take long to realize there was never a relationship to begin with. There were many times over the course of my pregnancy when I didn't know where he was. Even with all of this happening in my life, the biggest challenge I was facing was raising my daughter alone. As a young girl growing up, this wasn't the vision I had, and it certainly was not the example my parents set.

My daughter became the focus of my life—everything I did, I did for her; all decisions made were made with her best interest in mind. I wanted to be the best parent I could be. I was determined not to become the stereotypical "single mom." I successfully managed to complete my first semester of college, only missing a few classes toward the end of my first semester when my daughter was born. After the birth of my daughter, I continued as a full-time student until the fall of 1998.

I began my professional career in the winter of 1998, putting my educational goals on hold. A job with stability was all that mattered at the time. I clearly remember on my first day of work, after providing my new hire documents, I ran into the ladies' bathroom and thanked God. I said a prayer because God knew what my heart truly called for, I thanked God because I would be able to provide for my daughter in the manner I always wanted, and I thanked God for keeping me focused during what felt like the most difficult time in my life. Yet it was only the beginning.

A year after my daughter was born, I started a new relationship with a wonderful person. He treated my daughter well and always treated me with respect. Four years into our relationship, our son was born. Everything was going great. I was in a new, happy, and healthy relationship, my daughter was five years old, I had a great job—everything appeared to be fine. Still a single parent, now with two children, I wanted more than ever to complete my undergrad studies and obtain my degree. With the help of my family I went back to school full-time, worked full-time, and took care of my children. This was a lot to juggle, but I was determined and never lost focus. Completing my undergraduate studies and earning my degree was a huge personal accomplishment, and having my family and children there to cheer me on was a great feeling.

From the outside looking in, one would think I had everything in order, yet something was still missing. I wasn't living the life I wanted to live. I wasn't honoring myself and my accomplishments in the manner deserving of me. I felt I hit a roadblock and I didn't know how to move forward. Moving forward came in the form of a message I received—a message I needed to hear: "Pack your tent," simply put, but the message went further. Oftentimes we find ourselves in situations that are supposed to be temporary situations. Instead we hold on and make them a part of our long-term plans. The same holds true to people. Some people were only meant to be a part of our present, but we make them a part of our future. These simple yet powerful words resonated through me and changed my life. I began to reevaluate my personal and professional relationships. I let go of the relationships that were not meant to be a part of my future. I truly believe that we are put in situations to learn and grow. Challenges are placed in our lives to see how we handle them, to see if we give up, give in, or make something out of it. There were many days where I felt everything I was working for was in vain. I felt that my faith was being tested and no end seemed to be in sight. I knew there was a light at the end of the tunnel, but at times it appeared to be dim. I couldn't see the light at the end of the tunnel, partly because I wasn't living to my full potential. I let the challenges I faced consume my life instead of living the life I was intended to live.

I "packed up my tent" in 2007 in every area of my life—professionally and in my personal relationships. My relationship with my son's father was not progressing. We were together for ten years. I'm not the same person I was ten years ago; my needs, desires, and thought processes are not the same. Through it all we have remained friends. I made the decision to invest in myself, to focus on me and what made me truly happy. Looking back, I wholeheartedly know that I made the best decision. I truly feel that you have to be able to identify what doesn't matter most in life. For me, that meant letting go of a title, that of being someone's girlfriend. I took stock in myself and realized my true worth.

Presently I am the CEO of the Book Bank Foundation, where I manage the day-to-day needs of the organization for Glenn Toby, the founder of the Book Bank Foundation. I also work for the Juvenile Rights Practice of the Legal Aid Society, where we represent children in family court proceedings. For the Book Bank Foundation I plan community related events and do motivational speaking to other women when we have outreach events. I recently formed a women's group that meets on a monthly basis to discuss various topics on parenting, relationships, and business networking opportunities.

I have overcome many life challenges with the help and support of my family and friends. My children are my number-one priority, as is their happiness and well-being. I'm a single parent raising my daughter to honor and respect herself, to put herself and her future goals before temporary satisfaction. I'm raising my son to be an honorable, respectful, and responsible young man. One should never give in. Instead, look at each challenge that you are faced with as a learning experience. God will never put you in it if He can't see you through it!

Be blessed.

Jennifer Lewis is the CEO of the Book Bank Foundation.

No Mirrors

By Kayla LaShell Harley

For a long time, it had always been just my mama; Kisha; my older sister, Kiera; and my younger brother, Kameron. We adjusted to living in our two-bedroom apartment for a while, eight years to be exact. By the time I reached the peak of my high school years, at age sixteen, my family and I went through a series of tosses and turns, living in several different homes—well, places, rather. But we had each other then; living in those confined spaces brought us closer. We grew to appreciate one another. The importance of family and having a support system became clear to me as I matured as a young woman and an artist.

I actually fumbled into dancing as a young girl; I grew to love it, and with favorable opportunities, I've progressively become successful. Surrounded by family and friends who always have encouraging words and reassuring smiles to ease some of the pressures that are entangled in the road to becoming an artist, I excelled. The beautiful thing about artistry is that those of us who have been blessed with natural talents have some of the highest hurdles to jump, but when our feet touch back down onto the surface, we become greater than we were before.

I didn't understand this then. In fact, I never fully believed in myself or even recognized my own potential until around February of 2007, when I was accepted into the prestigious school, the Kirov Academy of Ballet. This multicultural school was established by former principal dancers from the Soviet Union.

I didn't even know that there were summer intensives for young dancers. My mama just pulled it up from the Internet one day. On the day of my audition, I was so nervous I had forgotten my tights and ballet shoes. I gave up then—I felt defeated. I could hear the voice in my head saying, "Who are you kidding? This fancy building, these clean white walls, and their crisp white skins. You're no match for this. Go home." This was the part of me that was afraid, but this also was the part of me that was trying to keep me from conquering what I had set out to do. In the midst of our scrambling, a parent happened to have an extra pair of tights, and another had an extra pair of shoes, all located within minutes of the beginning of the audition. Well, two right ballet shoes, to be exact.

In the days after that audition, I just kept replaying each and every moment of that experience, from my clothing mishap to the triple pirouette I pulled in front of the instructors for the first time. I thought of myself as silly most times, thinking about how I just didn't fit into the mold of that place and avoiding thoughts of greatness and prosperity, calling it "just being real with myself." Two weeks later, I received an unexpected letter from the Kirov Academy of Ballet saying—Congratulations! I just cried. It may seem like nothing to cry about, but it meant the world to me then. I couldn't even decipher just what I was crying about, happiness or my own disbelief. My faith in God's plan for me immediately stepped in and played its part at that point. Faith comforted me and eased my doubts when I looked at the expense of the tuition; faith was my motivation to find that money. Members of my church and those who were eager to support me, including the founders of the Chris Samuels Foundation, contributed graciously in response to my letters and flyers.

I had no idea what I was getting myself into when I began the first of my three weeks. I'd never had Vaganova ballet training before, so I knew I had to play catch-up. There was so much pressure, I felt, being the "darkest shade" in the room. And there I was, in the midst of my dream coming true, feeling unable, inadequate, and behind. I've always felt confident in anything and everything that I did, because I knew I had the potential to just be that good—but not that time.

My spirits were so low the first week. Discouragement began to overwhelm me, and now I was shy for the first time in my little life in doing the one thing I desired to do—dance. Not only that, but no one would talk to me, they would just stare. So many emotions and thoughts clouded my mind, and I became someone that I did not recognize. She was someone that was weak and she was someone that I could not recognize to be myself. For the first time, I had to act alone and be responsible for making decisions in my life that would determine my own destiny. But I knew I could not have done it completely by myself. So I turned to the one and only, and I released my worries and cast my cares right out on Him . . . and again He took care of me.

Looking back on that day, my audition day, I know that there was nothing "extra" or "coincidental" about it, but I see how God was setting me up for greatness at that very moment. It was me overcoming the first of many obstacles and seeing God work right in the middle of it, at a young age. I am privileged. My journey at the Kirov Academy of Ballet may have ended after just three weeks, but a part of Kayla that I did not know was there came right on home with me.

This experience has prepared me for many other challenges I have already faced, and still expect to face in the future. Being in a position of uncertainty really changed my outlook on the things and the people around me. It has strengthened my emotional and mental stability and allowed me to feed off the energies of those around me. My experience at the Kirov Academy invited me into such a professional atmosphere in which I found myself becoming more of a budding artist rather than a young girl in awe.

As a living testimony, and a continuing testimony, I'd like to reiterate that God is real. He is the best friend you never knew you truly had; He'll give you the desires of your heart, when you trust Him. And to all the young black girls who dance or are pursuing any career in an artistic field, it is important that we learn to humble ourselves. It's natural for us to carry this sort of arrogance and sometimes let our pride as black women get the best of us, but let us focus on who God wants us to be and allow that confidence to be an inspiration to someone else. And to those who may not quite have an understanding of the artistic realm, just continue to be supportive of those who are engaged. We are more powerful united than we could ever be trying to do things all on our own.

Throughout my senior year of high school, I've participated in some excellent programs, including the Alvin Ailey American Dance Theater Intensive as a fellowship student; the National Foundation for the Advancement in Young Arts Scholarship Week Winner in Miami, Florida; a prospective Juilliard School student / dancer; and in the fall of 2009, I will begin my freshman year of college under Alonzo King's LINES Ballet BFA program at Dominican University of California.

Kayla LaShell Harley, a high school graduate, is an aspiring contemporary / ballet artist. Kayla was inspired by some of the greatest pioneers in dance including Alvin Ailey, Gillian Murphy, and Julie Kent. She calls life her teacher and is excited about continuing to learn and grow.

Moving Beyond Labels and Boxes

By Desiree Hulen

As I stepped foot in my college classroom for the first time, I had no idea how quickly my first year would go by, nor did I anticipate the challenges I would face or the lessons that I would learn. Thinking it would be easy for me to balance my schoolwork and all of the social activities, I was in for a big surprise. In high school I had special education teachers (SETs) who helped me in all my classes, but I did not want that type of help in college. I just wanted to experience college life like every other student on campus. For once in my life I was finally on my own, and I didn't want to depend on any adult to help me get through the experience. In high school, it took a while for me to move beyond the fact that I was dyslexic, and I didn't want to have to think about it or deal with it in college. However, it didn't take long before I learned that my journey with my learning difference was far from over.

I remember one specific week very clearly. My mother kept calling me multiple times a day asking me if I had gone to the Services for Students with Disabilities office to self-declare as a student with dyslexia. I got an attitude every time my mother called and would sometimes ignore her phone calls. I just wanted my mother to leave me alone and allow me to go on with my new college life. When I did answer the phone, I made multiple excuses. I would tell my mother that I had too much to do that day and didn't get a chance to go, or that I would go another day and handle everything. It wasn't that I felt that people would make fun of me; I just wanted to prove to myself that I was able to get through my classes without any help.

In high school I used my dyslexia as a way to get by in my classes without having to do much work. It wasn't that I couldn't do the work, I just thought that if I had an easy way out, why not take it. But by my senior year it became annoying to me, and I did not want to deal with or work with my SETs anymore. I knew that I didn't want the same treatment when I got to college, so I set out to change things. When I got to college, I believed that I would not need to get extra help to get good grades. I had to prove to myself that my dyslexia would not hold me back in this new setting and that I could and would succeed on my own.

I soon discovered that my plan wasn't working. By the time I recognized that there was a problem, midterms had passed and I was failing my classes. My parents began to grow frustrated with me and decided to take matters into their own hands. My mother found the name and number of my academic adviser and spoke to her about the situation. When I received a phone call from my father, I knew they were upset. I knew that I had gone too far because my mother stopped calling me and my father began to take control. I received a couple of calls from my father and I quickly learned that he was aware of my every movement in the situation. He would ask me questions about school and would already know the answers to them. I knew I could not respond to my father the same way I would to my mother. My father gave me an ultimatum and told me I had until the end of the week to see my adviser. The more I was told to go to her office, the more I didn't want to go, but my father told me that I had been given enough chances to do it on my own and had failed to handle it. I knew it was a lost battle, so I just gave in.

When I walked into the adviser's office, she already knew who I was. She shared that she had had many conversations with my parents. I was unaware that they had spoken. I was so upset that my parents took things into their own hands and called my school. I felt that if they had taken the time to call the adviser, then they should have taken the extra step and called the office for the Services for Students with Disabilities and taken care of everything. What did they need me for?

My adviser explained the situation and stressed the importance of me going down to the office to self-declare my learning status. We then went over my grades, which were not the best. I was embarrassed and I tried to explain that I could have done better. She then asked me which of my classes I was having the most trouble in, and I told her psychology and French. We started with psychology, because that was my declared major. I told her that the class readings were holding me back and that having to read chapters consisting of twenty or more pages was a lot for me. I was not used to reading large numbers of pages, comprehending them, and then taking specific notes on their content. As a person with dyslexia, reading and vocabulary was challenging for me, so these tasks were overwhelming.

My adviser told me that because of my dyslexia, I could get a reader who would read my textbooks for me, in any subject, and help me take notes in class. When she told me this, I immediately felt that by taking these services I would appear as if I could not read on my own, which was not true. I felt hurt, but I did not say anything about it. I was hurt because I did not feel like a regular student and I felt that I was letting myself down by utilizing the services. However, I realized that not speaking up did not help matters either. Avoidance had become a pattern for me.

After we discussed my options for psychology, we reviewed my status in my French class. Everyone knows that learning a new language is challenging; however, I had convinced myself that despite my learning difference, I could do well in the class because I was motivated and had always wanted to take French. The adviser told me that if my teachers knew that I had dyslexia, they could change the grading system and modify the tests for me. This bothered me as well, because I looked at this as a form of cheating and did not want my teachers treating me any differently than the other students in my class. Now as I reflect on my reaction, I realize that it was irrational. I overlooked the fact that this had not been a problem when I was in high school. In the past, anytime my mother told one of my teachers that I had dyslexia, they all had the same response: "I did not notice that Desiree was dyslexic."

Even though I agreed to follow my adviser's suggestions, I was still upset about having to declare myself as a student with a learning disability. Toward the end of the first semester of my freshman year, I lost my motivation and began to give up. I would sit in my classes and think about everything else. I stopped studying and looking over my notes. I didn't care how late I was to class. Something came over me during finals week and I started shifting gears. I began doubling up on my note taking and studying, especially for French class. I realized that if I did not change, I would let myself down, and I couldn't live with that. When I received my grades after finals I was surprised when I got a C in French. I know that a C isn't something to celebrate, but I really felt that I was going to fail that class because of my posture during the semester. Miraculously, my grades in my world history and freshman orientation classes picked up as well. This shocked me, but I was relieved that I had turned things around and I wouldn't disappoint myself or let my parents down. I was upset about how the semester played out, but I was glad that I made my mistake in my freshman year and had time to salvage things so that my college career wouldn't be ruined.

Before finals I went to the office of Services for Students

with Disabilities, on my own, to turn in my Individualized Education Plan (IEP). I spoke to a representative in the office and realized that I had overanalyzed and exaggerated everything. I also talked to my friends about it and everyone laughed because they could not see why I had made such a big deal out of the situation. They even joked around and said that we all have a slight case of dyslexia. They asked me questions about it and wanted to know why there is such a stigma attached to it. I honestly don't have an answer to this; however, I do realize that being diagnosed with a learning challenge or difference is not the end of the world. You can live and thrive with it as long as you accept it. My mom always reminds me that many celebrities have the same learning challenge and they are doing very well. The fact that I am not the only one helps a lot. I also recognize how important self-acceptance is.

Desiree Hulen is an eighteen-year-old native of Brooklyn who is currently a sophomore at Morgan State University in Baltimore, Maryland. She is majoring in psychology.

The Best Medicine

By Robin E. Wilson

I'm too young for this crap. Life is serious business. Business is serious. How did my life get to be so serious? Everything seemed to be crashing in on me at once.

I knew that at some point I would have to learn to laugh at myself, or I would lose my natural black mind. God has a sense of humor, right? He must, because far too often it seemed like my life was the punch line.

At the ripe old age of twenty-seven I was going through a really tough time. My life had gotten very serious. I found myself at the end of a seven-year relationship with my daughter's father, and I was devastated. I decided to focus on raising my daughter and taking care of my business. I wasn't interested in anything else. I couldn't handle anything else.

Each day I would follow the same routine: get dressed, get my daughter dressed, drop her off at school, go to work, pick her up, go home, feed her, get ready for bed, and do it all over again the next day. Oh, and just for fun I would get to pack my daughter up every other weekend so she could spend time with her father and his new girlfriend. I was miserable.

One Friday while my daughter was off with her father and the soon-to-be stepmonster, my grandmother asked if I would drop some food off for her on my way home. I agreed and went about my day. I remember that this particular day I had on my usual uniform as a hairstylist: scrubs.

The scrubs I had on were about two sizes too big, but I didn't care because I wasn't paying much attention to what I wore anyway. I wasn't at all interested in appearing attractive. The last thing I needed was to attract male attention. That's how I got hurt in the first place. So after finishing up my clients and tidying up the salon, I visited the ladies' room. I tied up my scrubs (not a double knot like I usually do), washed my hands, and headed off to Captain D's to get my granny's food.

I sat in the drive-thru line for what seemed like an eternity. I decided to go inside to order because the line wasn't moving fast enough for me. I was very impatient and wanted to hurry up and get home so that I could be miserable in my own place. I jumped out of the car and started toward the door. I hadn't taken a good three steps when my pants fell all the way down to my ankles. I screamed! I had to bend over, reach down, and grab my pants with both hands to hoist them back up.

I ran back to my car and grabbed the door handle, trying to make a quick escape. Unfortunately, I always lock my doors. I had to find the key while panting and looking around to see if I had been spotted. I finally managed to get into the car and speed off.

My first reaction was to cry from the embarrassment: *I'm pathetic.* It was then that God spoke to me. Right there in my car. He showed me how serious I had become. How I would go for days, weeks, months without laughing or smiling. He told me that He missed my smile. He even showed me how ridiculous I must have looked in the parking lot, with my pants down around my ankles, wearing polka-dot cotton bloomers (it was laundry time). It was there in my car, with my daughter spending time with her other family, with life as I had planned it shattered, that I did the most bizarre thing. I laughed. I laughed hysterically. I laughed a good old-fashioned belly laugh. I laughed until tears ran down my cheeks and formed a puddle under my chin. I laughed until other folks in traffic thought I was having a nervous breakdown. I laughed until I got tired and then . . . I laughed some more. I laughed until I was gasping for air. I laughed until I couldn't keep the car straight. I laughed until it hurt. I laughed and it felt good.

It was from that experience that I realized that I may not have a choice about the things that happen to me, but I do have a choice about the way I respond. So now when I find myself feeling burdened by real life, I ask God to teach me the lesson and to show me the funny. When I returned to the salon on the following Saturday, I was still laughing. I shared my breakthrough, my revelation, my awakening (whatever you want to call it) with anyone who would listen, and we all laughed together.

This past Thanksgiving I was at a friend's house enjoying dinner when another guest spoke to me and called me by name. I didn't recognize her, but obviously she knew me. She told me that she remembered me from the salon where I used to work. It had been five years since I'd seen her. She told me that she has a son now and had recently gone through a divorce. She also reminded me that she had been there the day I came into the salon talking about how my pants had fallen down at Captain D's. She told me that while going through her divorce, that was a story she called on to remind her to laugh. We laughed again together. Life had taken its best shot and we're still standing. Standing and laughing.

Go on and laugh, girl. If you're anything like me, laughter is the only abdominal exercise you get.

Robin E. Wilson is a teacher, healer, and seeker. Robin travels and collects experiences that make great stories that she can share with her daughter, her friends, and the world.

If I Knew Then What I Know Now About Life's Challenges . . .

Greatness is not measured by what a man or woman accomplishes, but by the opposition he or she has overcome to reach his goals.
—Dorothy Height

How great are you? Have you learned from the opposition you have faced, as Dorothy Height said? We all have proverbial stumbles in our lives, but it is how we face those spills and tumbles—how we get back up again—that determines who we are as women. Whatever your challenge may have been, is, or will be, love yourself through it. Know that you are capable of managing the situation with grace and dignity. Decide to succeed and be in charge of how you feel about the challenge you are facing. Know that challenges are temporary and what is everlasting is the lesson.

THE PRESIDENT OF ME

By Lalah Hathaway

I have a song on one of my CDs called "Learning to Swim." It really applies to my life, both literally and metaphorically. Throughout the history of my life, I've had like fifty friends try to teach me to swim. And through all those swimming lessons, I never get the actual top of my head wet. I have this weird block about swimming. I'm constantly learning to swim, but I still don't know how to swim.

I realize that in my own personal life, I'm a student all the time. I'm always relearning things or learning them from a different perspective, again and again and again. One thing that I'm learning to do is trust my intuition. It's huge. Particularly as a young woman, you're socialized to believe what people tell you: trust authority; trust people in your field, they know what's best for you.

Start trusting your intuition now. Whatever you are, wherever you are, start believing in the woman that you are right now. It's vitally important. Even if you make a mistake, you made a mistake because it's something you believed in.

I used to do a lot of things by committee. If I'm going to buy a house, I've got to call my manager, talk to my mom, my girlfriends, the guy I'm dating. I try not to do so much by committee now. You need to trust the voice in your head and the gut feeling you have instead. I have realized some of the worst decisions I have made in my life were counterintuitive and blew up my face. In the beginning of my career, there were decisions made without my involvement, everything from my hair to what kinds of songs I'd perform, even the tempos. Some of those decisions I was not happy with, and I had a hard time justifying my own inner voice.

I have my hair locked now, and that was a big deal. They didn't want me to lock my hair; it was too African American, it wasn't the hip thing to do. I had to learn the hard way that no one does me better than me. I am the president of me, the CEO of me. Young women have come a long way in the twenty years since I've started making music. I look at Beyoncé and Rihanna. They understand what their power is. Even when there are people pulling the strings, I think that young women in the music industry are a lot more self-possessed. It might be self-absorbed, but the result is the same. When I was younger, I didn't realize that my gut instincts were right on.

When I personally don't trust my intuition, I always end up feeling shitty, no matter how it goes, because I let someone else navigate my life. Women are socialized to look outside for answers. The double message you get as a young woman is to stand on your own two feet as long as everyone else is standing. I am now over forty, and with time and experience you become aware and self-aware. At this point, I'm willing to go down in flames.

Now, sometimes it's hard to differentiate between your intuition and that negative, fearful voice. To me, you're motivated by one of two things. There's fear or love. You either do things out of fear, or you do them out of love. All these not-so-nice things that we do, not being kind to others, not trusting our intuition, that's all fear. I'm really working on listening and differentiating. Sometimes even when I hear that fear voice, I follow it. I'm working on it. The important thing is to realize you are a work in progress. You're a work in progress and you're going to learn, and relearn.

Once you let yourself flow with what your real intuition tells you to do, you're flying. Once you start doing it, you can't stop. I recently went to Hawaii and got in the water and attempted to learn to swim. This time I got in and let go—there I was in the ocean, swimming. You can too.

Lalah Hathaway is the talented daughter of the R&B icon Donny Hathaway. Lalah attended Chicago's Performing Arts High School, then graduated to the famed Berklee

College of Music in Boston. At the age of twenty-one she signed her first record deal. Lalah would like to leave a legacy of music that makes women and people really feel something, whether it be happiness, sadness, grief, or heart-ache. Her current album is entitled *Self Portrait* and is a "look back" over her life and the lessons she's learned.

Your Soul's Sustenance

We all know that there are challenges in life. You will have to go through some stuff to get to the best woman you can become. That stuff makes you and isn't meant to break you. Once you understand that, you will be challenged and you can move forward prepared. The preparation is mental, physical, emotional, and spiritual. Fortify yourself so you are up to life's challenges.

Your Personal Book of Revelations

- *Have you felt like things are too hard to handle?*
- *Is your first instinct to meet your challenges or to retreat from them?*
- *How can you fortify yourself mentally, physically, emotionally, and spiritually?*
- *Have you had a particular challenge that has made you feel defeated? What can you do differently to tackle this challenge?*
- *Have you had a challenge success story? Briefly write it down and read it back out loud whenever you feel another challenge on the horizon.*

VII

Isms

I miss the seventies where you had shows like The Jeffersons *and* All in the Family, *where black people could be black and white people could be white. Racists could be racists, and non-racists could be non-racists, but it was talked about.*

—Queen Latifah

We already have three strikes against us: racism, sexism, classism. Now more prevalent than its predecessors is a fourth: *colorism.* In your lifetime, if you have not already, you will experience all four. Racism is a set of beliefs put in place for economic benefit. Angela Davis said it best: "I see racism as being more dangerous in the latter nineties than it was in the fifties and sixties. For one thing, it is more structurally entrenched in the economic system, and so the globalization of capitalism has led to racism structure that we often do not recognize as racism."

As women, we experience this every day—the systematic way in which one group keeps limited natural resources from another. It happens in corporate America when you are hired and your male counterpart will get paid more money than you because he has a family to take care of. It is the denial of credit, the predatory lending rates even though your credit is stellar. The experience of being pulled over for a routine check that we call "driving while black," or racial profiling or losing a loved one due to excessive force by the police.

Sexism is also as relevant today as it was thirty years ago; it is just done more discreetly. Regardless of your professionalism, skill, education, and best intentions, some men will mistake your interaction with them as sexual. Candace remembers being at a ceremony and a gentleman who was high up in a local organization spoke out about the famous fish fry that the group hosted at least twice a year. Candace said, "Boy, I would really like to try the fish because I have heard about it from so many others in the community." He then said, "I am sorry, I don't think my wife would like that. I am married." He then proceeded to show her his wedding ring. Clearly he has an enormous ego, not to mention the need to flatter himself over a public fish fry.

Classism and the seeking of status have become a societal driving force. Music has had a great influence on how we look at poverty and property. The fast cars, the MTV cribs, the seeming overabundance that puts you in a place that may make you feel inadequate when you can't compete with the images, and compels you to ask, "What am I doing wrong?" It's the bling-bling era, a phrase coined by Lil Wayne and adapted by hip-hop artists after the clinking sound of jewelry. If it's not shiny and expensive, then you are not elevated in the eyes of others. African Americans are the largest consumers, spending billions of dollars on luxury items each year. All that glitters is not gold. Camille Cosby said, "As long as you are consumers, you are a beggar. You must become a producer."

Items of luxury are nice when you would like to reward yourself for accomplishments and milestones. Unfortunately, as women, we utilize luxury brands as descriptors for who we are and what we stand for. It's the one-up factor women engage in, the bragging rights; flaunt it if you got it. Instead of values and ways we can empower ourselves through building businesses, we look to global designers to do it for us through the right handbag, shoes, jewelry, and clothing, making us as black women the *ultimate beggars*.

Good news. The posturing and positioning is exhausting, and the pendulum is swinging back because as our economy has been give a sobering wake-up call after massive layoffs, losses in the financial markets, and a crashing housing market, the era of bling has taken a dizzying fall from popularity because it is hard to keep up with the Joneses when your own home is in foreclosure and your company just closed.

We have lots to work through, but our own worst enemy is ourself. We do it to ourselves by creating decisive ways to keep each other down from assumptions based on color, to the labels on our clothes and the cars we drive. It is a shame after all of the hard work of some of the amazing women in the twentieth century that as young women today, we are reduced to mistreating one another based on superficiality.

There is a brand-new era being ushered in that reflects on social values, where we are going as a people, and the changes we need to make to get there. We can't stand idly by as we let others define who a young black woman is, or let someone else fight our battles for us. This section will help us to choose our battles, whether it be in the public spotlight or quietly behind the scenes, by hearing the stories of inspiring women who have made those difficult choices, and ultimately giving each of us one less battle to fight.

LITTLE BLACK MINISKIRT

By Ashley Foxx

Every now and then, when the weather is warm and enticing and I'm feeling confident, I'll still slip into a dangerously short miniskirt. My closet still contains a colorful collection: zebra print, khaki, country-club plaid, and plain black. The rush of summer air tickling my bare legs, however, always brings a bittersweet feeling. I tend to cringe because I can't help but remember my first black miniskirt and how it ended up in the trash the same day I bought it.

At fifteen, a miniskirt was the perfect temptation. It was my rebel cry. When teen girls are in the thick of adolescence, nothing is more deliciously disobedient than a short skirt, high heels, and bare legs—not even "forgetting" to clean your room or sneaking on the phone past midnight. The first time I wore it, I felt a gleeful surge of satisfaction as I looked up from applying my third coat of ninety-nine-cent "very cherry" lip gloss. Over my shoulder, I caught a glimpse of my mother's disapproving reflection in the mirror. I could see her mentally picking her battles. It had been a war zone lately; we fought about everything: my 11:30 curfew, the "tone" I took when she got on my nerves, and of course, my wardrobe selection. However, this time I had recently brought home a spotless report card, my room was clean, and I bought that skirt with my own secret monetary stash. She could sense that I was not merely getting ready for a party this time, I was making a point: I was fifteen and, yes, I wanted to wear a miniskirt.

Plus, this was no ordinary party I was attending; no pin-the-tail-on-the-donkey or musical chairs shenanigans. I was going to an upperclassman's birthday bash at a club in downtown Memphis. Even though it was just local, there was something incredibly chic and sophisticated about a party "in the city" for a fifteen-year-old girl whose family had moved on up to the middle-class suburbs. So for this party, I transformed into a Maybelline misfit: painting my face with dollar-store cosmetics, covertly spraying on my mother's designer perfume, and sliding my slender thighs into a little black mini that I bought with my own money. The rebel in me just loved how a beautifully made-up face, a skirt that skimmed the borderline of provocative, and a party thrown in the wilds of downtown Memphis could create such alarm in my mother's face. We shared a cool silence as she drove me to my friend's house. Her eyes kept averting from the road, to my brown legs spilling from beneath the polyester, and back to the road again. The creases of worry on her broad forehead deepened and the veins on her hands made patterns as she gripped the steering wheel. She didn't completely buy the idea that my pals and I were just going to continue our obsessive primping. She knew (and I hated that she knew) that we were joining forces to plot, but she remained silent. At the time, I thought her warning eyes and tight-lipped consent made the party all the more inviting; but, as I found out years later, the only reason she was silent was because she was praying for me.

I kissed my mom on the cheek and grabbed my purse the second we pulled into the driveway. My mother touched my arm as I reached for the door handle and said, "Ashley, remember who you are and whose you are." Ever since I hit puberty, before I could even get out the door, my parents' cautious words would always meet me at the threshold. They were so ingrained in me, I could mouth them in unison or sometimes beat them to it with a rushed, "I know, I know. Remember who I am and who I belong to." As I hurried out of the car, I nodded a flippant yes to her request and sauntered inside to meet my two comrades. We examined each other's outfits, made suggestions, and then finally gave approval in the skillful way only fifteen-year-olds can. Finally finished, we piled into her uncle's car. She had easily convinced him to take us to the party, and although he was forty, he was a much more acceptable chauffeur than our parents. He had an expensive, long, sleek black car with a leather interior, and we giggled at how jealous we would make our enemies when we pulled up to the party.

I was about to slide in the back with my friend when her uncle asked me to sit in the front. For a split second, the offer struck me as odd, but I masked my concerns with a naïve smile. After arriving at the party, I quickly realized that the momentum leading up to the event caused more excitement than the actual festivities. It was overcrowded, hot, and too dark for anyone to even notice my miniskirt. So, when the clock struck 11:00 P.M., I hurriedly kissed my friends good-bye and made my way through the crowd to the street. All my friends were staying put at the party, but I had an obligation to make my parents' curfew. I could have called them for a ride home, but that would have defeated the purpose of the whole night; it was a declaration of independence! Consequently, when my friend's uncle offered to take me home earlier that evening, I had eagerly accepted. I quickly found his long black car parked on a side street. He had been waiting for me the whole time.

He turned the radio dial and smooth, slow jazz filled the air. His long fingers touched the knob of the air conditioner and he asked if I was comfortable. I lied and said I was fine, even though the cool hum of air from the vents was giving me goose pimples. I tugged at my skirt and crossed my arms tightly to keep warm and hide my silly attempt at being polite. We slipped in and out of cordial conversation for the first ten minutes. Then the hints dropped. He liked my smile. My skirt was nice. Could a girl who was fifteen be this beautiful? I didn't quite know how to accept his flattery. Up until that moment, I had only dealt with the stammering rehearsed pick-up lines of high school boys. These compliments felt totally different. Still, I continued to play the part of the polite Southern belle. Even though

I was a little girl and felt like a little girl, I didn't want him to think I was immature or fearful. I was wearing a miniskirt and my mother's perfume, surely I could handle a little flattery—even if it was coming from my friend's forty-something uncle. Yet I knew I had ventured into totally foreign territory.

I watched his eyes—remembering my mother's—avert from the road to my legs and back to the road again. His hand was awfully close, and the way he was massaging the gearshift made me revert to my nervous habit of twirling my hair. I was so aware of everything at that moment, like how you remember a car crash or your first kiss, and how time slows down so you can consider every critical second. I heard everything he said even though he was whispering over the jazz. He told me I seemed mature and there was no need to beat around the bush. He wanted to make love to me. I knew textbook sex from homework I had in health class. Making love was something people only did in the movies or sang about on the radio at hours when I was supposed to be asleep. He would give me anything I wanted: expensive Thai dinners, trips to France where sex wasn't so taboo, money for more black miniskirts. I knew his words were only whispers, but I could feel every verb and noun creep up and down my skin. I was quiet for a moment, searching for something witty to say, but I didn't want to flirt this way. My speechlessness made me hate everything about that claustrophobic car. The air-conditioning now made the air stale and stuffy. The jazz music was harsh and unfamiliar. The leather seat was punishing the back of my sweaty thighs. In the moonlight, I could still see his hand slowly massage the gearshift while his eyes playfully bounced from street to legs to street.

As we turned onto the lonely road that led to my house, he eased off the gas and drove at an aggressively slow pace. "You know, we could pull over right now," he said, eyes no longer bouncing but gazing steadily at the shadow nestled between my young thighs. This was not what I wanted. I wanted to get the attention of this seventeen-year-old boy with curly hair and dimples that was at the party. The miniskirt was meant for him, not for some man I barely knew. I twirled my hair again and wiped my sweaty palms on what little fabric my clothes provided. Since I was without money or cell phone, I wasn't sure what I could do if he decided to stop. Thankfully, from somewhere deep inside, I found the right words to say: "Take me home." We continued to ride the rest of the way in silence. I thought I caught a slight smirk on his face but I didn't care. I was just grateful that his eyes were now solely focused on the road ahead.

When I finally got home, all of the fear and confusion from that night stirred within me. It had never occurred to me that I wasn't invincible, that I could be touched in ways that I did not want. I had been flirting with my sexuality, hoping to explore the beauty of French kissing and the art of covering hickeys. However, that night I wandered far away from the world of teenage puppy love into a grown-up game of sexual attraction, and it was my fault. I made the first move; I wore that little black miniskirt, despite my mother's disapproval.

Safe inside my room, I stood in front of the mirror and let the tears wash away the drugstore mascara and wiped the last trace of lip gloss from my mouth. I closed my eyes for a minute, letting the "what-ifs" and "what could haves" rattle me. When I opened my eyes, I saw my mother's reflection as she stood there watching me silently. She knew (and I'm blessed that she knew) that I needed her arms around me. The events of the night spilled from my mouth and she just listened and held me tight. Her silence that night meant much more to me than her words. I know now that it was her silent prayer that saved me, and it was her peace that comforted me then in just the right way. When the tears subsided, she wiped my face with her warm hands and helped me into my soft cotton nightgown. Before bed, I crumpled up that little black miniskirt and threw it in the garbage. My mother kissed me good night and closed the trash lid.

That night, of course, didn't completely eradicate miniskirts from my closet. Throughout the years, I still have slipped into one or two. Now that I'm much older, though, itty-bitty minis have definitely lost most of their appeal (I'd trade them for a good pair of blue jeans any day). However, that night taught me a powerful lesson about remembering "who I am and whose I am," my parents' favorite little pearl of wisdom. So, "who I was" then was a fifteen-year-old girl, although I was trying to expedite my years by masquerading behind miniskirts and make-up. I, like so many young girls, naïvely sent a message out into the world and I wasn't ready for its consequences. Although women should be able to wear baggy sweatpants or a miniskirt without being objectified sexually, the cruel reality is that this world is a very visual place and our choices—fashion and otherwise—send messages to men, colleagues, and peers. Yes, young women deserve to be respected regardless of what they're wearing, but it's much easier to demand the respect of a first lady, like Michelle Obama, if you look the part. Today, I have grown confident in knowing "who I am" and just "who I belong to," and consequently, I try to project my inner light outward. Whether in jeans and sneakers or a dress and heels, I am a beautiful, black woman that is fearfully and wonderfully made. I define the clothes; the clothes, the men, this society, do not define me. With that affirmation, I look in the mirror every day, get artfully dressed, and dare anyone to misinterpret the message.

Ashley Foxx is the creator of Foxxology Report (foxxology.com), an online destination for media, marketing, and advertising professionals of color. Prior to launching the Foxxology Report, she held various positions in marketing, public relations, and professional development within the magazine industry at key companies such as Magazine Publishers of America, Hearst Magazines, and *Black Enterprise*.

In 2005, Ashley received a bachelor of arts dual degree in communications and English from the University of Pennsylvania (UPenn) and will receive her master's in digital media from Columbia University Graduate School of Journalism in 2010. She is originally from Memphis, Tennessee, where her parents, Brett and Lela Foxx, and her sister, April, still reside. She currently lives in New York, although she will always and forever be a Southern belle.

The Black Girl

By Bianca Payton

My high school career carries some of the most vivid memories of my life. My mother moved me from South Carolina to Bernardsville, New Jersey, a beautiful suburb that is considered horse country. The school system is one of the best. Yet I felt as though I was on a constant roller coaster, changing personas with each school term. I was one of three African Americans who attended the school, and I evolved from being known as the quiet and soft-spoken black girl to being defined as a "real" black person. I was friendly, witty, not afraid to speak my mind, and I was friends with everyone. My popularity came to a screeching halt when more and more people began using my race as a way to define me or predict my behavior and responses. When I realized that there were a large portion of people that not only knew me as Bianca, but as that *black* girl Bianca, I became a Menace to Society.

As any revolutionary would, I felt as though it was me

against the world; my back was against the wall. Even though this might not have been the case, I spent over a year convincing myself that it was. From fistfights to near expulsion, it took the glory of God in the form of my precious grandmother to teach me that the power of God's love can destroy any hatred inside my heart. I was taught that I should love my enemies, not hate them. Things of this nature are not pleasing to God, so I was therefore missing out on my own blessings. I am intelligent, above average, and destined to do great things. It was the experiences from high school that have molded me into the person that I am today. Four years of Bernards High School taught me life lessons that I could *never* learn from a book.

My personality started to really develop when I was in middle school. I was living in South Carolina with my grandparents at the time, and stayed there for grades five through eight. I was outgoing, charismatic, and "fun." Even though I was young, I have always been wise beyond my years. I had a personality that drew people to me.

People from the South hated and isolated those who were different. Being from up north made life much harder for me. At such an impressionable age, I thought it would be better for me to blend in and not draw too much attention to myself. I changed the way I dressed, often discarding the brand-name clothes, shoes, and accessories that my mother sent me from New York City. Having a mother in the music and fashion industry made it hard for me to blend in. Honestly, it was hard pretending to be "regular."

And had I not been one of three black kids in my high school, I probably would have continued down this same path.

I'm almost positive that my whole outlook on life changed in the beginning of my tenth-grade year, within the first two weeks. I can remember sitting in my sociology class, talking to a girl named Gaby. She was Hispanic, from New Rochelle, New York, and I felt like I could connect to her a lot more than the other people in my school. We would trade stories about living in New York, how it was so much better than New Jersey. I do not really remember the extent of the conversation that erupted in class, but it was quickly switched to the issue of race. Race and religion were subjects that I liked to stay away from because the chance of offending someone is so prevalent. There was another Spanish girl in my class named Elaine. Gaby and Elaine were from the same country, Paraguay, but Gaby didn't even consider her Spanish. Elaine hung out with all the white girls and made sure she stayed away from people of color.

While having a friendly debate, I could feel the tension rising in the room. There were a couple of boys in my class, including this Jewish boy, who tried their best to make me feel uncomfortable. Why, I cannot really explain. I was able to sense the change in the atmosphere. I braced myself because I knew what was coming next. I had heard of little snide comments being made, but no one had ever blatantly disrespected me. Until this day. I think that the teacher asked about the factors that contributed to the high crime rate and violence in urban cities, or something to that effect. Whatever the question was, I knew that people in the class would use this as a way to attack minorities, black people specifically.

Elaine decided to comment. This was a ploy, no doubt, to receive praise from everyone else. It was always a contest to see who could push my buttons and how I would respond. Elaine said that racism was something that was constructed a long time ago and no longer applied. She said that she also thought that a lot of black people used racism as a crutch to dignify their actions. The entire time she was talking, all eyes in the classroom were on me. I wanted to be careful in how I responded to her. My emotions were too out of control. I jumped out of my seat and asked her what the hell she knew about being a black person. Feeding off the excitement, she decided to try to argue with me. I wasn't in the mood to argue, though. I wanted to fight. I lunged at her while my teacher, holding a baseball bat, threatened to expel us (me) if I ever jumped out my seat again. I looked at my entire class, knowing that I had changed that day.

From that point on, school became a daily battleground for me. As far as I was concerned, it was me against the world. I had a daily routine of going to school and not talking to anyone unless they talked to me. I would walk down the hallways waiting for someone to say something, look at me funny, or run into me. I was feared. Hated. Despised.

The last racial incident that I encountered was different. One day in my United States history class, this girl commented that it smelled like a "black man" in the room. It was at this moment that I felt the most alone. I knew she had made a racial comment (I was used to them by now), but the silence in the room told me that it made a big impact. I approached her and asked her what she said. She told me that she said something really stupid and she was really sorry. I looked at her, my peers, and my teacher. Everyone was on pins and needles, waiting for my reaction. At that exact moment, I felt like I could seriously kill her. Seriously. Instead, I turned around and walked straight out of the classroom.

My high school experience equipped me to better deal with the problems that were to come in my future. One of my closest high school friends, Lizzie, has an Italian background with family from the woods of Kentucky. It was her family that made it clear that they would rather her not be friends with a black girl. Despite the adversity, Lizzie and I grew closer. There are many things about me that she does not understand. From time to time, she even cracks jokes on the whole white versus black thing.

I slowly came to realize that I was only punishing myself. My grandmother was instrumental in helping me look to God for my problems. Once I was able to do that, my life began to turn around. Pent-up hatred in my heart would only hurt me in the long run. I will miss out on my blessings and all the Lord has in store for me. I realized that I had to change my life, my behavior, and my attitude.

Bianca Payton is a student at American University who volunteers her free time for women's empowerment projects and plans to get her law degree and practice crisis management.

Thanksgiving Day

By Nicole Paultre Bell

It was an extra-special Thanksgiving Day for me. Family was everything to Sean and me, and we chose our wedding day—Saturday, November 25, 2006—so that we could make it a long weekend of activities. The weekend was finally here, and after all of the planning, I was about to get married in just two days, and I could not keep the smile off my face. Forget about being exhausted, I was working on 100 percent adrenaline. As I helped prepare dinner that evening, Sean was fielding calls from all of the friends and family that were traveling into town.

I was living my dream. How many women actually get to marry their high school sweetheart? Sean had caught my eye. I was a straight-A student and he was a baseball player at John Adams High School in New York City. Sean was handsome and sweet, and we had so much in common. We would talk on the telephone for hours, go out on dates to the movies, and think about what our future would bring.

I was one year behind Sean, and when he received a baseball scholarship to a local community college, we were elated. I had planned to go to college, but then I got pregnant. Sean left school and worked as many jobs as he could to take care of us. He loaded trucks for a local newspaper company and a dairy plant. After seven years of being together and the birth of our second daughter, we were going to get married. The night before our wedding, my mother hosted a bridal shower for me at her home, and Sean headed out for a bachelor party with his friends at a local club. I kissed him good-bye and I went to bed.

There was a missed call on my cell phone from Sean at 1:00 A.M. and I was awoken at 4:00 A.M. by my mother. Something had happened to Sean, we weren't sure what, and I raced to Jamaica Hospital. When we arrived at the hospital, the New York Police Department officers were cold, as if Sean had committed a crime. They gave us absolutely no information for the first hour. Finally, after I begged a security guard, he led me to a room and said a doctor would be with us shortly. I was in denial; I thought that they were going to tell us that he was in a car accident.

Just then my brother in-law came in and told me what the police had done to Sean. There were fifty bullets, killing Sean and severely wounding his childhood friends Joseph Guzman and Trent Benefield.

What? *Dead, this can't be! Today is our wedding day*. I cried so loud and hard. The pain in my chest and my head was just unbearable.

It took seven more hours before they let me identify

Sean's body. How could this happen? The police assumed that Sean and his friends were armed, yet they never found a gun. Why would they shoot fifty bullets? The late Reverend Timothy Wright, who was part of my extended family, reached out to activist Reverend Al Sharpton of the National Action Network, who arrived at the hospital and never left my side.

This was racism at its finest, and I needed to make sure that there was justice and that no other family would have to go through this. Sean was a father, a son, a friend, a person, and my soul mate. Mourning Sean's death was and is an incredible pain and heartache I would never wish on any human being; I knew that I did not want his death to be swept under the rug. I prayed to God every day to give me the ability and strength. I had absolutely no experience with community activism, but I was about to learn. When was the excessive force utilized by police departments around the country going to end, and who was going to end it? How many more Amadou Diallos and Sean Bells does it take before policies are changed? How many families, mothers, fathers, wives, girlfriends, sisters, daughters, and sons are going to suffer silently as black men become victims?

I petitioned to change my last name to Bell to honor Sean's memory, and I won. We organized vigils and marches. Three of the five detectives involved in the shooting went to trial on charges ranging from manslaughter to reckless endangerment. Each day I would go to court, and people would stand silently outside the courthouse. Some of them would even do it every day before they went to work. As I walked by I would hear prayers being whispered. There would be handmade signs of support.

After a difficult six-week trial, the verdict rendered by Judge Arthur Cooperman acquitted all three officers. I had to be carried into a side room because I could not even walk. I was confused. *Where is the justice? Sean is dead! My daughters have no father, and no one is responsible?* The pain was unbearable. I wept along with my family, friends, and the people who have supported us as a family.

Have you ever been in a place in your life where you have a decision to make and it could alter the lives of not only you but everyone else around you?

That was my moment. On the morning of April 25, 2008, I had to make a decision. When I walked out of the courthouse that day, hand in hand with Reverend Sharpton and the rest of our family, it was for our daughters, for all of the wives, mothers, and families who have suffered devastating loss due to excessive use of force by police departments around the country. It was for Sean's legacy.

The Bell family and my parents, sisters, cousins, and neighborhood friends all became one, and we never wavered. Together we marched and organized a series of protests and slowed down the city that never sleeps. At one such protest the crowds made their way to the streets, stopping the flow of traffic. The police arrested over two hundred people, including my parents, Trent, Joseph, Reverend Sharpton, and me.

We approached Congressman Gregory W. Meeks, and

along with numerous members of Congress, asked for an investigation. The U.S. Department of Justice announced that its Civil Rights Division would conduct an independent review of the facts and circumstances surrounding Sean, Trent, and Joseph's malicious attack. There were hearings by Congressman John Conyers of the Judicial Committee, and the investigation is still ongoing.

Then I began to see the small miracles in this tragedy. Young men who would never speak to one another began to embrace each other as brothers, regardless of race or ethnicity. Racial profiling of brown and black men was openly discussed. Policies began changing.

I also found myself in a place where I needed to forgive. That was tough, but in order to go on for my daughters, I needed to provide them with a mother who would not be bitter. I needed to come up with ways to educate young people about their rights if and when they are stopped by the police so that we can prevent another Sean Bell tragedy. I started an annual event, the Sean Bell Conference: Minority Men and the Police, to help young people understand their rights and responsibilities if and when they are stopped by a police officer. We enlisted the help of the police department, attorneys, civil liberties activists, and elected officials so that we can all have an open dialogue on how to work with one another. In addition, we launched the Sean Bell Little League, developing sportsmanship and leadership in young boys and girls. One of the most important lessons we as a community have learned from Sean's death is, we no longer can be silent and hope this doesn't happen to our family.

Nicole Paultre Bell is a mother of two daughters and a college student who is currently managing her nonprofit organization, When It's Real, It's Forever. Nicole and Sean's parents, William and Valerie Bell, family, friends, and elected officials were able to successfully rename a stretch of three blocks of Liverpool Street, in Jamaica, Queens, near the site of the shooting, to Sean Bell Way.

If I Knew Then What I Know Now About Isms . . .

I don't judge people by their sexual orientation or the color of their skin, so I find it really hard to identify someone by saying that they're a gay person or a black person or a Jewish person.
—Diana Ross

Any type of ism, whether it be sexism, racism, ageism, or any other ism, is an insidious practice of oppression. We must work toward erasing the world of isms, and that work starts with us. We must realize that isms work both ways—we cannot complain about being marginalized and then turn around and make a racist comment toward someone else. Isms are embedded in our society and are pervasive. The one thing we need to remember is that we are humans and our humanity is connected and far greater than any class, ethnicity, age group, or womanhood.

VIII

I'm on Top of My Game

I'm extremely ambitious. I don't know why people are afraid to say that. I won't sell my soul to the devil, but I do want success and I don't think that's bad.
—Jada Pinkett Smith

What does it really take to make it? How do I choose the career that is right for me? The job market is dwindling; will I ever get my foot in the door? How can I transition from college to career, or do I have leverage where I am in my career to get to the next level? Long gone are the days that your first day of the job is met with enthusiasm and after twenty-five years of service you retire with a gold watch and a lifetime of great memories. The job market has changed. Between mergers, downsizing, outsourcing, booms, and busts, as well as the economic up- and downswings, the job market can be unpredictable.

Although it may sound bleak, in every situation, regardless of how difficult, there always lies an opportunity. America is built on small businesses that have grown into mega enterprises, and great wealth has been accumulated based on individuals or partners coming up with an idea that fulfills a need. It is Madam C. J. Walker, Oprah, Steve Jobs, Bill Gates, Edward Lewis, and Robert Johnson. Whether they are hair care, television programming, computers, networks, or a publication that catalogs it all, these companies change the way we live and the way we look at ourselves.

There is now a growing number of black women who are CEOs or at the top of the management levels at major Fortune 500 companies. There are opportunities everywhere. Some women will take the job for right now, others will swing open their own business, others will opt out of the career track and seek raising a family, which is a job in itself. Then there is a group of women who, after years of strategic thinking, will get the position they have always wanted and in turn bring other women along.

Regardless of the path that you choose, if you want to be successful, you will need to take risks and face challenges at every level and step out of your comfort zone. Risk comes with sacrifice and a price that some of us are not willing to pay.

We have news for you: A successful career or business is built with time, tenacity, relationships, and the best lessons learned from failures. Success is certainly a journey and not a destination. If you rush it, you will miss all of the exit signs that take you to valuable lessons needed for your next step in your career and life. The women in this chapter share with you their experiences and what it takes to get to where you want to be in your career.

GOAL DIGGER

By Rashana Hooks

I am a goal digger. I am a woman who is attracted to success and in love with hard work.

My love affair with goals is no secret. I make it very clear and obvious that I'm here to succeed.

I wish I had an astounding story to tell the world that gives a reason for my drive and determination. I have no rags-to-riches story, this is just who I am. It's ingrained in my DNA, it's my essence and my life. In my eyes there is no such thing as average or complacency; therefore, I don't settle for anything less than the best in everything I do. I set both personal and professional goals so I cannot only better myself, but set examples for others.

In theory, all of those things may qualify me as a goal digger, but what truly makes me one is the passion that burns inside me to be successful in my career and the commitment I make to myself to achieve it despite the obstacles and challenges that may come my way. You see, the three things that make me and every other successful woman out there a certified goal digger are the three Ps—passion, perseverance, and positivity. These three elements are ingrained in my mind, body, and soul. My passion ignites the fire, my perseverance keeps me fanning the flames, and my positivity protects me from any negative damage. Out of the three, I would have to say my perseverance is the biggest factor in my success. My tenacious and persistent mindset is what keeps me up way past my bedtime to meet deadlines and provide my best work possible. My perseverance has also caused me to create opportunities for my goals to be achieved even when there weren't any present. Not matter how hard it seemed, I created opportunities for myself through my exemplary work ethic and fearless nerve.

Life as a goal digger is a nonstop journey to success. Each and every goal set and achieved is a stepping stone to the next. Although I find myself in a happy place most of the time, I worry that I will never be "satisfied" or take the time to celebrate the many achievements I set for myself. I remember as a young girl my mother would always tell me to "keep your eyes on the prize, Rashana." Her words spoke volumes about my academic achievements in my schooling to my current achievements as a writer and marketing specialist. Ever since she gave me the words of wisdom, my whole life has been about seeking "prizes." Once I identified what they were, I would remember her words and remain focused on achieving them, refusing to allow anything to get in my way. Since I learned early in life, through observation, that many of us women fall victim to distractions (i.e., men, children, and personal issues) when it comes to our dreams and aspirations, I made a conscious effort and vow to allow my goals to dictate the choices I made. Be it a man or the party of the century, I refused to allow anything in my control to jeopardize my dreams. By putting myself and my dreams first, I was able to accomplish my goals successfully and without regrets.

One of the things I do to motivate myself and remind myself of my goals is create a vision board. I'm a firm believer in the power of visual actualization. If you can imagine yourself living your dreams, it makes it so much easier to achieve them. My vision board includes various clippings of things that inspire me, encourage me, and empower me. Many of them are pictures of women whom I admire and consider fellow goal diggers. Others are material items and experiences, such as my summer home or dream vacation, that will remind me of the rewards I can have if I work hard enough. Another good habit I have is writing everything down. When I write my goal down on a blank sheet, my goal immediately becomes real and I feel a level of commitment to achieving it simply because of its existence. Also, when writing the goals down, I incorporate time lines or deadlines to give them even more credibility. A goal is worthless if it does not have a plan of action attached to it. I believe when you give life to a goal, its "date of birth" is important to track its progress and celebrate its success.

I also live by a few principles in the world of goal digging. One is having a personal agenda. No matter what my goal is, I have a clear understanding of why I'm doing what I'm doing and what I want to get out of it. An agenda serves as my road map to keep me en route to my destination despite the detours and roadblocks that may appear. Another principle is embracing sacrifice. Being willing to give up or pause some of the things I enjoyed doing in order to achieve my goal was a necessity. I remember being faced with some hard choices and opting to chose my "prize" because my success meant more than anything. Erasing fear is another important trait I live by. I always told myself if fear did not exist, what would hold me back from achieving my goal? The answer always remained the same—nothing! Once I realized that not being afraid of failure or success was the biggest battle, the road to my goal was less bumpy. I also learned to use my fear as fuel to drive my goal digging deeper. Knowing my worth and not being afraid to communicate it is another principle I live by. In order to reach any goal, you must take full control of your destiny, know your worth, and be able to communicate it thoroughly. Lastly, having resilience and strength is important, especially because when you're a goal digger you are vulnerable to being misunderstood and unsupported. One of the hardest things I had to accept was that not everyone is going to congratulate me on my job well done. There were many discouragers or what I like to call haters who tried to break me down because I served as a reminder of the person they could have become. Being a goal digger means you may have to stand alone at times. Family and friends may not always see your vision. Being a goal digger is being strong.

I know there are thousands of other women out there like me whose sole objective is to live their best life ever. From assistants working their way up the corporate ladder as they envision themselves as the CEO of the company one day, to the Debra Lees of the world who are constantly setting and achieving new goals to take their careers to the next level. That's why I make it my goal every day to reach back and forth as I achieve my goals. Goals diggers are not just women who care only about their goals. They care about helping others reach their full potential as well. I make it my priority to mentor and encourage other young women to reach for the stars. Goal diggers come in all ages, colors, and passions. No matter where they are in life, they are always digging for the better.

My goal-digging traits have proved time and time again that I can do anything I put my mind to. This lifestyle has afforded me great satisfaction and fulfillment not only as a career woman but as a woman overall. I truly believe my authentic drive to succeed is God's work. Once God places a purpose in your life, your success has already been planned. My ability to see no limits and achieve great things can only be a blessing from above. And with His blessings I believe I can achieve every dream I have imagined and more. But with God's blessings also comes balance. I'm a firm believer that every goal digger can have it all, just maybe not all at the same time. All goals can and will be accomplished if we work hard enough, yet focusing on multiple goals at a time usually leads to incomplete and unachieved goals. Why? Because contrary to popular belief, we ladies should not multitask—we should focus on one goal at a time.

The important thing about achieving goals is having a plan and following that plan one step at a time. Although you can achieve goals simultaneously, I don't suggest you act on them simultaneously. What I've learned is to focus on one goal at a time instead of having multiple goals and objectives and trying to reach them all simultaneously.

I know I will forever be a goal digger. It's in my DNA. Just like I'm confident Michelle Obama and Oprah Winfrey will be as well. Because goal digging comes from the heart, it is a passion, it is a lifestyle, it's me.

Rashana Hooks is a marketing specialist for a popular cable network and is currently writing her first book on women and their careers.

Loving the Skin I'm In

By Donja Bridges

I am an eighties baby. Brown lady. Do you like me? Circle yes, no, or maybe so. Interestingly enough, I was told at an early age not to worry about other people's perceptions of me. I was taught to love the skin I'm in by a community of resilient women who are equally responsible for placing me on my cyclical journey of self-discovery, self-confidence, and self-love. According to them, I did not need anyone to like me as long as I loved myself. Such a strong message was not so easy to swallow by a young girl who at the time had a throat more interested in candy necklaces, Kool-Aid, and McDonald's fries. Yet this community of women, comprised of young, old, and middle-aged wisdom, saw in me the potential that has now come to manifest in my passion as an educator, in my love for the power of words, and in my hope for young people and others to see their true potential as well.

I was born in the month of March to a strong mother who claims she had no problem giving birth to me naturally. From birth through adulthood, my mother raised me to be independent, and she always valued the power of education. Full of faith and fire, she is a praying mother who will give you the shirt off her back if you need it. But understand, she is not the one to cross. Brought up in a household that restricted her self-confidence and was void of hugs and kisses, my mother loved me hard and wanted nothing more than for me to have the opportunities she was unable to attain for herself. I was her first child and the first niece and grandchild in the family. I was also a daddy's girl who received plenty of attention from my father, who could not deny me if he tried; I was his little twin. My parents were very instrumental in keeping me well rounded, and to this day, I believe the value of having a two-parent home is priceless.

Growing up, I spent a lot of time at my grandmother's house. Being surrounded by women on a daily basis had a big impact on my perceptions of beauty, womanhood, and responsibility. My grandmother was thoughtful and loving. She seemed so proud to have me as her granddaughter, and she always made me feel safe. I still call her my angel. She kept a clean house, food on the table, and a warm demeanor. I do not recall ever hearing my grandmother say a harsh word to me. She is a gentle spirit and I credit her for my optimism.

My aunties were like my sisters. My mom is the oldest child of four, and her two youngest sisters were teenagers in my youth. "Cool" and "fly" are the words that come to mind when I think of them. Although they did not always like it, I held on to their coattails wherever they went. I looked up to them and wanted so badly to be like them when I grew up. One of my aunts is a diva in her own right, and her style and confidence has had a tremendous influence on why I have always and continue to dream big. My other aunt is down-to-earth and street-smart. *Yo! MTV Raps* was always playing in the basement rec room, and she always taught me the newest dance moves and fads. For my rebellious spirit and love for those in the struggle, I give her props.

These women, who looked like me and took care of me, set high expectations for a young black girl who had her entire life ahead of her. Both of my aunts went to college, so college for me was not a choice but an expectation. Certain standards were set, like chores before fun, books before boys, and marriage before children. I naturally began to develop into a headstrong young lady who was not afraid to speak her mind and had solid self-esteem. This was not always the best attribute to have as a young girl; my mouth still can get me into trouble at times, but this confidence would come in handy as I began to find my passions and figure out my life's pursuits.

Reading and writing has always been something that came natural to me. My mother kept my bookshelf full of literature, and these stories helped fuel my imagination. To keep myself busy as an only child for the twelve years before my younger sister was born, I entertained myself by writing short stories and making up song lyrics for Whitney Houston's next single. It was fun and fulfilling. How would I know that this gift would stay with me and find its way back into my life at a time when medical school and science courses seemed to be the best option toward a career?

I was not looking to be an English major when a black woman professor with locks and a divine demeanor walked into my class my freshman year of college. She was intelligent, strong, and glowing in her love for black literature. Here was a woman at a predominantly white institution of higher education that represented a space of power that I envied and admired. She was a mere reflection of where I came from and who I could be; another woman who would have a lasting impression on my abilities and aspirations. My experience with literature became more personal during this time, and I discovered that although I had invested much time into the idea of becoming a doctor, it did not stimulate my mind and creativity in the way that literature and writing did. Using writing and literature as a form of self-expression was a strength that got me through much self-doubt during my undergraduate years, and my relationship with this professor / mentor reminded me that I come from strong stuff.

I finished college with the ambition to be a published author and / or a magazine editor. I did not see the point in going back to school for a higher degree, although my mother insisted that I do so. I was ready to get my hands dirty and be a part of the real world of writing. My naïvety became quite clear when I received no response from the many articles I sent out to publication after publication.

When I applied for writing positions, I was either under-qualified or did not have enough experience. I became very discouraged during this time and began to wonder if I would ever become the successful, career-driven woman I always envisioned myself to be.

"This too shall pass" are the words that come to mind when I think of this trying time in my life, and these words have become a personal mantra to remind me that all things happen for a reason. I learned very quickly that my dream job was not going to happen overnight, and now when I look back, I realize that at that time, I was not ready for the demands that such a position would require. Every successful woman I look up to did not become successful without hard work, preparation, and time. It is obvious to me now that I needed to plant my seed in order to reap the harvest. All of the women who were and still are inspirational in my life were placed around me in order to keep me faithful in God's will for my life. He was preparing me for what was ahead, and although it was not the path I anticipated, it was the path that was necessary for me to grow and blossom into the woman I am today.

Just like my mother predicted, I went back to school and received my master's degree in education. I never thought I would be a teacher, but I am and I love it. After substitute teaching in high school classrooms for a few months, I found that I enjoyed working with young people, and this propelled me to continue my education so that I could give back to the community that gave so much to me.

There is nothing like being around young people every

day who remind you of how you once were and how important it is to be a positive force in their development into adulthood. I feel a natural kinship with young adults that keeps me innovative in my approach to teaching literature and writing. As an advocate of incorporating more cultural literature into the classroom, I have used my education in African American literature and my experience as a black student who rarely saw myself in the literature I read in school to build a curriculum for a black literature course in my current school district in hopes that more students will see the beauty of black culture and use that knowledge to broaden their thinking of themselves and the world around them. I also urge students to look at writing as a form of expression and to appreciate the power that words can have.

By infusing my love for literature and writing with my passion for enlightening and inspiring young people, I have been able to create an environment that is the best of both worlds. Young adults have fresh perspectives on life, are outspoken, and give me the opportunity to effect change in a powerful way. Through my goal of inspiring them to go after their dreams, they in return inspire me as well to never give up on mine. I am now currently studying toward my doctorate degree and continue to write in the belief that I will be a published author and successful writer.

I reminisce on the love that the women in my life gave and continue to give to me so unselfishly. As this community of women believed in my capabilities to do great things, I now pass on the same encouragement and unwillingness to accept failure in my students, friends, and community. Although challenges have and will continue to come along the way, I believe it is all about the approach you take in dealing with those challenges. The jeweled words of wise women that told me to never give up, to always believe in myself, and to stay strong in the midst of the storm never rang so true as they do now. The lessons I learned and the valleys I've had to experience have only made me more confident in who I am, where I come from, and where I'm going. I am young, powerful, educated, inspiring, courageous, and fearless in the face of doubt. I'm an eighties baby. Brown lady. Do you like me? I love myself and that's all that matters!

Donja Bridges is currently working toward her doctorate in education at Ohio State University. She is an English teacher and aspiring writer.

DANCING MY WAY TO FINANCIAL FREEDOM

By Shamony Makeba Gibson

Ring! Ring! I brace myself as I hear the sound of the bell indicating that my lunch period is officially over. It is time for me to morph into dance mode, and I drag my feet as I walk up eight flights of steps to the studio. As I prepare myself mentally and physically for the forty-five minutes of torture, I begin thinking of an excuse to get my dance teacher to let me sit this one out. An excuse quickly comes to mind. "I'll tell her that my stomach hurts and I can't dance. Better yet, I'll tell her I have cramps. No, I can't tell her that. I used the cramps excuse last week."

I enter the girls' locker room, open my locker, and begin searching for some "appropriate" dance attire to wear to class. I look for a band to pull my hair back and I search deep within myself to find the motivation to take a step into the dreaded classroom yet again. Before I cross the threshold, I shift into my "ballerina posture." I lift my head up, pull my stomach in, which is very hard to do after a big lunch, and I squeeze my buttocks tight. Just as my cheeks take their proper places, I hear the voice of my ballet teacher shouting: "Ready, class . . . and one, and two . . ." I take a deep breath, step into the line of dancers, and pray that today I won't be critiqued about my back being too arched, my legs being hyperextended, or my turns being too black. Oh, did I say that?

I spent a good portion of my life believing that my true passion and life's vocation was dance. From the time I was seven, I was told by teachers, family, and friends that I was a great dancer. I enjoyed dancing, especially the feeling that I got when I was onstage connecting with the audience through the movements of my body. I would dance for several hours a day. It was my life and the life of the people around me. I mention the people because they were the main reason why I continued to dance long after I lost my passion for it. My entire circle of friends were dancers and, at the time, I felt like I had to be one as well.

It wasn't until I auditioned, was accepted, and started attending LaGuardia High School for the Performing Arts that I realized the level of competitiveness that existed in the world of dance. I also recognized how time consuming it was and how it could take over your entire life. Both in school and outside of school I was bombarded with dance terminology, rehearsals, shows, and conversations that consisted of nothing but dance. I also grew weary about talking about body parts, dance tricks, and people's dance accomplishments. It became apparent to me that while I had a dancer's body, I wasn't built for a dancer's lifestyle. For one, I was never aggressive when it came to dance, and I was definitely not competitive. For two, I had the ideal body type but didn't possess the esteem to match it.

As my interest in dance began to diminish, at the same time, I discovered that I had another interest that brought me great happiness: doing hair. Yes, I said doing hair. When I was a young teenager, I started braiding and styling people's hair. My friends and family members would let me practice on them and I was always amazed at what I could create with my hands. One summer before I entered the eleventh grade, I got an opportunity to work in a salon called Locksmyths in Brooklyn. The owner, Ona Maat, took me under her wing and allowed me to be her receptionist and apprentice. During my time there, I learned the fundamentals of natural hair care and how to run a business. I never forgot those lessons, and I am grateful to Ms. Ona for being a role model for female entrepreneurship.

I made the connection early on that the state of a person's hair could affect their attitude and self-esteem. I enjoyed the fact that my work with hair could change the way a person felt about themselves. For example, my mother always wore her locks toward the front of her face. She kept her hair this way because she was very self-conscious about her forehead and had been that way since childhood. It wasn't until I started styling her locks and pulling them up into beautiful buns that she allowed her face and forehead to be revealed. My gift and creativity allowed her to appreciate her beauty on another level and release her negative beliefs. I guess she returned the favor by being my walking advertisement, because her hair brought me many customers. Everyone wanted to know who did her hair. This helped me to learn one of my first lessons about business: Good advertising leads to more clients and more success. I would also get a lot of attention about my own hair. It is my belief that my hair should always look good, because a stylist should be a walking advertisement of her skills and abilities. With this in mind, I strived to do my best work on my hair and the hair of my customers, because you never know who will see the finished product. I'm sure we will all agree that there is nothing worse then a hair stylist with bad hair. It makes you wonder, "With hair like that, what can you do for mine?"

Thanks to the power of black women and the magic of word of mouth, at the age of seventeen I had more clients than I could manage and was making more money then most of my friends and some of the adults that I knew. This expansion happened due to the fact that I offered my clients "at home" service. This allowed people to have their hair pampered and styled within the comfort of their own homes. This is rare in the field of hair. In the beginning, I was just moving through the process, operating unconsciously. Then, as time progressed, I began creating my life and business plan. After all, in order for any business to grow and thrive, there has to be a plan. My mom encouraged me to give my business a name, and in 2005, Afro-Centrix Natural Hair Care was born.

I feel that everyone should be doing something that they love. I'm devoted to, and I get rewarded for, helping people feel good about themselves. This work has created a great deal of joy in my life and has been the key to my happiness. I am now competing with myself and I am able to create my own schedule, which helps me to stay motivated and to produce great work. Great work makes for happy customers.

In my opinion, the perfect ingredients for a successful business are one spoonful of idea, a dash of motivation, a half cup of skill, and a gallon of love. As T. Harv Eker says, thoughts lead to feelings, feelings lead to actions, and actions lead to results. This means that whatever thoughts you have in your mind can be empowered by your actions, which can result in victory. I am now dancing my way to financial freedom, and I encourage every young woman to begin thinking in the same way. Growing up, both my father and my mother stressed that I should start my own business. They believe that this will allow me to touch the world through my "hair artistry" and to pass a legacy on to my children.

Shamony Makeba Gibson is a twenty-year-old entrepreneur who owns her own freelance hair-care business called AfroCentrix Natural Hair Care and works part-time as an apprentice in a salon in Queens, New York. She prides herself on being a "healer" of hair who uses her hands to transmit light and healthy energy into the hair and scalps of her clients. Shamony is also a performance artist, dancing, singing, and acting her way into the hearts and spirits of her audiences.

If I Knew Then What I Know Now About My Career . . .

I love to see a young girl go out and grab the world by the lapels. Life's a bitch. You've got to go out and kick ass.
—Maya Angelou

What a powerful quote from a powerful woman. As you see, many of the women who have shared their stories about their careers had to do exactly what Dr. Angelou suggested. They first needed to know exactly what it was they wanted to do and put themselves in a position to do it. But what if you don't know what you want to do? Let's hear from a veteran what can happen if you are heading down a career path that might not be the path paved for you.

Running into a Brick Wall

By Georgia Woodbine

It's one thing when you don't know what else you can do, but once you know what you can do, you just have to do it. That's the crossroads I found myself at, late into my second lucrative career. I had it all, but I didn't want what I had. Every day, I woke up and wondered where things went wrong. When I was younger, I used to tell myself that I wasn't good enough. It took years for me to work past that fragile little girl to be a confident woman who had tackled two different careers in very demanding industries. But on one particular day, I was reduced back to my former self, a scared little girl, alone and worried about what was coming next. Even though I was a grown woman, I found myself crying just like a teenager who had run from bullies in the high school hallway. I was sobbing uncontrollably at my job, right before work, in the women's bathroom. I laid my head against the side of the cold steel door and just cried.

I didn't see a way out, and I didn't mean out of the bathroom stall. For a moment, that square area was my temporary solace from a job that I no longer enjoyed and that was draining me professionally and, little did I know it, physically.

It wasn't unusual for me to feel dread going into work or to have crying fits. Someone might think that it showed in my performance or on the job, but it did not. I kept it tight at work. I left my expression of emotions for my cathartic bathroom crying ritual. After I had cried I could walk out of the stall and leave all my stress there. Or so I thought. I thought that crying was just a symptom of the stress that I was under for working a job that I no longer loved. But my crying bouts were not just symptoms, they were a signal, a clanging alarm and a blaring alert, that something was wrong.

I ignored it and went about my day. There were many days that I cried thinking about the day ahead and many nights that I cried thinking about the day after that. I still went to work, I still made my numbers. But every day I would wake up and dread going to that dark, burdensome place. For years I worked in a job that helped to raise the value of my bank account at the same time that it was draining my energy to focus on what I truly valued: making an impact. It was so hard to let go of what people called a "good job" because being in that environment no longer felt good to me.

I knew about making transitions from working in the entertainment industry with the best of the best and the biggest names in music. But I left that behind once I saw all the lovely young women who would do, and in fact some of them actually *did* do, virtually anything to be a part of the music world. Regardless of the role that I played, I felt somehow contributory to what these women were faced with. So I left that world and began to work in the pharmaceutical industry. It was a good job with great pay and awesome benefits. But it still wasn't for me. I missed the entertainment industry, and I got enough requests for my services as a consultant to know that I was still missed in a field of work that I enjoyed. I tried to compensate for it by hiring more people to help me with my marketing consulting practice. But the guilt of not doing the work that I knew I could do saddened me, and when I started to turn down projects that I loved in favor of assignments that I felt no passion about at all, well, that downright depressed me. I was sick, sad, and overwhelmed. I didn't know it, I am not sure if my friends or family could tell it, but my body knew it.

I knew that someday I would move back into a line of work that I felt passionate about and that it would take time for me to get there. It turns out that time was something I did not have. I always thought a going-away party and my announcement about the next stage in my life would mark my last day at my corporate job. But it didn't happen like that at all. My last day at work I didn't go out with a bang—I went out in an ambulance.

The morning before I collapsed at work, I felt this feeling that I just couldn't shake. I literally felt trapped with no way out, and I honestly couldn't figure a way out of my trap. I arrived at work and found that it is one thing to be sick of a job and quite another thing to be sick *because of* the job. I had both. The pressure of working a job that starves your spirit can make you physically sick. Add to that the fact that I had sleepless nights worrying about the next day, and there was no respite for me to deal with the fact that even though I was emotionally unhappy, I was also physically overworked.

Normally when I had my crying spells in the bathroom stall, I felt like I had relieved a buildup. By crying I was able to gain some temporary relief before I could move forward. I didn't see this as a weakness; I was just tired and knew that something needed to change. I knew I needed a breakthrough. Crying was a way to express that. The silent alarm that my crying represented signaled the beginning of many exits: an exit out of the bathroom crying, an exit out of that job, and an exit out of the constraints of working in a job that was bringing me down.

But if someone could wave a magic wand and make it all go away, I wouldn't want that to happen. I believe that the pain that I went through was for a reason. It served a purpose. I believe that pain anoints you to do things in ministry, teaching and helping others. After I recovered from my medical setback and the separation from that job, I began to evaluate my life. I moved back toward my value and purpose by teaching others through my workshops and books. Knowing what I know now, I wouldn't change a thing.

I am grateful for every moment. If it hadn't happened, I wouldn't be who I am today—a wiser, stronger, more spiritual woman.

Georgia Woodbine is a motivational speaker and author of the national best-selling book *How to Make Big Bucks Without Selling Your Soul,* as well as other motivational products that empower many in communities near and far.

Your Soul's Sustenance

Some of us get in our own way of success, through our fears and notions before our careers ever start. At our roundtable, one young and ambitious college student said her mother told her when she goes into the corporate arena to never make friends with any other black women at her company because she may need to take them out. Can you really come into a company and start figuring out who you can take out? It actually happened to Candace when she asked a young employee to let her show her the ropes. The employee said, "I don't have to listen to you," and didn't. This young person felt that if she could outshine Candace and run her over, then she would get all of the accolades. The young lady still is struggling to find her footing. What she failed to realize was that Candace was giving her the gift of mentorship. If she wasn't so wrapped up in going from assistant to president, she would have seen the value in the guidance Candace was offering.

Career coach Dee Marshall shares her experience: "Young Savvy, it was a painful season in my career. One day I'm on top and the next day I was out. All the work I had done to win the respect of some of the most intelligent, educated, seasoned, and successful people was no more. I was no longer the go-to girl, no longer a leader, no longer a 'high-potential' and no longer referred to as 'one of the best.' Why? I was standing in my own way, which is typical of some of us brown girls. While I had earned the support, respect, and favor of my colleagues at a prestigious

Wall Street firm, my reaction to organizational change was a major blow. Me standing in my own way—being negative, having a bad attitude, controversial, vocal, loud, you name it, it cost me a big opportunity early in my career.

"However painful the season and embarrassing it was to me personally, I have no regrets, because life's greatest lessons come in our biggest setbacks. There are no mistakes in life, only lessons, and lessons will repeat themselves until learned. Once I accepted this theory, whatever challenges life threw my way, I became anxious to learn the lessons so I wouldn't have to repeat any classes.

"What was the lesson learned? I never once thought about the work it would take to stay on top. I knew enough about creating a roadmap to success and climbing to the top, but I didn't have a conscious thought as to how I would maintain my status once I 'arrived.' Now, years later, having had a successful career on Wall Street and running my own coaching practice, I offer you this: *get out of your own way* and remember these critical success factors for navigating your way up the ladder and staying there.

"*Maintain consistency.* Whatever it is that got you to your ideal career, whatever worked for you, you must continue and consistently deliver. So make it your practice to reflect on what things you can attribute your success and let it be your guide, your playbook.

"*Be flexible.* Whoever it is that employs you will most certainly change their course at some point—business objectives, strategy, structure, and leadership—however, you must remain flexible. Adapt with change or you will be left behind. Make it a point to become relevant and so necessary you're viewed as the 'most valuable player,' and your sponsors and supporters will go to bat for you.

"*Never stop learning.* Learning does not end after college. In order to stay fresh, stay sharp, increase your marketability, and stay competitive, continue to develop yourself. Make it your practice to create an individual development plan listing your areas for development and an action plan that includes specific steps for how you will hone those areas whether it's formal education or informal seminars, workshops, conferences, certifications, designations, volunteer opportunities, or simply getting in conversations over your head.

"*Develop a quality image.* Presence is everything. Be clear that your image, your look, your walk, your talk, your message, your content, your circle—matters. It represents your personal brand. It's your unique selling proposition, the thing that will distinguish you from the rest. So please smooth your rough edges and polish yourself off. Learn business culture, protocol, etiquette, and common courtesy.

"*Grow your EQ.* Dan Goleman says 80 percent of success is attributable to emotional intelligence, and I am a witness! While it is necessary in this day and age to have formal education beyond high school, I encourage you to balance your technical skills with your soft skills; that is, how you manage yourself and how you relate to other people. Your ability to communicate, to problem solve, to resolve conflict, to follow and to lead, to engage and influence others are nonnegotiable competencies and key ingredients to long-term success.

"*Know who you are.* Your ability to climb the ladder, kick down doors, punch in the glass ceilings, break barriers, deal with all the challenges, obstacles, and ups and downs, and not lose yourself will heavily depend on your sense of self. I encourage you to self-discover, find out who you are, why you are here, and where you're going. If you don't know, no worries; just make it your business to work toward defining yourself detached from all things external. If someone asks you, *Who are you?* you ought not to attach your employer, your job title, your companion, your children, your car, your fur coat, your house, your organization, your fill in the blank—know who you are and remain true to *you*.

"See you at the top; raise the bar!"

Your Personal Book of Revelations

- *What are you willing to do to achieve your dreams?*
- *Do you know what your passion is?*
- *Do you have a plan for your career?*
- *Do you have a network of positive people who support your career vision?*
- *How are you going to achieve your goals?*
- *Where do you see your career a year from now? Three years? Five years?*

IX

Got Faith?

I meditate and pray all the time. The faith and respect that I have in the power of God in my life is what I've used to keep myself grounded, and it has allowed me to move away from the storms that were in my life. I'm still a work in progress, but I know that as long as I stay close to God, I'll be all right.

—Halle Berry

Faith is a powerful lesson in your life's experience. No matter where you place your faith, you will at one time or another have to rely on it. Faith for us is an understanding that there is a power much greater than us at work that guides our lives. We place our faith in God and, regardless of the situation we face, we thank Him for the opportunity to learn what He would have us learn.

Oftentimes, people consider faith as an expectation for things hoped for in their lives. Faith is not you hoping for something and receiving it; faith is the quiet space in which you center yourself and know that whatever the outcome may be in any situation, you are covered. What we mean by covered is that you are where you are supposed to be at that moment to learn the lesson you are meant to learn. Faith is knowing that the outcome is the intended outcome and you are well equipped for it no matter what it may be.

Many women may think this is easier said than done, but if you think about it, what do you really have control over but your reaction and actions in a situation. You can choose to be miserable or you can choose to be happy. You can choose to seek out the good in a situation or you can choose to see the misery and despair. With faith you only have the option of choosing to see the best in any situation. Live your life with faith, knowing that you are traveling on the road in which you were meant to tread.

Fear and Faith Can't Exist in the Same Space

By Kimberly N. Cooper

One of my favorite timeless scriptures is Ecclesiastes 3:1: *There is a time for everything, and a season for every activity under heaven.* Time is one of those things I had no concept of as a teenager. I just wanted to live. Be me, do me! There were no consequences except the ones my parents imposed. Time was this barometer that measured how long I needed to be in school—four years in high school and four years in college. Anything after that was suspect! God was in my life—kinda. I mean, I knew He existed, but I didn't have my own personal relationship with Him. I wasn't really thinking about God all that much, to tell you the truth. He kind of was this omnipresent being.

Whenever something affected me, I'd call it my conscience, not the Holy Spirit. My mom called it vibes. I also knew early on that she was spiritual. This is not to say that my teen years were void of God's presence, but I pretty much wouldn't say that my faith was the substance of things hoped for or the evidence of things unseen. So suffice it to say, I was kind of just moving through life doing what I was "supposed" to do: get an education. But the real deal was, all this life was happening around me and I identified only my parents as the controllers of my destiny. I was one of the lucky ones who had two parents who were married to each other. I definitely didn't consider myself a Cosby kid, but I was pretty blessed, not realizing I was an anomaly. I had a quiet expectation that this was how life worked—I would be taken care of forever, or at the very least my parents would be around for a very long time. This is what I believed; however, at a very early age, my beliefs got shaken.

Let me explain.

The Beginning—Hope

Romans 12:2: *Do not conform any longer to the pattern of this world, but be transformed by the renewing of your mind. Then you will be able to test and approve what God's will is—his good, pleasing, and perfect will.*

By the time I was twenty-two, both my parents had passed away from cancer. My mom passed a week before I went away to college and my dad passed a year after I graduated from college. I was raised an only child, only to find out soon after my dad passed that I had an older sister. I was quietly uncomfortable about being alone in this life. Even with the introduction to my sister, without my folks I felt abandoned and alone. I was just plain old scared of life without my folks.

Being out of college for a year at that point, professionally I had just begun my career in the music business. A friend invited me to visit his church in Brooklyn. Now, I am a Bronx girl, so the thought of hiking to East New York on the A train for an 8:00 A.M. church service was not exactly exciting. I figured it was my twenty-third birthday, so what the heck, and it has turned out to be one of the best decisions I made, and it's ten years later.

Back then, I was apathetic about my relationship with Christ. I was almost angry that He took my folks away. I kind of knew everything happens for a reason, but wondered what made me get the short end of the stick with no parents at the beginning of my adult life. I had to grow up faster than my peers who still had a mom or a dad around. In the span of five years I went from two parents to no parents, but life still had to move on—right?

So even though I was disconnected from everything except my career, I was really digging this pastor my boy introduced me to at his church. From the pulpit Pastor A. R. Bernard talked to me about God in a way that appealed to my practical and intellectual nature, and it resonated with me long after I left Sunday service. I got excited about hearing the Word of God and identifying how to apply it practically in my own daily life when I attended service at Christian Cultural Center.

What I loved equally was seeing people who were just

like me in church. I'm kind of cool. Quiet as it's kept, and I wasn't raised in the church. But I had a perception about church people as stuffy and overzealous. I didn't grow up getting spiritually fed, so going to church on a regular basis was something I grew to enjoy as a young adult. The music was contemporary and the service kept me engaged, with praise and worship through the message. But that was on Sunday. Monday through Friday I was filling my time with wrong influences and being engaged by my surroundings and living the music video lifestyle—champagne wishes, caviar dreams, and a whole lot of trying to keep up with the Joneses.

It wasn't all bad, but clearly it wasn't all good. Application is the evidence of learning, and I was not applying what I was learning about God to my everyday lifestyle. The funny thing was, when I didn't do the right thing, I could feel something stir inside me. By this time I learned it wasn't a hunch, it was the Holy Spirit. God was with me the entire time; even if I didn't identify or recognize Him, He was always rocking with me. How refreshing is that? But to keep it all the way real, I was constantly tested.

My relationships with my friends and family, my professional life, and my personal life were constantly being challenged. I was like, "Dang, God, I thought we was all good now?" That's when he hipped me to this, Jeremiah 29:11: *"For I know the plans I have for you," declares the Lord, "plans to prosper you and not to harm you, plans to give you hope and a future."*

That's when I had to start checking myself. I wasn't quite

full of faith, but I was getting warmer. I was learning that in order to have faith, you often literally have to go through the fire of life to develop your own personal relationship with Him.

The Journey—Requires Faith

2 Corinthians 5:7: *We walk (live) by faith, not by sight.*

The more your faith grows, the less physical evidence you need. God had continually blessed me. Personally, I was learning to adjust my perspective and attitude. Professionally, even though I met a few challenges, I was considered successful. My professional relationships grew and so did my profile. The companies—*Honey* magazine, *The Source,* BET—celebrities, parties, title changes—executive assistant, coordinator, marketing manager, editor-in-chief, managing editor, talent booker—it was a pretty okay time to be Kim Cooper. Even when I got laid off for the first time, I wasn't thrown to pieces, I just started my own company and utilized my gifts, talents, and abilities to keep the lights on. I became an entrepreneur. BG Unlimited was birthed from necessity, but clearly it came from a spark that my man G-O-D ignited within me.

Fast-forward. Then life happened as it always does. Those can be simply identified as the seasons of our lives. We all go through them. How long we stay in them depends on our obedience. After a breakup a couple of years ago, my heart was broken and I was devastated. I cried for days on end. Couldn't eat. Couldn't sleep, just a hot mess.

I was already on my path with the Lord, but I had gotten knocked down—badly. My emotions connected this particular breakup to the loss of my parents. The really big difference was at all points I knew God was present. Even though I had developed my own personal relationship with Him, I really couldn't see the light at the end of the tunnel and I was in His Word daily. And when I was not dwelling on how I was feeling at any given moment about my circumstances, when things weren't going 100 percent, this situation wasn't my entire life, just a piece of it. But you couldn't tell me that. For months I was just hurt. *God, how could you let this happen? Why me? It's not fair. . . .* A lot of self-pity going on, which in the moment just feels like I was letting it all out.

Philippians 2:12–13 (NLT): *Dear friends, you always followed my instructions when I was with you. And now that I am away, it is even more important. Work hard to show the results of your salvation, obeying God with deep reverence and fear. For God is working in you, giving you the desire and the power to do what pleases him.*

God is in control and He's our source. When we focus our faith in Him, no matter what the circumstances or the situation, He will make apparent the steps to direct our path. You just have to believe. It took a while, but I finally started to really believe God again. I knew He wouldn't bring me this far to leave me. I really began to identify what it meant to diligently seek Him. There was a real desire and fire for Him. To be comforted by Him and to know Him was challenging and amazing at the same time. That was a very real experience that I believe we all deserve to enjoy, but you have to go *there* and dig deep. You're going to be stretched. The pain of your past or even your present circumstances do not define you. Consider them character-building exercises that God has us go through to get us where He needs us to be.

At any given time, I've wanted to be a million different places and things—actress, lawyer, talk show host, executive. I've almost never been fully comfortable in my present and am always looking for what's next, but once I really started exercising my faith, it was finally becoming clear that it is all to the good. Life isn't perfect, but it absolutely could always be worse. When I look at TV, there's so much negativity and heaviness in the world. So I'm thankful for each day and I keep on pushing when the going gets tough, prayerfully looking forward to another day.

The Growth—Desires Patience

Psalm 37:7: *Be still before the Lord and wait patiently for him.*

I wrote this piece at a particularly empowering time during my healing from depression.

"Now" July 1, 2008
The time
The season
Is upon us.
The reason to commit

To trust
To depend on Him
The One who guides,
Is now.
Now
We surrender to life
Surrender ourselves
To obey the calling upon us.
The temptation that exists
Between spirit and flesh
Will not rest
Protest
Confess
Pray.
I say
This day
A way
Will be made
I'm in a sentimental mood
Feeling subdued
Contemplating the framework
Upon which my mental is situated
I've been inundated
With heaviness about this world we live in.
I've been stressed
Depressed
And often not focused
On the shifting dynamic that plagues my situation

I've made bad decisions
With my indecision
In the midst of a circumcision between
My wants
My desires
My reality.
Now
I figured
I've triggered
The sensibilities
For my ability
To deal with the situation.
Contemplation
About moving forward and leaving behind
The residue that caused chaos
In my mainframe
Time to change game
Change clothes
Refocus
Get noticed
For the righteousness that exudes from within.
The line is thin.
The duality that exists between present and past
The last
Shall be first
The thirst to quench
Drench
In the unconditional dichotomy

Of reality
Love is the center of this oneness
The time is
NOW!

Everything is destined to reach its maximum level of productivity. My pastor, A. R. Bernard, teaches us that we have two choices on how we live—either by sight, sense, and circumstance, *or* by faith, spirit, and Word. Each depends on our level of maturity, but God is interested in our success. And you can't have a testimony without a test.

I'm a survivor. A few years ago I would have never identified myself as such, but what didn't break me made me stronger. I've learned that we cannot grow in isolation, so I try hard not to separate myself to figure it all out. First, I've learned to consult with God. I must check in with Him first. Now I have an amazing man that I'm clear God presented to walk back into my life last year. God has positioned my fiancé to be my accountability partner and requires me to do the same for him. Beyond that, I write to express myself and share my story with others I feel may have an opportunity to benefit from it.

Everywhere we turn, there's a potential opportunity to connect with Christ. Sometimes we have to seek Him out, but there's also always an opportunity to connect with and touch other human beings. We all have choices to make. Crosses to bear, if you will. Life is only a montage in memory—everything else is hard work. So faithfully navigating through this life terrain one day at a time and identifying those moments when you connect to Him through our everyday experiences is what life is all about.

The Bible is my source of faith and rule of conduct, and it keeps me refreshed with the stories of men and women who were inspired by JC just like I am. As a writer I continue to dig deep and allow my stories to be shared so that others will prayerfully be inspired. I encourage everyone to seek Him and know that He is always with you. We are all works in progress—fearlessly and wonderfully made, with amazing stories to share and tell.

Kimberly N. Cooper is a seasoned mass media professional with a proven track record as a writer, editor, copywriter, marketer, and producer across various communications platforms including broadcast, print, radio, and online / digital. An astute entrepreneur, Cooper owns BG Unlimited, Inc. The gifted writer and editor's byline has been spotted on the pages of *Essence, Playbill, The Source, the Amsterdam News, NV, Scratch, YRB, Savoy, Smooth,* and *Honey* magazines. As a copywriter and producer, Cooper's taglines, scripts, and creative executions have been seen and heard regularly on Black Entertainment Television (BET) through a variety of promos, print ads, online, radio, and consumer marketing initiatives. Cooper can be found developing her gift to communicate as a voice-over talent, currently for the BET J weekly series *MPR: Profiles of Urban Entrepreneurs*. Cooper received her BA in government from Wesleyan University in Middletown, Connecticut, serves on the advisory board of Hip Hop 4 Life; as a national officer on the executive committee for the National Association of Black Females Executives in Music & Entertainment (NABFEME), and is a member of New York Women in Film & Television (NYWIFT). Part of Cooper's professional journey has been documented in the recent Hachette Book Group release *Put Your Dreams First: Handle Your (Entertainment) Business*.

Being Twentysomething

By Diera Shaw

When I turned twenty-seven last year, I realized that the phenomenon they call the "quarter-life" crisis was real. In case you haven't heard of it, here's a brief synopsis:

According to Wikipedia, this is a term applied to the period of life immediately following the major changes of adolescence, usually ranging from the early 20s to early 30s.

UrbanDictionary.com says "the quarter-life crisis occurs sometime in your twenties, a few years out of school when you still feel as though you're waiting for your life to begin."

In general, it's an age when we start developing a more realistic outlook on life and begin feeling as if we haven't accomplished certain things in life we thought we would have accomplished by now, and that we may never accomplish them (which is absolutely untrue and there's still a long time to attain our goals).

I don't like the term "crisis" to describe this natural progression or transition that we make in life. It's rather an "awkward" time, kind of like an adult version of puberty. (And by the way, I'm still struggling with acne!)

This awkward time for me started around age twenty-three, when the reality of being an adult and all the responsibilities that come with that began to set in. Even at twenty-seven, I've still been a child longer than I've been an adult. At the time, I had completed my undergraduate degree and was in graduate school and working part-time as a residence hall graduate assistant. I remember thinking and feeling that I was just pursuing a master's degree for the heck of it. It wasn't really fulfilling, but yet I wasn't ready to work a nine-to-five. I had always been an overachiever, so being a professional student worked for me.

This was a lonely and uncertain time in my life. Because of work and school, I had been displaced from my hometown where all my friends were. And I hadn't quite settled in to make connections with new friends. I was battling with confusion, depression, changing relationships, identity, and self-esteem issues. It was an emotional roller coaster—one moment I was on the peak of my climb, feeling quite content with life, and the next moment at the bottom of the dip, feeling empty and lost.

I was also coming to terms with my feelings of abandonment from the unhealthy relationship I had with my father and the impact that was having on my adult relationships. I was so desperate and longing for a man to love me to fill this gaping hole in my spirit that it resulted in a series of unhealthy relational and behavioral patterns: chasing and pursuing relationships in unhealthy and unbeneficial ways;

using alcohol, men, and partying to numb the pain of loneliness; confusing sex for love; and misinterpreting lust and infatuation for genuine interest. My adult life quickly filled with broken relationships, low self-esteem, and self-destructive patterns. I thought I would have been married with children by twenty-four, and in hindsight I'm so happy that I wasn't! In the last few years, my life and perceptions of reality have so drastically changed, I'm not sure what type of relationship I would have gotten myself into. Certainly not one that was healthy and stable.

When it is all said and done, I attribute my ability to come out of that foglike state to one thing, rather, one person, and his name is Jesus Christ. In the midst of all my insecurity and disorientation, I found a Savior who became all that I was looking for in the world around me, even though society was telling me something different. We are bombarded with messages that say if we just find the right job or the right mate, we will find true happiness. And that couldn't be further from the truth. I've had my share of relationships and jobs, and none of them could do me like Jesus did!

The Bible teaches four principles: (1) delight ourselves in the Lord and He will give us the desires of our hearts; (2) Jesus came so we would have life more abundantly; (3) God is able to do exceedingly and abundantly above all we can ask or think; and (4) if we ask, we will receive; if we seek, we will find; and if we knock, the doors will be opened.

It's a shame that more young adults don't believe in the validity of the Bible and treasure of having a relationship with God. I know firsthand how difficult it is to be a twentsomething! I'm still twentysomething! But I also know the burden that is lifted when you yield to faith in Jesus Christ and learn to trust and obey Him. There's no promise of "happily ever after," but there is an inner peace and joy that I have learned to draw from that helps me remain balanced and puts life's challenges into perspective.

Today, I am a minister-in-training at my local church and I am taking steps to pursue the full-time calling on my life for ministry. In 2007, I was blessed to purchase my own home and now I am in the process of starting my own business. As Paul says: *Not that I have already obtained all this, or have already been made perfect, but I press on to take hold of that for which Christ Jesus took hold of me.*—Philippians 3:12

Diera Shaw founded Winning Image Consulting because she believes that faith, a positive self-image, and refined leadership and interpersonal skills equip young women for success. Diera holds a master's degree in professional communication from LaSalle University, and graduated cum laude with her bachelor's degree from Seton Hall University. She has accumulated over twelve years' experience in the hospitality, pageant / beauty, and entertainment industries. She has experience coordinating trainings and workshops on the topics of personal image, self-esteem, interview preparation, customer service, and diversity.

Deliverance Allowed Me to Discover the Real Me

By Nicole Sallis

I woke up to a plush pillow and the warmth of the sunshine hitting my eyelids. I smiled, but when I looked around, I realized I was in an unfamiliar place. Not only that, but I was lying next to a guy I didn't even like or care anything about. We both realized after the first couple of conversations the only use we had for each other was *sex*. At this point in my life I was fine with that and feeling liberated, but secretly using sex for many reasons that stretched beyond the obvious. I found comfort in the fact that last night's sexual excursion was a conquering point for me with this guy, and I felt a strange sense of accomplishment.

I got up, took a shower, got dressed, and headed to class like nothing ever happened. I was taking a fashion illustration course, and in this class we used a drawing instruction workbook to assist us in learning drawing techniques for drawing women's bodies, facial features, and so on. So we had one of our final assignments due, and me being the Queen of Procrastination, I waited to the last minute to complete it. Though I created my own clothing designs, I used the body drawing I created in the class to save time. While eagerly awaiting the great grade I knew I'd receive on this assignment, the professor's aide pulled me out into the hallway to say my project would not be graded and "we have a serious problem." She went on to say that my women's facial features were too close to the instruction book and not only was she failing me for this assignment, but she was also planning to report this as a case of copyright infringement that would most likely result in me being kicked out of school. Now, I'm a senior, thousands of dollars invested, the first girl in my family to graduate from college, and I was set to move to New York to pursue my fashion / entertainment career. What was I going to do? I started to panic and immediately went to the bathroom and started to pray; I am and was then a Christian, so that's all I could think to do. I started to cry and begged God to help me out of this situation. Just then I heard so clearly, "You know the Word, does your lifestyle line up with what you say you believe?

"Do you recognize you've allowed sex to become an idol in your life, and I will have nothing, not even your own selfishness, in front of Me. Do you ever think on those nights like last night, and while you are willfully and boldly disobeying Me and My word, that a situation like this would be unfolding outside of your knowledge? You went from disrespecting Me to asking Me for help; where are the men and all the things you put before Me in this current situation?" Have you ever heard the saying "God's goodness will convict you?" That's exactly what happened in the process of Him delivering me out of this situation and allowing me to eventually graduate from college. He started showing me, me. I *never* looked at myself, my willingness to give myself away so freely, or my relationship with God the same after that day. God started revealing the reality that I'd given away so many pieces of myself, I was broken and tainted. Furthermore, only He could restore me.

I was overly stressed about college. I needed to carry twenty-four credit hours for the next two semesters in order to graduate by the end of that year, not to mention I was dealing with money issues and an unfamiliar family brokenness. I had just recently broken free from an abusive relationship, and let me just say once you've lost control, been oppressed, or had someone abuse their control over you, when you're free you desperately seek to regain a sense of power in any area in your life. In my mind, sex gave me power over men. If I could get them to truly lust after me, I had power over them. At the time I was also diagnosed with depression due to a chemical imbalance, and I was sad most of the time with constant suicidal thoughts. I had terribly low self-esteem and I used sex among other things to replace the negative feelings I was experiencing with a temporary falsified sense of love and acceptance. God showed me how my desire to have sex increased whenever I was sad, lonely, depressed, or anxious.

I was too afraid to actually enter into a relationship because I'd had so many bad experiences and been hurt so many times by men through infidelity, but I wanted revenge! So I indulged in the relationship *games,* not relationships, but playing games, which totally revolves around sex.

Sadly, my sense of self was based on winning in situations, and I was good at sex, so if I can win in this area, "let's go." It was also an escape tactic. These sexual experiences and using my energy on finding ways to seduce or manipulate men through my sexual power gave me something to take my mind off the issues I so desperately needed to face. All that time I thought I had the power; in fact, I was suppressing my genuine need for love. I was attempting to replace love with fickle sexual relationships, which deep down further damaged my broken self-esteem. I'm a Christian, and I was living totally contradictory to the Word of God. Besides, realistically, a respectable woman can only fool herself for so long that she enjoys being a jump-off and the late-night creep. I was destroying the sanctity of my temple, which in turn hindered my relationship and ability to hear and obey God. On top of all that, I was creating unrecognizable unhealthy dependences.

Dependence can be physical or psychological. Very similar to habits, it can come from repeated actions. Oftentimes when it's psychological, it has to do with what emotion the action is connected to. For example, sometimes people are not hereditary alcoholics, but they can create unhealthy dependencies on alcohol based on their actions. Every time they get stressed, they drink; they become sad, they drink; they become lonely, they drink. At one point I had drinking dependencies, among other things; but in this case, sex was the escape, the perceived control like a drug. I've learned that without God, it's hard to find balance in life, to handle the tragedy and trials that are inevitable. Many times we don't connect our actions to the possible meanings behind them, and we create unhealthy dependencies we're unaware of. After continuously resorting to quick fixes, I not only developed dependencies, but I was deceived. I was in bondage and didn't even realize it. When I stopped having casual sex and God showed me the depth of me, He started showing me patterns, dependencies, and strongholds that I needed to purge from my life. A stronghold can be described as being constrained to a set of boundaries. It can be positive or negative. A good stronghold can be in the Word of God. When you desire to do something bad or sin, the stronghold constrains you in the boundaries of what you know to be true about sin. A negative spiritual stronghold, on the other hand, can be formed during casual sexual encounters when you are physically connected to someone you are not spiritually connected with. Let me stop and say sex is not a bad thing; it's great in God's eyes, but in the right context, in the safety of the person He has for you. It's not wise to be tied or open emotionally and especially spiritually to just anyone or in an unhealthy relationship for perceived physical needs. Think how many unhealthy relationships people go back to or operate in just to support the constraints of a conscious or an unconscious set of boundaries, and they may not even recognize it. When my eyes were opened to all my bondage and I let God deliver me with His word, I was able to see myself in a different light, the way God saw me. There are things about every creation that only the Creator knows. The closer I got to God, the more He started to reveal intricate details about me and heal my insecurities.

For me, one of the biggest things holding me back from wholeheartedly seeking God was sexual sin. What's holding you back?

I've gone from being sexually promiscuous and clinically depressed to healthy, happy, and abstaining for the last three years. I am being restored and free from the bondage of fear, sin, depression, and dependencies. I am waiting for my husband and walking in my divine destiny! No one can tell me God is not a deliverer, and remember, He's not a respecter of person, meaning He doesn't love me more than you. God is a respecter of *faith*. Today I'm closer to the center of His will for my life, and I'm discovering something more beautiful than anything I've ever seen. I'm discovering peace that surpasses all understanding; I'm discovering a defined, more confident assurance in the woman God is constantly pulling out of me, no matter what anyone thinks. I'm discovering pure joy, I'm discovering me.

Nicole Sallis is a writer and a poet.

When You Are Down to Nothing, God Is Up to Something

By Jasmine Jordan

Singer Yolanda Adams said it best in her song "Open My Heart." I was alone in my college dorm room freshman year. There was nobody there but me and God. I was discouraged; my heart had been broken by a man who was never supposed to break it, school was kicking my behind, and I was restless. Some days I took solace in food, and other days I had no appetite. I was doing things that were out of character for me and lashing out at people who were trying to help me. My social life became almost nonexistent. I began to weed through the many friends that I had and made my circle a very tight few. Those tight few rarely heard from me. The four walls of my room became my sanctuary and the only place I could almost feel any peace. I hated being in my room, but I didn't want to go out. Even when I went out, I felt alone in a room full of people. Cleaning my room made me feel better, so I cluttered it on purpose just to clean it up. When everyone else was waking up, I was just lying down trying to fall asleep.

Tears became an everyday occurrence. I couldn't explain to myself or to anyone else why I cried or what was wrong, because I didn't know and they wouldn't understand. When I wrote in my journal, my thoughts were like knots of thick rope tied around my wrists. My confidence was gone and it felt like everyone was watching me, waiting for me to fail. My heart was heavy and I was tired of pretending that I wasn't hurting or struggling. I was tired of wearing a mask, like I had everything under control, when I was fighting to understand who I was. I was also tired of hiding from my mother, who could read me like an open book. I needed to get some relief and I didn't know where I could get it from.

I finally broke down and called my mother. My mama is a very strong woman who, though she may not say it, can make what you are going through seem like it is all in your mind. Of course, like most mothers who are concerned about their children, she wanted me to come home. As much as I wanted to run to my mother and cry on her shoulder and wait for her to fix it, she couldn't fix this.

One night after I had done all of the rearranging and cleaning that I could do, I dialed all of the friends I could stand to talk to, and I cried on and off for the better part of an hour. A gospel song, "Stand," began to play from the play list on my laptop. My room had me closed in and I felt like I was fighting for air. I didn't know what else to do but scream out. "What is it? What is it?" The next thing I knew, I was getting up off my knees in my dorm room, face wet and hands above my head. It was as if God had been waiting on me to ask and I surrendered. That night I lay down and slept a little bit better. The next night I called on Him again, and the next night again, and on that Sunday, I got myself together and went to church.

The Lord led me right to my father's church. My father, the man I had been avoiding for the last few months and who had broken my heart beyond repair over the years, looked just as shocked to see me there as I felt to have actually shown up. I wanted to leave, but the Lord had other plans. What went on during that church service I can describe no other way than as a spiritual healing. It seemed like the song the choir picked was just for me. What the preacher said that day seemed to be just for me. A woman that was a member of that church pulled me aside and prayed for me. I was beginning to feel better and I got over some trivial things that I was hanging on to inside. The more the pastor preached, the more it seemed like he had a plate of food, and instead of giving it all to me at one time, he would give me a piece, then pass the plate right under my nose. Because I was still hungry, I continued to go back.

God showed me that my problem was that I always had to be in control and I wanted to be perfect. No matter what happened, whether it was to me or to my family, I had to be in control of that situation. I didn't want to let

Him help me or let Him in. So God took away my control and forced me to look at myself. I had no choice but to ask Him for help.

No one is perfect. We all strive to be a better person than we were the day before, and sometimes we become discouraged. People hurt us, we hurt others, and we hurt ourselves. We sometimes do the same things over and over, expecting a different result, because we don't want to admit that we need help. God sees all of this and simply waits for us to ask for His help. He wants us not to be afraid to need Him and not to be afraid to thank Him as well.

Because of His glory, I was better prepared for the passing of my father. I am nowhere near completely healed. I am a work of God in progress. I still miss church sometimes. Sometimes I get a little too "busy" for God and need a reminder of who He is. I still cry sometimes. I still shout and call His name, but the difference is, after we have had our moment, I can pick myself up and keep going. A storm doesn't last forever, and I know that God will never put anything on me that I cannot bear. He's my rock when I need something to lean on, my foundation when I am trying to stay out of sinking sand, and my doctor when my soul is broken. Whatever I need, I know God's got it. And unlike friends that don't answer the phone, I know I can call any hour and He'll always answer. I accept that it might not be what I want to hear all the time, but it is always what I need. Everything that God does, He has a divine purpose and plan for me. I see His miracles every day and know that I am one of those miracles because I made it.

I was lower than I had ever been in my life and He pulled me up, pointed me to a mirror, and made me see myself and who I was. And wouldn't you know it, when you're down to nothing, please believe God is up to something. I'm still one of God's works in progress waiting on direction. "What is it that you want me to do, God?"

Jasmine Jordan is a college student and a participant of the Passage and Leadership Development Institute, which provides long-lasting change in the lives of young people, families, and communities of color. She currently resides in Brooklyn, New York.

If I Knew Then What I Know Now About My Faith . . .

We all have a responsibility, and since I've been so wonderfully blessed, I really want to share and to make life at least a little better. So every chance I get to share the gospel or uplift people, I will take full advantage of that opportunity.

—Gladys Knight

Our faith is not a commodity to be held by us and us alone. It is our responsibility to speak to our soul sisters and others about how our faith has brought us through. Faith is an expression of who we are as a people. Our faith brought us through hundreds of years of slavery and bondage. Our faith was what held us over the roughest time in our individual and collective lives. Faith is not a secret to be kept in the dark, but a beacon to shine as a representation of steadfastness and character.

Your Personal Book of Revelations

- *Where are You, God?*
- *Why does God allow me to suffer?*
- *Is it okay to question God?*
- *Do I have to pray?*
- *Why is He always testing me?*

X

My Body, My Temple

For me, it's not about looking like a supermodel—it's about feeling good about who I am naturally.
—America Ferrera

When you're young, you believe you're invincible. Your health is the last thing on your mind unless you're exposed to illness early on in your life. Health concerns for women are almost always pushed to the back of our minds, and we have to ask, why is that? Our health should be a priority at any age.

No matter how you feel, there is always something you can do to tend to your health. Whether it be physical, mental, emotional, or spiritual, your health can always improve. There are some simple ways to stay holistically healthy. First, make sure you get a yearly physical. You should be seeing your medical doctor, gynecologist, and dentist at least once a year.

Your mental health deserves the same type of attention. Constant learning about your field of work, your leisure interests, and current events are ways to keep you mentally fit. Challenge yourself intellectually by joining a book club or investment club, or spending time engaging in a hobby that is both challenging and intellectually stimulating. Stress can come in many forms and oftentimes it creeps up on you and you just accept it as the norm. Ladies, we implore you to slow down and appreciate life. In this chapter women share their personal stories about their health challenges and victories.

BADGES OF COURAGE

By Samantha Wheeler

I have several nicknames—Sam, Sammie D, Baby Bear, Bright Eyes—and my family and friends typically call me by those. But whenever my mother calls me Samantha, my response to her is always the same: Is this bad news? Usually it's not, and mom gets on my case for overreacting. So it was no surprise that when she called me in the early evening of October 24, 2007, and referred to me as Samantha, I figured it was no big deal. I was sadly mistaken. While the exact details of the conversation are fuzzy, I recall a few key words: Father. Heart attack. Nothing major. Hospital. Get here. I sat at my desk, frozen. The phrases "heart attack" and "nothing major" should not be used together. Ever. A couple of my friends from the office came over—we had a routine walk to the parking lot together—and when I shared what my mom just told me, they looked at me in shock. "What are you still doing here?" they asked. "Go to the hospital! Are you okay to drive? Do you need a ride?" I'm not sure what kept me at work for a full thirty minutes after my mother's initial phone call; hindsight tells me it was a fear of the unknown.

The drive from downtown Los Angeles to the San Fernando Valley was inexplicably short that day; a ride that would typically take over an hour took a mere twenty-five minutes. As I parked the car and made my way into the emergency room, I tried to prepare for the worst-case scenario. My parents have a history of downplaying things to prevent me from panicking, and I was going to be as calm, cool, and collected as possible to face whatever presented itself in my father's room. Perhaps Mom was right. Perhaps this was nothing major.

And it seemed that way at first. When I walked into my dad's hospital room, he looked his usual self, despite looking a little tired and breathing a little hard. I asked how he was doing, and he turned the conversation back on me, asking how my day had been and telling me not to be concerned.

"It's no big deal, Baby Bear," my dad reassured me. "Papa Bear will be back to normal in no time. Don't worry about it."

As Dad spent the next few days in the hospital, I took off from work to spend time with him and Mom. And by being at the hospital, I learned a little more about my dad's health. Apparently, "nothing major" to my parents meant an initial diagnosis of congestive heart failure to the hospital staff. Dad's heart was functioning somewhere in the 20–30 percent range, and if it did not improve within five years, he might need a transplant. When he first arrived at the hospital, his skin was gray. After the nurses took one look at him, they immediately rushed him past the other emergency room patients. He seemed to take it all in stride, making jokes about the hospital food and how he could not wait to go home and eat some bacon. Mom and I did our best to joke along with him, teasing him about how he brought this on himself by smoking cigarettes his entire life. And he kept the nurses in stitches, developing a special rapport with some of them. We kept the mood light and uplifting, convincing ourselves that everything would be okay.

And everything was okay for the next month. Dad went back to work a week or so after returning home from the hospital and began taking better care of himself. He stopped smoking and drinking and stuck to a low-sodium diet. Despite the ongoing visits to the doctor and the daily routine of pills, everything seemed like it was returning to normal. So of course, if it's too good to be true, it probably is.

I came home from work the day before Thanksgiving expecting to help my mother with Thanksgiving dinner preparations. Instead, I saw two family friends at my kitchen table, and they nonchalantly informed me that my mother had taken my father to the hospital because he was complaining of chest pains. He assured me that it was no big deal and that he would be out of the hospital before the night was over. Unfortunately, the doctors did not see it that way; they kept him for observation for the next two days, causing him to miss Thanksgiving dinner. It was during that time we learned that my father would need to go back to the hospital in a few months for a defibrillator.

The following January, my dad went to the hospital for the operation. While his previous hospital visits had been at one location, the surgery would take place at a much larger hospital, one my family was quite familiar with. Some fourteen years earlier, I had open-heart surgery there. I was born with a hole in my heart that was growing quite rapidly. I was aware of the situation but did not think much of it; I would occasionally lose my breath when I ran, and I would have to take medication before dental appointments. Other than that, nothing major. Or so I thought. When I was around ten, my cardiologist told my parents that I would need to have open-heart surgery soon or else I might die of a heart attack before I turned eighteen.

My memory is cloudy on exactly how my parents broke the news, but I remember going into the situation as if it was no big deal. Aside from being taken out of school for angiograms and to donate blood to myself, the idea of open-heart surgery seemed like nothing to worry about. The surgery was scheduled for the summer, and the doctor proposed two options: They could make a horizontal incision under my bustline, which would take up to three months to heal; or they could make a vertical incision straight down my chest, which would take up to six weeks to heal. For this eleven-year-old, the choice was clear. Vertical incision meant more summer vacation. Even though the scar would be visible, I'd be able to play much sooner. Easy decision for me.

On a late June morning in 1994, I went to the hospital for my open-heart surgery. The doctors and nurses did an amazing job of making me feel comfortable and at ease, even down to playing my favorite Take 6 CD in the operating room. My memories of that week in the hospital are all pleasant, for the most part. My parents were there every day, my friends from school came to visit, and I got to watch anything I wanted on television. It was a worry-free time. When I was released, my parents and I made sure I took proper care of my scar and followed my breathing exercises, and by the end of July, I was back up and running around. I proudly displayed my scar as my badge of courage, knowing full well that after weathering open-heart surgery, I could do anything.

I was expecting my father's hospital visit to be significantly less dramatic than mine given that his procedure, while serious, was not as serious as open-heart surgery. The visit took its toll, however, as we waited a good six hours before my dad even prepped for surgery. At some point, we were notified that he had finally gone in. Now it was just a waiting game.

What was supposed to be a routine procedure ended up taking several hours; I lost count after hour three. Mom and I chatted about my operation and how waiting for Dad brought back memories of waiting for me. She started sharing other stories with me about my time in the hospital, recalling things a bit differently than I had. She shared that I almost died because of a staph infection. She mentioned that my first night in the intensive care unit, a baby had just died after having open-heart surgery, which made it difficult for her and Dad to keep their composure around me. My parents did not want me to worry about my operation. They knew if I understood the severity of the situation, I would panic. I knew then how worried about dad she was, even if she wasn't letting on. So I tried to do what our family does best—I tried to joke about the situation.

It seemed to keep our mind off things for a while. Pretty soon, we were told that Dad's surgery went well and that he would be okay to come home. I sat across from him in the hospital room, looking at the defibrillator in his chest. The first thing I remember saying to him was, "Nice scar! We're almost matching now." He smiled, because we were. Father and daughter with similar badges of courage across their hearts.

Sometimes we don't want our loved ones to worry any more than they have to. My father did not outwardly show signs of worry or fear during his condition, and my parents certainly did not outwardly show signs of worry or fear during my heart surgery. I have gotten through both ordeals because of my faith in God, naturally, but also because of the calm nature of my parents. They have made me feel like I can take on anything with no worries, and they're absolutely right. If I had that kind of courage at eleven, Lord only knows what I will possess in the future. All I have to do is look at my badge and realize that I will make it through anything that comes my way.

Samantha Wheeler is the daughter of actress Hattie Winston (*Becker*) and arranger / composer Harold Wheeler (musical director, *Dancing with the Stars*). She is pursuing a career in corporate communications. She holds a master's degree in strategic public relations from the University of Southern California and a bachelor's degree in economics from Drew University.

A Second Chance at Life

By Aleia K. Moore

If I could remember it like it was just yesterday, I would recall those events exactly the way they happened, but the head trauma I suffered caused me to forget certain events in that part of my life, so I can only tell the story as it has been told to me. My mother and father separated when I was very young, but my father and I remained very close. I was eight years old when my father passed; heartbroken, I wanted to die to be with him. Little did I know that death was lurking right around the corner. It was a Saturday afternoon, just a few months after burying my dad, and I, my mother, aunt, and two cousins were going shopping. My family lived in Newark, New Jersey, at the time and we were driving down the street. Just as my mother turned around to ask if I had my seat belt on, a car ran a stop sign and crashed into our car. My mother called out to everyone to see if they were okay; aside from minor cuts and bruises, everyone responded yes, except for me. My mother called my name but got no response, and she turned around to find me slumped over in the backseat of the car. She immediately knew that something was wrong, and directed my two cousins to get out of the car. Having worked for a major hospital in New Jersey, the University of Medicine and Dentistry (UMDNJ), for over fifteen years, and with some nursing experience, she carefully slid my lifeless body out of the backseat of the car and onto the sidewalk. As she called my name again, she saw my eyes roll in the back of my head and knew that I was unconscious. She checked to see if I was breathing—I was not! Luckily, she knew CPR and worked diligently to resuscitate her only daughter and youngest child. Once the ambulance arrived, they prepared to rush me to the number-one trauma unit in the state of New Jersey, located in Newark—ironically, UMDNJ—but not before telling my mother how, had she not performed CPR, I would've been dead on the scene.

Upon arriving at the trauma unit, I underwent various MRIs and CT scans to assess the amount of injury to my brain. The emergency room doctors informed my mother that I had sustained two hematomas, one on each side of my brain. Basically, I was bleeding in my brain. The impact of the car hitting ours caused my body, which was unrestrained because I was not wearing a seat belt, to sway from side to side, hitting my cousins, which caused the hematomas. This would also explain the knots on the lower right and upper left side of each of their heads. I was transferred to another hospital for further care. It was a grueling sight for any parent to see; I had ventilation tubes and IVs coming from everywhere. Due to my head injury, I suffered from seizures, was paralyzed on the left side of my body, was in a coma, and according to the report the doctors gave my mother and stepfather, there was not a good chance that I would come out of that state. In the event that I did awaken from my coma, the doctors said that my parents should be prepared for me to be in a vegetative state for the rest of my life. This would also mean that my honor roll days in school were over. To them, none of that mattered; they wanted me in whatever state I was in, as long as I was alive.

My parents took turns spending the night at the hospital, each day hoping and praying that would be the day that I would wake up. The end of the week was approaching, and the nurse was doing her normal rounds when she heard something. She leaned into me and then ran into the waiting room to get my father; my mother had gone to the cafeteria to get something to eat. When the nurse and my dad came into the room, she said, "Shh, listen, she's whispering something . . ." He leaned in and said, "No, she's singing." In a very low voice, I was coming out of my coma singing, "Jesus Keep Me Near the Cross," which is what my dad would sing to me in my ear each night that he stayed with me in the hospital while I was in a coma. By this time, my mother was back and the next thing I said was, "I want some pancakes!" (Please don't ask me why . . . smile.)

I was awake, but not in the clear just yet. I was transferred, yet again, to another hospital, Children's Specialized Hospital, in Mountainside, New Jersey. There, I continued to take medication for my seizures and also had to go to physical therapy. Although I was eight years old when the accident happened, I reverted back to a three-year-old, so I had to learn how to talk, and with the paralysis, I had to learn how to walk and use my extremities again. There was progress each day, but by this time I was also getting tired of being in a hospital. However, it did have its perks. Every Friday, my therapist and I would go to Friday's for ice cream, and as part of my therapy, I'd have to calculate how much change I would get back. Another really cool feature at the time was the Ronald McDonald phone. Because of the physical therapy, I was able to get in and out of my bed and walk down the hall unassisted and use the phone to call my parents. The conversation was the same all the time: They would ask how I was doing, I would ask them when they were coming, then follow it up with, "Can you bring me a cheeseburger Happy Meal from McDonald's?" Depending on whether I read all the books she brought me, I would ask my mother for some new books (perhaps that's why I'm an avid reader now) and would close the conversation with, "When can I come home?" It pained them to leave me there, as much as it did me to have to stay there.

My parents, in their infinite wisdom, decided that since I could walk around and talk on the phone, I should get a tutor so I wouldn't fall too far behind in school. As much as I disagreed then, I appreciate it now. This whole situation gave me a much brighter outlook on life. It wasn't until I was a little older that I could fully grasp what I had actually gone through. This single event was the catalyst that catapulted me to soar beyond what some thought was impossible. To date, I don't have any bodily injuries as a result of that accident, nor do I need to take any medication. I've maintained the academic standard that I had prior to the accident all the way through college, and am currently pursuing my master's degree. I value my life, and strive every day to do something better than I did yesterday, to raise the bar for myself a little bit higher, push myself to go just a bit further, and hopefully inspire someone along the way. I am a living witness of what can be accomplished when you have faith and determination. As fate would have it, I should be dead or a vegetable, but I've beaten those odds!

Life knows no boundaries, no limits, only we, as humans, do. It will take you as far as you're willing to go, so . . . *aim high!*

Aleia K. Moore, twenty-six, is an actress, author, poet, motivational speaker, and business owner. To contact her, e-mail moore2lifemotivations@yahoo.com.

Luckier Than Most

By Hydeia Broadbent

My life didn't start out looking very promising: I was born with HIV. My birth mother abandoned me shortly after my birth. I was three when I was diagnosed with AIDS. Doctors said I wouldn't live past five. At the time, they weren't giving children infected with HIV / AIDS any medicine. So basically, I was given a death sentence at birth.

But despite all this, I was luckier than most: I was adopted by my parents, and they fought for me. They fought for me hard. My mother started going to conferences, lobbying to get people to change their laws, advocating for me because I couldn't advocate for myself. I watched her and I kind of picked it up along the way. From her, I learned to be an activist. I got my inner toughness from my mom. She didn't raise me thinking that anything was wrong with me. She raised me with the idea, "This is something that we're going through, that you have to deal with. You can't change it, so why not deal with it."

Growing up with this disease, I had to rely on myself,

to not listen to what other people said. People would look at me like I was weird or like something was wrong with me. I had to believe in myself: There's nothing wrong with me. People don't understand what AIDS is, and that's why they act ignorant. I learned at a young age that I can't let people's fears or negative thoughts affect me.

When I was in kindergarten, my parents sat down with my teacher. They told her how to deal with my blood, what happens if I get hurt or something. They tried to educate her about universal precautions. One day I remember I sneezed, and boogers came out. She panicked and got out the bleach. She sprayed the air around me, and it got in my eyes. I was only in kindergarten, so I didn't really understand. But at that moment, I felt kind of weird because everybody was looking at me. To me, all I did was sneeze; I didn't understand why she was reacting that way.

By the time I got to middle school and high school, it was obvious because I had been on TV, doing different things, advocating for people living with HIV / AIDS. It was better that way. I didn't have to lie about where I was when I missed school. That was the best thing for me. A lot of kids living with the disease have to lie about why they're absent from school, why they're always going to the doctor. I feel bad for them. Not everyone is comfortable enough to say, "I'm infected." They don't know how to speak up for themselves. They're afraid that they'll be discriminated against.

Besides my kindergarten teacher, I didn't have issues

until high school. There was one guy who was kind of afraid to be around me. He didn't understand the ways you could get AIDS. He wouldn't say things to my face, but I would hear it from other people. So I would go around him more, make him have to deal with the fact that I'm here, and I wasn't going anywhere. And another time, I was dating someone who couldn't deal with the fact that I have AIDS. It took me a couple of years to figure out that was the problem. It hurt. But you live and you learn. I realized that I'm always going to have AIDS; there's nothing that I can do about that. I just had to learn to let it go. I realized my issues weren't my issues; they were other people's issues. I realized that I didn't care what anyone said. Now I have a really good boyfriend, so I don't really harp on the negative.

It's hard to find someone who is secure enough with himself to deal with an illness like AIDS. People are going to have questions; their families are going to have issues. He has to be strong enough to deal with his own issues. When we first started dating, my boyfriend said he was afraid. We started dating in high school. We were friends and I asked him to the prom. And then we started getting closer. But he was afraid. So I took him with me to my doctor's appointment. I explained what was safe and what wasn't, and I guess that opened him up some more. He's become really strong.

I want to get married, have kids, and buy a house. I look forward to my future. I'm planning for my future. I want to write my memoirs. I've been a professional speaker almost all my life. But now I want to figure out what else I want to do—before it's too late.

I have a good life, but living with AIDS isn't easy. When you get older, you have to watch your body. I'm always trying to find the perfect balance for my medications. It's hard, but you have to do what you have to do.

I've learned to use tools to get me through the hard times. I rely on myself, my family, and my friends. I believe in God, but I'm not religious to the point where I'd have to drop to my knees and pray. Basically, I just call on my family and friends. When I'm in the hospital for a short period of time, sometimes I don't even tell anyone because it's not a big deal. But of course my family is always there for me.

I've learned that every choice you make today is going to affect you in the future. So you really have to think about the choices that you make. A lot of people jump to make quick choices to deal with the situation that's in front of them. It's okay not to know the answer. It's okay to ask for help and guidance from somebody. I'm twenty-five and I know I don't have all the answers. Sometimes I have to ask. You shouldn't be afraid to ask for help. You've got to think. The choices that my birth mother made affect me to this day. The choices that we make will affect tomorrow. We have to think about what we do. We have to think about our actions.

Hydeia Broadbent became known as a teenage AIDS activist. She contracted HIV at birth from her drug-addicted biological mother and has battled the disease ever since with the help of her adopted parents. Hydeia began speaking publicly about the disease while assisting her mother's activism, and now travels the country educating people of all ages about the dangers of AIDS and how to protect themselves from contracting it.

Don't Wait for the Weight

By Monica Marie Jones

This morning I almost got discouraged when my weight had increased by five pounds from yesterday's reading, but then I had to catch myself and remember how the scale can be a true setup. Several factors contribute to the many reasons why our weight on the scale may fluctuate from day to day and sometimes throughout the day. From my research, I have found that our true weight is the weight that we see first thing in the morning after we have used the bathroom. We also must keep in mind that different scales are calibrated differently, thus giving us a different reading. Don't pay so much attention to the number. Pay attention to the gain and loss, and try to stick with one scale. No matter what actual weight any scale may say, if you lose five pounds, you lose five pounds, just as five pounds of feathers weighs the same as five pounds of bricks.

I came to the conclusion that my weight had increased

so rapidly due to two factors. One was that I had not used the bathroom yet, as I always do when I wake up in the morning. The other factor was that the day before I had consumed far less water and far more sodium than I usually do; thus, I was suffering from water retention. This is another reason why we should not rely solely on the scale as a measure of our progress, because oftentimes the change that we see is a water weight loss or gain, not fat. I like to measure my progress by keeping track of my inches, gauging how my clothes feel, and measuring my body fat percentage. This helps me because I carry weight much differently than most. When asked to guess my weight, many guess an average of 140. When I reveal to people that I am hovering around 180, they usually don't believe me. When I was hovering around 140, I began to look too skinny and I had lost all of my womanly curves. Thus I have come to the conclusion that 150 is the ideal weight for me. I believe that I tend to weigh more because of the fact that muscle weighs more than fat. I have a lot of muscle, primarily in my legs.

Yesterday I made the conscious decision to enjoy and love my body as it is in the present. I will continue to work out, eat right, and strive to increase my quality of health and level of fitness, but I will not wait until I reach a certain goal to do everything that I want to do. I hear people saying that they want to wait until they shed the pounds to take pictures, put on a swimsuit, or perform in a show. I used to be the same way. There is a fat gal's voice that continuously lives inside my head. . . .

A fat girl lives on the inside of me
Although I've shed the pounds I'm still weighed down
By insecurity
Mannerisms are meek and mild
Characteristics of my inner fat child
The scale and the mirror are my two biggest enemies
The scale measures failure and the mirror deceives
I don't see what others see 'cause
99 percent of losing weight is psychology
It has been a challenge physically
But has been more taxing emotionally
Confusion, stress, and strain afflict my psyche constantly
Put the pounds on now the weight's gone
My life has become an oxymoron
When I was large I was invisible
Now that I'm small I cannot hide
At size 16 when it came to men, I was virtually unknown
At size 6 when it comes to men, they won't leave me alone
I can't help but wonder, would they have acknowledged me the way I used to be?
For the majority, attraction is based solely on what they see.
Fat jokes told in my presence offend me and confuse me even more
Then I realize they're not meant for me, but for those who look how I looked before
Why is it, then, that they cut deep and still affect me so?
Because the fat child housed within refuses to let it go
When I shop through the aisles and look at small clothes

My inner fat child screams, "Leave those alone!"

When I try on those clothes I cannot believe

How they all fit me with elegance and ease

When I meet a new man that I catch feelings for

My inner fat child says, "When he finds out that you were fat he'll head straight for the door."

With reluctance I reveal my past to that man

Using pictures as my evidence of my wide waist and hip span

I prepare for him to leave as she said that he would

When he surprises me by saying, *"Girl, you still used to look good!"*

"Don't believe him, he's just saying that now, if he saw you back then he would call you a cow!" my inner fat child says with fury and spite, putting an immediate damper on my feelings that night.

My past and my present in a constant tug-of-war

Making it hard to appreciate all I've worked so hard for

My will was strong, but I could never win

Unless I confronted my demon within

I said, "Fat girl, would you please just let me be? Just let me enjoy my new healthy body."

She said, "Girl, don't forget that you used to be fat. You drop a few pounds now, you think you're all that? Just as you lost it you can gain it all back!"

I said, "I'll never forget what I used to be. I've only changed externally. Who I am inside is the same and will always be. Now one thing's a fact, I won't gain it all back; I'm committed to keeping my lifestyle on track."

She said, "You say that now, you gluttonous sow, but I'll be here laughing when you finally back down."

I said, "I know that you thrive on my fear and self-doubt. I've conquered those things, so now you can get out. Your nourishment comes from my insecurity. Now I am secure, so you can just leave. You used to control everything that I'd do; now I'm in control, so I rebuke you!"

I was prepared for her response filled with vengeance and rage

After listening closely, silence was all that I could gauge

Then suddenly I heard a surrendering sigh

That escalated into a defeated child's cry

Those cries and small footsteps began to slowly fade away

I never heard from my inner fat child again after that day.

When I was 150 pounds, I felt fat; now I would give anything to be back down to that. When I was 140 pounds, I felt too skinny, missing my womanly curves and feeling like I was shaped like a little boy. Now I look back at pictures and see how beautiful I was at every moment of my life, even when I was 214 pounds.

I could not deal with the constant voice that would creep up every morning. I woke up one morning and put the fat girl to bed. I'm not sure what triggered it, but it felt good.

When you believe that you are beautiful, you exude a confidence that is magnetic. Now that I do not have the fat girl in my head, I will not wait to do a professional photo shoot, I will not wait to wear a two-piece swimsuit, I will not wait to get another tattoo, and just live life.

Monica Marie Jones is an author whose published works include *The Ups and Downs of Being Round, Taste My Soul,* and *FLOSS*. She is also a contributing author in *Chicken Soup for the Girl's Soul, New Directions for Youth Development,* and several publications and youth development training materials for the High / Scope Educational Research Foundation. She has worked as a columnist and freelance writer for the *Michigan FrontPage* newspaper and is an active member of the Motown Writers Network.

Struck with Kindness

By Sasheer Moore

I began my third year of college in a cloud of angst. At the end of my second year, I found out that my roommate and close friend of the preceding two years was deceitful and hurting herself and the people around her with her behavior. She was beyond any help I could give her, and she did not want any of my help. My father was in the midst of his fourth marriage (the second after my mother) and there was tension between his new wife and me whenever I visited the house, due to misunderstandings and miscommunication. I was growing tired of confusing, false, and superficial relationships and I did not want to start the school year continuing any of these relationships.

I began to withdraw from social interactions to avoid potential awkward or stressful encounters with people. But this antisocial state did not last long. A car hit me shortly after the school year began. On that sunny afternoon, I was walking through a line of traffic to get back to my dorm when a car from the end of the line sped around the other cars and through the turning lanes and struck me. I was in the crosswalk, and he was driving too fast. I backed up enough so I only caught the front corner of the truck. I bounced off the hood, spun in the air, hit the back of my head on an adjacent car, and landed on the asphalt. When I landed, I could see my bloody arm in front of my face, and beyond that, I could see the driver running to me with a terrified look on his face. The paramedics arrived and took me to the emergency room. I was not able to contact anyone while I was incapacitated and waiting to see a doctor. I thought I would have to face this event on my own, until an unexpected visitor arrived.

An acquaintance of mine witnessed my accident and biked to the hospital to see me. He came to my room and kept me company while I waited for treatment. He called more of my friends to let them know what happened. I knew this student through shared friends and organizations, but we were not close friends. Despite our unfamiliarity, he stayed with me for all six hours I was in the hospital, and held my hand while the doctor pulled the glass from my arm. His support amazed me. And he was not the only person to show his concern for me. I received numerous caring calls and e-mails from strangers and affiliates. This show of love made me realize how I underestimated the value of other people. I believe that young man went over the call of duty as a friend. His compassion, and other people's kindness, restored my faith in humanity. I value people and their company more than I did before the accident, because I will never know what will happen to them, or me, the next day.

The goodness in others surpassed the drama that was depressing me. I found happiness from this event, and I plan to spread it to others. Don't wait for a traumatic incident to make you value others, or to make you understand how others value you. You will encounter many people that will drive you crazy, but there are so many other people who can brighten your life if you let them. I hope that there are days when I can be that person who exhibits a good example of what the human spirit can do, and that is something we should all strive for.

Sasheer Moore recently graduated from the University of Virginia with a B.A. in drama. She plans to move to New York in January 2009 to act and apply to graduate theater programs at New York universities. Sasheer did not receive any broken bones or lasting injuries from the car accident, and has been safely crossing the street ever since.

Health Crisis

Personal Book of Revelations

- *Do I take my health seriously?*
- *Will I inherit all the same illnesses?*
- *How much effort do I put into staying healthy?*
- *Do I practice safe sex?*

XI

It's So Hard to Say Good-bye

When Michael Jackson died, the world gasped—mostly out of disbelief. Actor, singer, and songwriter Jamie Foxx took the stage at the BET Awards just a few days after his death and said, "We are not going to be sad, but just celebrate the life of this black man."

If you have ever gotten the news that your loved one is gone, the feelings of denial, emptiness, anger, disappointment, hurt, grief, and mind-numbing pain are insurmountable. It is like a bad dream, and you just want to wake up. The pain further intensifies when it is a cruel and senseless death.

After the shock has set in, you will eventually get to a place that you can celebrate, but for some it can take a while to get there. We are all interconnected, and yet we take for granted the role that people play in our lives and believe that tomorrow will happen—but in reality, each morning that we arise is a special gift.

The gift is simply a realization of who you are and what

you represent to one another. At one point in your life you will be the first, the only, the most; the liberator, the blessing, the glue, the strategist, the resource, the grace, the innovator, the strong, and the organizer, just to name a few. If you have not stepped into that position, you come from a long line of women who have stepped into those shoes. Willingly or not, they did what was necessary to move their generation and their families forward.

Everyone has a story of how they came to be and the sacrifices they made in order for you to be where you are, and we could never wrap our heads around it. The ultimate thank-you is creating an opportunity to be supportive of your loved ones in their older days. Making someone's last days on this earth happy is powerful. Even if you are the only family member willing to step up to do it, you will never regret the time spent and the special moments between you and your loved one. It is an enriching experience that will enhance your life and better prepare you to fulfill all of your dreams and aspirations, because there is a legacy that lives within you, your children, and the work you do on this earth.

The essays in this final section will help you change the perception of death. The women in this chapter share their insight that there is no time to waste, but only time to love.

Loving Myself, Releasing Him

By Tameka L. Cage

She called in her soul to come and see.
—Zora Neale Hurston, *Their Eyes Were Watching God*

When I was seventeen, I landed a competitive job at LSU Medical Center for the summer, working as a research assistant for a program that investigated the connection between illiteracy and breast cancer among poor African American women. On the first day of the job, I met a boy who seemed to be my equal. He was smart, tall, and witty. I learned over time that he didn't believe himself to be handsome, but I thought he was appealing and adorable. We both loved Michael Jordan and savored intellectual conversations. He wanted more from life than what Shreveport-Bossier had to offer, just as I did. I liked him instantly. We quickly became friends, and I, just as quickly, began to want more. Over the course of the summer, my feelings deepened, and I thought I was in love. Though I now realize what I felt was desire and something as far from love as the Earth is from the sun, no one could have told me he should not be my partner forever, that we should not have babies, that we should not build a life together and break the cycle of poverty that had colored our lives, and travel the world as a successful African American couple that had "made something" of ourselves. I thought he was someone special, and having never been properly validated, loved, or treasured by my father, who was never validated, loved, or treasured sufficiently by his father, I craved his attention and hoped beyond hope that he would not only like me, but that he would love me fiercely. That he would say I was the person he had been waiting seventeen years for, and that he would ensure his heart only to me.

Looking back, I realize I was naïve. And desperate. In my naïveté, I expected a seventeen-year-old boy to know what he wanted out of life and to make an unyielding commitment to me, when in truth, there was no way I could have known what I wanted. We were, after all, young adults still becoming; our destinies had barely been revealed. I was desperate because I wanted him to think and say I was beautiful, to think and say I was important, to think and say he wanted me. I felt on some level that if he would love me, my entire self would be validated, that finally, I was worth something. But he could offer only some of what I thought I could receive only from him, in part because he needed someone to say it to him, too. After all, he was just as emotionally bruised and broken as I was, just as needful of validation, support, and approval, just as ravenous for someone besides his mother—perhaps his father, who had abandoned him and his mother early in his life—to say he was handsome and wanted, and that his efforts to be the best at absolutely everything would get him out of the projects and on a fast track to his dreams. If there was ever a "what-I-know-now-versus-what-I-knew-then" revelation, it is this: He could not give me something he did not have, and I hurt myself by asking of him what he could not give, and by thinking his love could replace me loving myself. It could not.

But even when considering all this, I realize I was not desperate for him. I was desperate for love, and so hungry for outside approval that I willingly allowed this young man to break promised phone calls and dinner dates, only to end up sitting by the phone, hoping that it would ring, or dressed in an outfit I had labored to put together to look my very best for him, searching for his headlights, and listening for his car in my mother's driveway. I opened the door for him to walk in and out of my life at will—even after he told me that he didn't want me to wait for him, and even after he confessed to me that he was "not a nice guy," and that he was not the grand person I had imagined. But I think I needed that image. I needed a wonderful man to find me to be wonderful, so I privileged that false narrative over what was true and what was smacking me over and over again, across my right cheek, then my left. It was true; he was not a nice guy.

This lasted over the course of about four years. The cycle was unending: we'd have a beautiful night, taking a walk or spending time with his family, and I'd think that maybe, hopefully, this was the time when he would finally return my feelings. On a given night, perhaps he had actually kept his promise and we'd gone out somewhere, and he'd treated me like I mattered for a few hours, and I would add magic, romance, and power to that fact and create something that was not actually there. And I'd end up right where I'd started: crying, by myself.

During that time, I put up no protective barriers. I did not guard my heart. I accepted his half-promises as truths, knowing all along they were lies and that he would let me down. We never even had a relationship. The one time I thought we did, I discovered he was telling another girl the same thing he was telling me: I love you. I feel certain that she believed him, just like I did. The reason I know this is because he had a charm about him, a way that was easy with women, but not necessarily slick or trying too hard; he seemed innocent, though I knew innocence could never hurt me like he did.

Now that I've met the true love of my life, my fiancé and life partner—who is a king in my eyes, and who relishes all aspects of me, from my ebony face to my strength to my fragility—I realize how true a friend's recent comments are, that there's a stark difference between charm and character. The young man I was willing to give my heart to could captivate me with his charm, but it is my soon-to-be husband whose charm is but one lump of sugar compared to his integrity, loyalty, and character, and those things combined with the raciness I feel when I'm with him are why I'm thankful God has blessed me with the gift of his companionship.

Two years ago, the young man I thought I loved so fiercely, beginning when I was seventeen and ending five years later, was killed while training aboard an Air Force Black Hawk. The aircraft crashed just miles from where it had taken off. I discovered he was dead when, after teaching a composition course, I checked my messages and heard my sister's voice saying she wasn't sure if it was him, but based on the description she heard on the radio, it sounded like this was the same man who, for so many years of my life, I agonized over and beat myself into near depression because he didn't love me. I listened to the message at least three times before I called my sister. After we talked, I called information to get his mother's number. She confirmed that he was dead. We cried together, and I shared some memories of some of the good times we had—and there were some, like the time when I was eighteen and he picked me up and ran through a neighbor's sprinklers during the evening because it was July, and Louisiana is fiercely hot in July. That was fun. But now he was gone, and I was no longer mourning a friend or would-be boyfriend, for we had lost touch several years prior. I was, instead, trying to figure out who exactly I was missing. All I had were memories. I did not know the person he had become—a husband, father, and captain in the U.S. Air Force. But I grieved for a life gone so soon, and for someone who, at one point in my life, not only meant the world to me, but on some sad level, had become my world.

During a recent talk with my fiancé, I began to realize that even after all these years, though I've earned a doctoral degree, traveled the world, and fallen in love with him, who loves me back in the strongest, purest way I could imagine, something inside of me still wanted the young man from my past to feel for me what I had felt for him. I still wanted to hear him apologize for being irresponsible with my feelings. I still wanted him to say that I was wonderful, amazing, beautiful, special, and rare. And that has absolutely nothing to do with him, and everything to do with me. In that place where I still need closure from his mistakes, I remain the little girl who longs to be kissed by her daddy before she goes to bed, as opposed to wondering where he was and why I had not seen him in so long. In that place I still need to hear my father tell ten-year-old me that no matter how bitterly I am being teased about my dark skin—which I am now embracing and learning to cherish—I am beautiful, and smart, and talented, and when God made me, He gave me all that I would need to live, love, and be loved.

This proves to me that I am still on a journey of self-love. I am not certain if the journey will ever end, or if it will need to. After all, I will be on a journey of love with my partner, our not-yet-born children, probably, for the rest of my life. Why should I not also be on a lifelong journey to love myself whole, beautiful, full as I am? And it is in that place, that place alone, where all I need is self-love and the gratification from knowing I am well loved by those who can and do return love to me. After all, self-love is one of the best things humanity has got going for itself, and if we spent as much time working on loving and embracing who we are, and celebrating that person in all our glory, we would scarcely have time to worry over whether someone who can't love us will ever do so. It has taken me years to learn this, and now that I have, I'll never let it go. Not for anyone, not for a second.

Dr. Tameka L. Cage was born in Shreveport, Louisiana, and received her bachelor of arts degree from Dillard University and her PhD from Louisiana State University. Her dissertation investigates discourse and female circumcision in a transnational context. She currently teaches in the Africana Studies Department at the University of Pittsburgh and is the theater critic for the *New Pittsburgh Courier*. She is working on her first novel, *This Far, By Grace.*

I WASN'T RAISED TO RUN

By Jessica A. Robinson

I will never forget November 3, 1993. In fact, I remember it just like it was yesterday. My day started out just like any other day. I did the usual things I always did. I went to school, came home and did my homework and played with my Barbie dolls. My father was in the hospital battling pancreatic cancer, and since my twin brothers and I were so young, my mother had no choice but to work and take care of us.

While my mother was cooking our dinner, our kitchen phone rang.

My mother answered in her usual pleasant tone. "Hello, this is the Robinson residence. How may I help you?" After that, my mother really didn't say anything else. I could tell that whoever was on the other end of the phone was saying some very important things, because my mother had stopped what she was doing to focus her full attention on the phone call.

"Excuse me, what did you say?" She asked the person to repeat what they were saying.

"Okay, I'm on my way up there right now. Thank you." My mother hung up the phone and then in an instant picked the phone back up and dialed what looked like my uncle's number.

"Denis, the hospital called, and they said that Dwight has taken a turn for the worse. We have to get up there now," she said as she turned off all of the burners on the stove.

"Okay, I'll drop the children off with Sandra. I'll be there in a second." She set the phone down in its cradle. Although I was only ten years old at the time, I knew what a turn for the worse meant. I knew exactly what that meant. It meant that there was a health emergency happening that could cause him to get worse, and I knew that when the doctors and nurses used those words, it was very serious. The minute my mother ended the call with my uncle, I was in her face asking a million questions, like, "What's going on with Daddy? Is he going to be all right? Can I go with you?"

My mom didn't answer any of those questions, but she grabbed my hand and led me out of the kitchen.

"Honey, your father is not doing too well. Your uncles and I are going to the hospital, and I have to take you to your aunt's house. Go and get your brothers so we can go." I knew by the intensity and tone in her voice that she meant business, so I wasted no time in getting my twin brothers ready to go. We were only going around the corner, so we just threw on any clothes we could find.

My mother dropped us off with my aunt and cousins, and she was on her way to see about my father. While I was at my aunt's, I did what any child would do. Even though in the back of my mind I knew that my mom said my father wasn't doing well, I still managed to have fun and play with my cousins. I was playing and having a good time, but every time the phone rang I couldn't help but wonder who my aunt was talking to. I think she kind of knew I was on edge about the whole situation, because after I ran into the dining room she told me to relax and try not to worry. Twenty minutes had gone by and the phone rang again. The past couple of calls I had let go and I didn't check to see who she was conversing with, but this time for some particular reason I found myself in the dining room staring directly in her face.

Something about the ring of the telephone and then her facial expression had let me know exactly what was going on. I already knew that my father was gone even before her lips parted to tell me.

Experiencing the loss of my father at such a young age was very rough. After he passed, I knew I had to step in and be strong and help my mother. I not only wanted to help my mother out, but I had to be strong for my little brothers. I had always been my mother's helper, and nothing changed that. The grieving process was tough to go through, but with time I was able to pull through and deal with the situation.

The next date that changed my life forever was recently, on October 22, 2008. This day happened not too long ago, but the events that took place on this day will be forever etched in my mind. I went to work and came home just like I did every day. Around seven thirty in the evening, my mother came home from teaching at school and was complaining of a backache. I offered to take her to the hospital, but she said that she was going to stay home and rest. I ran her a bath, and after she lay down, I went up to check on her and she was gone, just like that. I tried to wake her but I could tell that she wasn't breathing, so I immediately did CPR until the paramedics came, but they were unable to revive her.

Never in a million years would I have thought that I would bury both of my parents by the age of twenty-five. It's just hard to believe that two of the most important people in my life are not here to share my life with me. Although I'm grieving all over again, I'm reminded of the legacy that both of my parents left. No matter how hard life gets, I cannot quit. No matter how rough the situation may get, I have to keep going, because I wasn't raised to run.

Jessica A. Robinson is the author of the book *Holy Seduction.*

Sunrise to Sunset: How My Grandmother's Strength Reigns in My Spirit

By Alysia Satchel

Weeks before she died, the last thing my grandmother Leonila wanted was a fresh batch of chicken adobo—one of her favorite Filipino dishes.

My grandmother lived with Alzheimer's and dementia for eleven years, and during her lucid phases acted as sweet as leche flan—caramel custard from her homeland in Manila, Philippines—and behaved as feisty as the tangy kick in her adobo.

Six months before my grandmother's health took a devastating turn, I was relaxing poolside in the sweltering Atlanta heat. I had no idea that God was going to flip my life upside down and inside out. After graduating from Ohio State University, I decided to drop everything and move to

Atlanta to pursue my dreams as a journalist. I lived there for a year to get my foot in the door with internships and was enthralled by the sea of successful black professionals. I lived with my cousin Kim, who graciously gave me a place to stay with her, and her eleven-year-old daughter. One summer day, we received news from our family in Cleveland that my aunt, Kim's mother, needed help with caring for our grandmother because she was experiencing difficulties with her congestive heart failure. My aunt worked as my grandmother's caretaker for over ten years, but the time had come for someone to do the same for her. One month later, we moved back to Cleveland to put the pieces of our family back together.

After returning home, I searched for a job week after week, but couldn't find any opportunities to help pay my loans or skyrocket my career. With my degree in tow, I soon grew frustrated within each interview and the unresponsiveness of potential employers. This disappointment coupled with the stress of questioning why God would place me back in Cleveland, when my cousin and I were succeeding in Atlanta, boggled my mind countless times a day.

My aunt remained in the Cleveland Clinic hospital for nearly four months. I visited her every day to keep her company and pray with her. When I would return from those visits, I cooked dinner for my grandmother, bathed her, and helped her get ready for bed.

Soon our family couldn't give my grandmother the care she needed, and we had to make a difficult choice. We decided to place her in a nursing home. We were dedicated not to act as an absent family, and we all took shifts visiting her throughout the day, every day. I washed her clothing, read her the Bible, and rolled her hair (she's always been such a diva) during my visits.

Months later I began to realize that my purpose for being home was much greater than landing a job or an internship. God showed me how to cherish moments—even the most heartbreaking ones with your family—because you don't know what you can be taught, especially in your darkest days. I learned great humility and patience while I cared for my aunt and grandmother, and I carry it with me everywhere I go.

In every chapter of my grandmother's life, I can undoubtedly see the strength that God blessed her with to live a full life of eighty-eight years.

I remember my father telling me stories when I was younger about how they struggled growing up in the projects in a one-parent household. After arriving in the States as a war bride in 1946, my grandmother became a widow when my grandfather Edmund died in 1966 from congestive heart failure. Although she grappled with her English, my grandmother intently read books and newspapers daily to strengthen her dialect while educating herself. When my grandfather died at age forty-three, my grandmother knew that his death resulted from his military service during World War II. For two years, she wrote several letters to former Ohio senator Howard Metzenbaum to review my grandfather's case. The case was initially denied, but my grandmother fought tooth and nail to have her voice heard. After requesting my grandfather's medical records and tirelessly writing letters, the case was reviewed again, and the Supreme Court ruled in her favor. This lesson taught me to continue to push forward in the face of any adversity, because if God has favor over you, His grace will be sufficient. While supporting her five children alone, my grandmother also worked as a nurse's aide for many years. Any time in life that I ever feel tired, I always think about how exhausting and challenging her life must have been during that time.

My family experienced great tragedy and struggled with their health throughout the years, but that also taught us to give people their roses while they're here with you.

I learned this lesson early, at eight years old. In 1976, before I was born, my uncle Sandy lost his battle with congestive heart failure at age twenty-nine. Years later, in 1992, my uncle Sherman died of a brain aneurysm at forty-one years old, and within the next year my aunt Shirley died of lupus at age forty-two-years old. In 1998, my cousin Romanial was brutally murdered in Cleveland by members of the Latin Kings gang. As catastrophic as these events have been for my family, I've learned that you can't question God's purpose for allowing these things to happen. Our family hasn't been the same since each of these losses, but I rest in the comfort of knowing that I loved them each day, and maintain peace that I will see them again.

The inconceivable fervor my grandmother portrayed during each of my family member's deaths is a quality I pray that God instills in everyone. She wore the armor of God every day to maintain peace and sanity within our family during these difficult times.

Besides being a peacemaker, my grandmother acted as a phenomenal cook and prayer warrior. At her funeral, Ralph Hughley, pastor and family friend, spoke about my grandmother's mentality of community, which meant if she had a loaf of bread, everyone ate.

This concept planted a prophetic seed, as I recall watching her prepare dishes for our family during the week like it was Thanksgiving or Christmas.

Throughout the births and deaths, the trials, tribulations, and triumphs that our family has endured, my grandmother upheld her faith through the peaks and valleys. She taught me how to act as a prayer warrior, by putting God first in everything I do. My grandmother was raised Catholic and married into a Baptist family. In every home she ever lived in, I remember how diligently she prepared her altar with crosses, small ceramic statues of Mary and Jesus, her alabaster box, and candles to light during prayer. Since age eight, I've maintained a small altar that has grown with each year, because she demonstrated the importance of honoring the Lord.

During my grandmother's last days of life, I read her favorite psalms and listened as she hummed and sang her favorite hymn, "I Surrender All." I knew her life was coming to a close. As gut-wrenching as this realization was for my family, we knew that we loved her, but God loved her more.

I keep all the values my grandmother instilled in me close to my heart, like: to always act like a lady, to take pride in my appearance, to fight for what I believe in, to know how to prepare a succulent meal to bring my family together, to always to be humble and gracious, and most importantly, to never lose faith, because God is on the throne.

During my time spent in Cleveland caring for these two special women in my life, God confirmed to me how He blesses us in what will seem like the most inopportune and challenging circumstances. I applied to graduate school before my grandmother passed, and was blessed with an assistantship that paid for my tuition. Weeks after starting my classes, my father called to let me know that my grandmother was losing her eyesight and her doctors didn't know how much longer she could hold on. When I began to fear that I wouldn't be given a chance to say good-bye to my grandmother in her last days, God spoke to me and told me not to move my feet. I finished my first summer session and arrived home to visit with her before my birthday. I sat with her every day during my two-week break before fall classes began, and she surrendered her spirit to the Lord two days after my twenty-fourth birthday.

This tumultuous year made me really see life visibly. I've realized God places us in the most incomprehensible situations, because He knows that we will persevere. But it's up to us to get up every day we have a breath in our bodies and do something great. I fought being home out of the apprehension that my success wasn't in Cleveland. Soon that selfishness faded away, and I saw that God ordered my steps so that I could honor my grandmother and take care of her, like she did for me all of my life.

Since my grandmother passed away, I've cooked chicken adobo more than usual, just to go back to the time we spent together. When I inhale the pungent scent of the vinegar, soy sauce, chicken, and white rice brewing and it hits my face, it's like she never left.

Alysia Satchel is a master's degree graduate of the S. I. Newhouse School of Public Communications at Syracuse University. She contributed to *Jezebel* and *Skirt!* magazines in Atlanta as an editorial assistant before landing in upstate New York. She hopes to keep her grandmother's dreams alive by composing a cookbook of her grandmother's recipes, passing on her lessons about life and love, and always maintaining the faith of a mustard seed in the face of adversity.

PRIORITIES

By LaShieka Purvis Hunter

My sister called me while I was in the midst of planning my birthday party at a chic Manhattan lounge to tell me that my grandfather only had a week to live. The words came as no surprise, because he'd been suffering from cancer for a couple of years and his health had deteriorated drastically over the last few months. She told me that they were moving him to a hospice and she asked when I would be coming down to Jersey to see him. I told her that I had some deadlines at work, but would come at the end of the week. After we hung up, all I could think about was how I was going to be inconvenienced by having to deal with the rush-hour traffic from Long Island to southern New Jersey. Then, can you believe that I actually said to myself? *Okay, he has a week to live. Today is Tuesday; I can go down there after work on Thursday, go to the hospice, spend a little time with him, and make it back for my party on Friday night. Yeah, that'll work.* As I write this now, recalling my thoughts, I am disgusted that something like that ran through my mind—that I was actually trying to work out the logistics of having a party around the inevitable passing of my grandfather.

The next day my father and sisters called me to give an update and tried to put my grandfather on the phone so I could say hello to him. My grandfather could barely speak, and the sound that I did hear was barely audible, almost childlike. Was this the big man with the booming Southern twang (although he had moved to New Jersey from down South decades ago) who'd always had a cigarette dangling from his lips, who loved working on his car, and loved a drink just as much? Was this my grandfather, who hunted and fished and had bear meat and turtle feet in his deep freezer, the man who could cook a pig a hundred different ways—yes, from the rooter to the tooter! (As a child and way before I gave up pork, you could find me and family at his kitchen table enjoying his tangy BBQ pig ears.)

Over the phone I told him I loved him, and my sister said he smiled when he heard that. Later, my mother admitted that he didn't look good at all. She also wanted to know when I was coming to Jersey. I think tomorrow, I told her. I had the audacity to ask her if I should still have my party, and she was quiet, as if trying to process how, at a time like this, partying was on my mind. Then she said that she didn't know what I should do. But then she finally said, "Maybe that's not a good idea." On my way home I started to think about how much of an inconvenience (me and these damn inconveniences) it would be to call the club promoter and cancel my party. But then I started to think about one of the last conversations I had with my grandfather. I had tried to connect with him the last time I was in Jersey, several months earlier. I told him I was coming at a particular time, but didn't go, and spent that time with friends. When I did go over there, he didn't answer the door although I saw his car sitting in his driveway. Perhaps he didn't hear me knocking or the door bell ringing? He was, after all, sick and almost immobile. Or maybe he was mad at me for telling him a certain time but just showing up when I felt like it. He didn't like when people said one thing and did another.

But he did call me the next morning while my husband and I were getting ready to head back to New York. I was short with him, telling him that I stopped by the day before and nobody answered the door. He apologized, saying he didn't hear the door, and even then I could hear his voice fading, but I think I tried to ignore it. He said that he was home now and I should stop by before we leave.

"No, we really have to go," I told him. "I'll see you the next time I'm down."

"Okay. Listen, Shieka . . ."

"Yes?"

"I love you."

"Uh, I love you, too, Granddaddy."

It was the first time I could remember my grandfather saying that he loved me. Sure, we had had great meals together, he had told many funny stories, but we weren't the tightest grandfather and granddaughter team around—especially after I got older.

So as I recalled that conversation, during my drive home from work, I began to realize that my party and a little traffic was nothing compared to him. Yeah, so what if we weren't that close, he was still my grandfather and deserved more than what I was giving him. The next day I called the party promoter, canceled the party, and headed down to Jersey.

When I got to the hospice, my heart shredded. At seventy-six years old, my grandfather was in the bed, motionless, half his size, eyes yellow and glassy, and cheeks sunken in. I kissed him, sat down next to him, and held his hand. I immediately hated myself for being so selfish, so inconsiderate, and so juvenile. My father suggested that I give my grandfather some water, and my hand shook as I tried to give it to him.

The next day, Friday, around the same time that I would have been getting ready for my birthday bash, my whole family, including cousins, aunts, and uncles, all piled into his room laughing and talking. A lot of us hadn't seen each other in years. My grandfather lay in his bed, quiet and still. My sisters and I sat in front of his bed chatting with cousins, looking at vacation photos from my uncle's digital camera. I looked up from the camera and over at my grandfather and he was staring at me. Just staring at my face, taking it in. I felt like leaning over to one of my sisters jokingly to say, "Granddaddy has an eye problem." But I didn't. And I saw him give a little smile and then cast his eyes over to my sister and then a cousin after that.

I left the room to get some air and went down to the

kitchen after a relative told me there were some delicious vanilla ice cream cups in the freezer for the families. I came back and chatted with a few cousins when suddenly my mom and sisters ran out of his room, crying.

"He's gone!"

I hurried into the room, and sure enough, he was gone, his eyes still open, but now focused on nothing in particular.

Among the many tears that broke out in the room and family members clutching each other, I sat there, quiet. I had never been in the same room with a person who had just died, and I guess I was in shock. I thought about my husband, a cop, who'd seen dead people and seen people die many times and was probably immune to it now.

I began to wonder what my grandfather's last thoughts were. Was he scared? Was he telling God that he wasn't ready to go? Asking for more time? I suddenly figured out the reason he was staring at me and the rest of his family members. He was probably examining our faces, taking in every crevice, each eyelash, and remembering a special time we shared with him. Maybe a time when he tried to get us to eat fried squirrel or some other crazy game meat in his fridge, and we squealed and ran away laughing. He was storing us and those delightful times in his mind, reflecting on the life he lived and the experiences he shared with each of us.

I finally got up and went over to him and kissed his forehead, which was surprisingly still warm, and then I touched his hand, which was remarkably cold. With tears trickling down my face, I silently apologized for being selfish and asked him to forgive me. I silently said I was sorry for not stopping back over to his house a few months back. And as I sat back down to let another family member kiss him and hold his hand, I realized that there was no other place I wanted or needed to be that Friday night, the night before my birthday. I didn't need to be at some dark lounge, drinking lemon drop martinis and dancing the night away. I needed to be right there, where I was, with my grandfather, to say good-bye and let him take one last look at my face.

LaShieka Purvis Hunter is a former assistant health editor at *Essence* magazine and a former researcher for *Honey, Savoy,* and *Heart & Soul* magazines. Her work has appeared in *The Source, Seventeen, Real Health, Honey, Savoy, Heart & Soul, ColorLines, NMA Healthy Living,* and *Essence* magazines. She is currently a staff writer for St. Francis Hospital on Long Island, and a freelance celebrity and corporate bio writer.

My Sonny Boy

By Evelyn L. Williamson

My Sonny boy came into my life on a beautiful fall day at the end of September, and it felt right the moment he shook my hand. If there is such a thing as soul mates, we were it. So imagine the irony, that he left this life and my world the end of September, eleven years later. He has been like a fixture in my life, in my children's lives, and at times for my friends and family members. He was my rock and anchor on my journey, and in the midst of this wild ride called the Campaign for Change.

Even though our conversations were brief while I was on the campaign trail, we spoke often, and the quality of our talks was good, special, and full of laughter. We looked so forward to picking up our lives and moving forward with each other after the campaign was over, and that fact alone was like jet fuel for my spirit. I smiled to myself whenever I thought of him, reminding myself how lucky I was to be loved, supported, and respected by the only man on this earth that at times could see into my very soul, who valued my opinion and called me his hero. I now look back, and I sometimes took our time together for granted to a degree.

The day that I got the call that crushed my heart, spirit, and soul, it was a rainy, cold Saturday morning, and I was campaigning for change hard in northwest Philly. Sonny boy died the morning of September 27 of a heart attack. My life and commitment to the Obama campaign had shifted into overdrive. My long sixteen- to eighteen-hour days, as usual, were filled with a hundred crises that needed to be managed and resolved all at the same time. I welcomed the distraction and the chaos that only a presidential campaign of this magnitude could deliver. In the midst of this storm called life and politics, I nursed and sheltered my grief as if it were a priceless jewel that had to be handled with delicate kid gloves. I was on an hourly mission to successfully complete the task and job that I had been chosen for. There were hundreds of volunteers that needed organizing, and as a general in this movement I had to lead the eager troops into a daily battle. There were goals and milestones that had to be reached.

At times I felt like I was on automatic pilot while my appetite for success, or just self-preservation, if you will, led my every move. My days were long and endless, and my nights were even worse because at night it was still and quiet, and my thoughts and memories of the love of my life consumed me. I told myself that work and daylight had no place for tears, pain, or grief, so I broke down every night alone in my bedroom, and tears along with my grief were my sleeping pills. With field reports and deadlines in one hand and usually a distraught friend or relative on the other end of my cell phone that I had to often talk down off the ledge of their own grief, I maneuvered through somehow. My children were in need of me to be strong and to be their safe place to fall; therefore, I was determined to be their quiet in this emotional and spiritual hell of life and loss.

I chose not to go back to Atlanta to the memorial service, because that would have destroyed me in so many ways. Besides, he and I both agreed that funerals were morbid rituals that survivors of departed ones needed to put themselves through only to get through. The day of the memorial, my day began at 5:00 A.M. and went at stealth speed up until 11:00 A.M. His memorial was at 11:00 A.M. I sat at my desk, frozen and unable to move one muscle. Even though the campaign office was bustling and busy, I didn't hear a thing going on around me. My best friend was no longer a phone call or whisper away. I left and drove around Germantown for a while, found a liquor store and bought his drink, Jack Daniel's and Diet Coke, went back to the supporter housing where I was staying, fixed myself a strong drink, went to my room, and assumed a fetal position. I felt him with me in my room that afternoon, and then I went to sleep.

Election Day and night came. We won my assigned state of Pennsylvania big. Barack Obama became the 44th president of the United States of America, our mission had been accomplished, and my Sonny boy was smiling down on me from heaven. Every once in a blue moon there is a perfect storm, a great love, and a realization of how strong you must be at the end of the day.

Evelyn L. Williamson is a political consultant and mother of two who currently lives in Atlanta, Georgia.

Your Soul's Sustenance

Losing someone you love is never easy; death is the second chapter in a person's life because the effects of their legacy are timeless. The pain may seem unbearable, but keeping your emotions inside will only add to the depression that could possibly come if there is no outlet available to you.

- *Writing about your loss in a journal will help you release some of the anger, pain, and resentment.*
- *As you go along with your daily routine, there will be opportunities for you to honor your loved one. Instead of tears, do it with laughter. It is a great way to work through the hurt.*
- *The question will always linger: Why me and my family? There will never be a good enough answer to this question.*

Your Personal Book of Revelations

- *Have you experienced a close personal loss? How did you cope?*
- *Are you letting people in your life know that you love them instead of waiting for their death?*
- *Do you have a plan in case someone close to you dies?*
- *What are your feelings about death?*
- *How can you move on?*

Resource Guide

People should know whatever it is you love to do. I am a living testament to the fact that you can do it. You can do whatever it is you put your mind to and you can do it in stilettos.
—Kimora Lee Simmons

Here is a list of books and some resources that will assist you in figuring out what you want to do and give you information to face the challenges life has to offer. Slide on those stilettos and know that you can be the great woman you are meant to be!

Books Every Young Woman Should Read

Act Like a Lady, Think Like a Man by Steve Harvey

A Random Walk Down Wall Street by Burton G. Malkiel

All Things Hidden by Judy Candis

The Purpose Driven Life by Rick Warren

The Alphabet Verses: The Ghetto by Jessica Care Moore

The Audacity of Hope by Barack Obama

Black by Tracy Brown

Black Firsts, 2nd Edition by Jessie Carney Smith

Black Girls Learn Love Hard by Ras Baraka

Black Girl / White Girl by Joyce Carol Oates

Black Pain: It Just Looks Like We're Not Hurting by Terrie Williams

Black Sexual Politics: African Americans, Gender, and the New Racism by Patricia Hill Collins

Black Women's Lives: Stories of Pain and Power by Kristal Brent Zook

Buffett: The Making of an American Capitalist by Roger Lowenstein

Butterscotch Blues by Margaret Johnson-Hodge

Change Your Thinking, Change Your Life by Brian Tracy

Chomsky on Mis-Education by Noam Chomsky

Choose to Be Happy: A Guide to Total Happiness by Rima Rudner

The Coldest Winter Ever by Sister Souljah

Color Coded by Kim Carter-Johnson

For Colored Girls Who Have Considered Suicide When the Rainbow Is Enuf by Ntozake Shange

Color of the Cross by Ayvee Verzonilla

The Color of Trouble by Dyanne Davis

The Conspiracy to Destroy Black Women by Michael Porter

Cracking the Corporate Code: The Revealing Success Stories of 32 African American Executives by Price M. Cobbs and Judith L. Turnock

Cut by Patricia McCormick

Double Outsiders: How Women of Color Can Succeed in Corporate America by Jessica Faye Carter

Dreams from My Father by Barack Obama

Encyclopedia of African-American Heritage by Susan Altman

The Gift of Fear by Gavin De Becker

The Girls' Guide to Hunting and Fishing by Melissa Bank

Glass by Ellen Hopkins

God Still Don't Like Ugly by Mary Monroe

Good Is Not Enough: And Other Unwritten Rules for Minority Professionals by Keith R. Wyche

He's Gone . . . You're Back: The Right Way to Get Over Mr. Wrong by Kerika Fields with an afterword by Janeula M. Burt, PhD

How to Get Over Him and Learn from Your Mistakes: A Survival Guide by Denician Angeleia

How to Hustle and Win: A Survival Guide for the Ghetto by Supreme Understanding

It Happened in Church: Stories of Humor from the Pulpit to the Pews by Patti S. Webster with a foreword by Pastor Donnie McClurkin

Lavina: The Saga of an African Princess by Author O. Wright

Letters to Young Black Women by Daniel Whyte III

Letters to a Young Sistah by Hill Harper

Letter to My Daughter by Maya Angelou

Life Lessons for My Sisters: How to Make Wise Choices and Live a Life You Love! by Natasha Munson

Life's Little Instruction Book by H. Jackson Brown Jr.

Longing to Tell: Black Women Talk About Sexuality and Intimacy by Tricia Rose

The Lovely Bones by Alice Sebold

Moneyball by Michael Lewis

Naked: Black Women Bare All about Their Skin, Hair, Hips, Lips and Other Parts by Ayana Byrd and Akiba Solomon

No Disrespect by Sister Souljah

Never Tell by Selena Montgomery

My Sister's Keeper by Jodi Picoult

One Up on Wall Street by Peter Lynch

Play Like a Man, Win Like a Woman: What Men Know About Success That Women Need to Learn by Gail Evans

Push by Sapphire

Racism in the Lives of Women: Testimony, Theory, and Guides to Antiracist Practice by Jeanne Adleman and Gloria Enguídanos

Riding the Bus with My Sister by Rachel Simon

Rich Dad, Poor Dad: What the Rich Teach Their Kids About Money—That the Poor and Middle Class Do Not! by Robert T. Kiyosaki

Sasha's Way by Scott Haskins

The Secret Life of Bees by Sue Monk Kidd

Our Separate Ways by Ella L. J. Edmondson Bell and Stella M. Nkomo

Shifting: The Double Lives of Black Women in America by Charisse Jones and Kumea Shorter-Gooden, PhD

The Souls of Black Folk by W. E. B. Du Bois

Souls of My Sisters: Black Women Break Their Silence, Tell Their Stories, and Heal Their Spirits by Dawn Marie Daniels and Candace Sandy

Souls Revealed: A Souls of My Sisters Book of Revelations and Tools for Healing Your Life, Soul, and Spirit by Dawn Marie Daniels and Candace Sandy with a foreword by Star Jones

Stolen Women: Reclaiming Our Sexuality, Taking Back Our Lives by Gail Wyatt

Why Is It Always About You?: The Seven Deadly Sins of Narcissism by Sandy Hotchkiss

Why Men Love Bitches: From Doormat to Dreamgirl—A Woman's Guide to Holding Her Own in a Relationship by Sherry Argov

The Words Don't Fit in My Mouth by Jessica Care Moore

The Will to Dance by Ebony Joy Wilkins

Women Have All the Power . . . Too Bad They Don't Know It by Michael J. Lockwood

When and Where I Enter: The Impact of Black Women on Race and Sex in America by Paula J. Giddings

Women and Leadership: The State of Play and Strategies for Change by Barbara Kellerman and Deborah L. Rhode

Women and the Leadership Q: Revealing the Four Paths to Influence and Power by Shoya Zichy

Tears to Triumph: Women Learn to Live, Love, and Thrive by Dawn Marie Daniels and Candace Sandy with Dr. Jarralynne Agee

Tears for Water by Alicia Keyes

Through the Labyrinth: The Truth About How Women Become Leaders by Alice H. Eagly and Linda L. Carli

News Article

"Black. Female. Accomplished. Attacked." by Sophia A. Nelson (*Washington Post*, July 20, 2008)

Soul Sources

Child Care and Elder Care

Care Guide
www.careguide.com

This online "personal care giving resource" provides directories, articles, a newsletter, and more about issues concerning dealing with older loved ones. There is also another channel that deals with child-care concerns.

Hospice
www.hospicenet.org

A site for patients and families facing life-threatening illness. It offers a great deal of assistance for patients and caregivers. It covers everything from resolving pain without medication to talking to children about death to preparing for approaching death.

Cyberstalking

The National Center for Victims of Crime is the nation's leading resource and advocacy organization for crime victims and those who serve them. Since its inception in 1985, the National Center has worked with grassroots organizations and criminal justice agencies throughout the United States, serving millions of crime victims.

National Center for Victims of Crime
2000 M Street NW, Suite 480
Washington, DC 20036
Phone: (202) 467-8700
Fax: (202) 467-8701
Website: www.ncvc.org

Cyberangels was created by the Guardian Angels and Curtis Sliwa in 1995. Today CyberAngels is one of the oldest and most respected online safety education programs in the world. Under the leadership of Anthony de Araujo and Katya Gifford, the program has expanded to become a virtual learning community—earning a prominent position among online safety education providers.

CyberAngels
P.O. Box 3171
Allentown, PA 18106
Phone: (610) 351-8250
Fax: (610) 482-9101
Website: www.cyberangels.org

Domestic Violence

DomesticViolence.com
www.domesticviolence.com

"You are not alone. You are not to blame. You do not deserve to be abused," says this website devoted to helping women deal with domestic violence. The site provides a "domestic violence survival kit" that provides everything from using courts to get orders of protection to getting help from the social service system.

National Hotline: (800) 799-SAFE

Divorcessource.com
www.divorcesource.com

This website provides valuable divorce-related resources specific to all fifty states. Included in the information provided for each state is a guide to divorce professionals in that state, an overview of divorce law in the state, articles on child custody, property distribution, and other issues. Numerous books are available for sale on scores of important topics.

EDUCATIONAL RESOURCES

United Negro College Fund. Having supported the studies of over 300,000 African American students, the UNCF is doing its valuable work every day. The UNCF is widely known for its popular tag line, "A Mind Is a Terrible Thing to Waste." If you are a student, contact the UNCF about ways they can assist you with your education. If you're not a student, a tax-deductible contribution would be a concrete way that you can assist in the UNCF's valiant mission.

United Negro College Fund
8260 Willow Oaks Corporate Drive
Fairfax, VA 22031
Phone: (800) 331-2244
Website: www.uncf.org

Health and Mental Health

American Cancer Society. The ACS is the foremost group in education and information on all types of cancer. The organization conducts a wide range of programs.
Phone: 1 (800) ACS-2345
Website: www.cancer.org

American Heart Association. The AHA is dedicated to providing education and information on fighting heart disease and stroke. Their website is a valuable resource for women.

American Heart Association
National Center
7272 Greenville Avenue
Dallas, Texas 75231
Website: www.americanheart.org

The organization is affiliated with the following hotlines:
Customer Heart and Stroke Information
(800) AHA-USA1
CPR Information
(877) AHA-4-CPR
Stroke Information
(888) 4-STROKE
Woman Health Information
(888) MY-HEART

Global Health Council is the world's largest membership alliance dedicated to saving lives by improving health throughout the world. The diverse membership is comprised of healthcare professionals and organizations that include NGOs, foundations, corporations, government agencies, and academic institutions that work to ensure global health for all.

1111 19th Street, NW, Suite 1120
Washington, DC 20036
Phone: (202) 833-5900
Website: www.globalhealth.org

Health Power for Minorities. The mission of Health Power is to improve the health of multicultural populations, and thus the health of society as a whole. Our mission is pursued through:

- *Production and dissemination of authoritative and culturally relevant health and health-related information.*
- *Promotion of health on communities of color, and among others in a position to have a positive impact on their physical, mental, and spiritual health.*
- *Provision of technical assistance to organizations serving multicultural populations for capacity-building, including the development and enhancement of culturally competent programs and activities.*

The hallmark of the Health Power approach is partnering with the public, nonprofit, and private sectors in planning, implementing, and operating customized programs and strategies for disease prevention, early detection, and control.

3020 Glenwood Road
Brooklyn, NY 11210
Phone: (718) 434-8103
Website: www.healthpowerforminorities.com

The National Institutes of Health (NIH), a part of the U.S. Department of Health and Human Services, is the primary agency for conducting and supporting medical research.

Helping to lead the way toward important medical discoveries that improve people's health lives, NIH scientists investigate ways to prevent disease as well as the causes, treatments, and even cures for common and rare diseases.

National Institutes of Health
9000 Rockville Pike
Bethesda, MD 20892
Website: www.nih.gov

Sickle Cell Disease Foundation of California has committed itself to "education and life-enhancing programs and services to individuals with sickle cell disease," to broadening public awareness about sickle cell disease, and to promoting medical research and education to ultimately find a cure.

6133 Bristol Parkway, Suite 240
Culver City, CA 90230
Phone: (877) 288-CURE; (310) 693-0247
Website: www.scdfc.org

SAVE (Suicide Awareness Voices of Education). The mission of SAVE is to prevent suicide through public awareness and education, eliminate stigma, and serve as a resource to those touched by suicide.

8120 Penn Ave. S., Suite 470
Bloomington, MN 55431
Phone: (800) 273-TALK
Local phone: (952) 946-7998
Website: www.save.org

The Sister Study is the only long-term study of women aged 35 to 74 who have a sister who has had breast cancer. It is a national study to learn how environment and genes affect the chances of getting breast cancer. In the next three years, 50,000 women whose sister had breast cancer, and who do not have breast cancer themselves, will be asked to join the study. Organizations that are in partnership with the Sister Study include the American Cancer Society, Sisters Network, Inc., Susan G. Komen for the Cure, and the Breast Cancer Network of Strength, as well as countless local community breast cancer support and advocacy groups.

Phone: (877) 4SISTER
For deaf or hard of hearing: (866) TTY-4SIS
Website: www.sisterstudy.org

Susan G. Komen for the Cure. The mission of the Komen foundation is to "eradicate breast cancer as a life-threatening disease by advancing research, education, screening, and treatment." The website offers a valuable array of information and support for people dealing with breast cancer. The foundation is best known for its annual Race for the Cure.

National Breast Cancer Helpline
(800) I'M AWARE (1-800-462-9273)
Website: www.komen.org

Internet Resources

About.com
The African American history section of about.com offers expert-guided Internet resources of interest to African Americans.

Google.com

The go-to search engine for every subject under the sun, including direct links to websites, subject-related videos, maps, photographs, news, and more.

BlackPlanet.com

Simply the best black online community on the web, with hundreds of thousands of members; you'll find lively discussions on just about any subject you can imagine.

BlackWebsites.com

Here is a collection of links to African American websites on every subject.

Netnoir.com

Netnoir is a very popular black website of general interest that boasts half a million visitors every month. Its channels include news, music, virtual communities, shopping, chat rooms, personal e-mail accounts, and much more.

SoulsOfMySisters.com

What started out as this book has become an exciting movement of sisters. SoulofMySisters.com is a community of sisters working together toward peace and healing. By sisters we mean women of color who share a kindred spirit that gives us strength and faith. The community is like a second home for its members. It is a community where women of color can come together for an intimate sharing of information and heart-filled support. It's like sharing secrets over a cup of coffee or having a late-night phone chat with one of your closest friends.

At SoulsofMySisters.com you can: get the latest information on your spiritual health and well-being, find out if you're truly in love, enter contests to win fabulous prizes like trips and spa days—and much, much more. Meet sisters like you who aren't afraid to tell their personal stories and to aid in the healing of women of color. SoulsofMySisters.com can start a spiritual journey toward healing you and your sisters.

Membership Organizations

The National Urban League. Established in 1910, the Urban League is the nation's oldest and largest community-based movement devoted to empowering African Americans to enter the economic and social mainstream. Today, the National Urban League, headquartered in New York City, spearheads the nonpartisan efforts of its local affiliates. There are over 100 local affiliates of the National Urban League located in 35 states and the District of Columbia, providing direct services to more than two million people nationwide through programs, advocacy, and research. The Urban League employs a five-point strategy, tailored to local needs, in order to implement the mission of their movement.

- *Education and Youth Empowerment: Ensuring that all of our children are well educated and prepared for economic self-reliance in the twenty-first century through college scholarships, early childhood literacy, Head Start, and after-care programs.*
- *Economic Empowerment: Empowering all people in attaining economic self-sufficiency through job training, good jobs, homeownership, entrepreneurship, and wealth accumulation.*
- *Health and Quality of Life Empowerment: Working to*

build healthy and safe communities to eliminate health disparities through prevention, healthy eating, fitness, as well as ensuring complete access to affordable health care for all people.

- *Civic Engagement and Leadership Empowerment: Empowering all people to take an active role in determining the direction, quality of life, public policy, and leadership in their communities by full participation as citizens and voters, as well as through active community service and leadership development.*
- *Civil Rights and Racial Justice Empowerment: Promoting and ensuring our civil rights by actively working to eradicate all barriers to equal participation in all aspects of American society, whether political, economic, social, educational, or cultural.*

The National Urban League
120 Wall Street, 8th Floor, New York, NY 10005
Phone: (212) 558-5300
Website: www.nul.org

The NAACP. The mission of the National Association for the Advancement of Colored People is to ensure the political, educational, social, and economic equality of rights of all persons and to eliminate racial hatred and racial discrimination. Some of the programs the NAACP offers include: economic empowerment, education, health, and many more.

NAACP National Headquarters
4805 Mt. Hope Drive, Baltimore, MD 21215
Phone: (877) NAACP-98
Local phone: (410) 580-5777
Website: www.naacp.org

The African American Planning Commission (AAPCI) Inc., is a New York City–based 501(c)(3), nonprofit organization committed to addressing issues of homelessness (domestic violence, HIV / AIDS, housing shortage, and unemployment) within the communities in which they live and serve.

African American Planning Commission, Inc., Corporate
P.O. Box 330-707
Brooklyn, New York 11233
Phone: (718) 218-7254
Fax: (718) 218-7115
E-mail: contact@aapci.org

AAPCI Program
Serenity House Family Residence
P.O. Box 330-704
Brooklyn, New York 11233-0704
Phone: (718) 218-7254
Fax: (718) 218-7115
Matthew Okebiyi, Director
Gladys Pipkins, Assistant Director
Website: www.aapci.org

F.F.A.W.N. (Foundation for the Advancement of Women Now)
145 West 45th Street, 12th floor
New York, NY 10036
Website: www.ffawn.org

MySistahs is a website created by and for young women of color to provide information and offer support on sexual and reproductive health issues through education and advocacy.

MySistahs
Advocates for Youth
Suite 750
2000 M Street NW
Washington, DC 20036
Phone: (202) 419-3420
Fax: (202) 419-1448
Website: www.mysistahs.org

National Council of Negro Woman
Founded by the legendary educator Mary McLeod Bethune, the NCNW is focused on the concerns of African American women. The NCNW is composed of 33 affiliated constituency organizations and 250 chartered sections.

National Council of Negro Woman
633 Pennsylvania Avenue, NW
Washington, DC 20004
Phone: (202) 737-0120
Website: www.ncnw.org

National Organization for Women (NOW). NOW's activism is apparent in the full range of issues of interest to women, from reproductive issues to radical and ethnic diversity.

National Organization for Women
1100 H Street NW, 3rd Floor
Washington, DC 20005
Phone: (202) 628-8669
Website: www.now.org

Money Resources

Black Enterprise
Black Enterprise magazine's website serves as a good financial homepage. It offers such information and market tools as stock quotes, tickers, and financial news. It also offers general news of importance to African Americans.
Website: www.blackenterprise.com

Debtors Anonymous
The focus of Debtors Anonymous is to help people "recover from compulsive debting." The only membership requirement is that you want to stop incurring unsecured debt. There are no dues and DA is not affiliated with any sect, denomination, or political viewpoint.
Website: www.debtorsanonymous.org

Political Organizations

Congressional Black Caucus Foundation, Inc. Established in 1976, the CBCF is a nonprofit research and educational institute that seeks to assist African American political leaders of today and prepare those of tomorrow.

Congressional Black Caucus Foundation, Inc.
1720 Massachusetts Ave. NW
Washington, DC 20036
Phone: (202) 263-2800
Website: www.cbcfinc.org

PROFESSIONAL ORGANIZATIONS

National Association of Black Journalists (NABJ) is an organization of "journalists, students, and media-related professionals that provides quality programs and services to benefit black journalists worldwide." Foremost among the goals of the NABJ is increasing the number of blacks in the media, especially in management positions. The NABJ also sponsors numerous informational and educational programs.

National Association of Black Journalists
University of Maryland
8701A Adelphi Road
Adelphi, MD 20783-1716
Phone: (866) 479-NABJ
Local phone: (301) 445-7100
Website: www.nabj.org

Black Career Women (BCW) is a national organization headquartered in Cincinnati, Ohio. Although the organization does not have chapters, its membership is national. The organization, founded in 1977, serves as a nucleus of support to identify and address the critical needs of black women in the workforce as it relates to their career mobility and achievement. BCW's members are diverse, representing aspiring and achieving women workers from entry level to executive level.

BCW's website was launched in 1997 and maintains priority listing on most national search engines. Over 140 visitors view the site monthly, primarily black women job seekers and job changers, professional women seeking to expand their networks, develop skills, stay informed, or share insights and resources.

Website: www.bcw.org

The National Organization for African-American Women was founded in 2007. The organization's goal is to provide a consistent and balanced voice for today's African American woman. The group's focus is geared around the issues and concerns of the condition of women of color. Our mission is to enhance the condition of women of color in America socially, economically, and politically.

The National Organization for African-American Women
P.O. Box 29579
Washington, DC 20017
Phone: (202) 529-5508
Website: www.noaw.org

African-American Women in Technology (AAWIT) is a nonprofit organization dedicated to the education, support, and advancement of African American women in the field of information technology.

AAWIT encourages, promotes, and serves the interest(s) of African American women in information technology, striving to help its members advance their careers and enhance their personal development through special resources and networking opportunities. AAWIT.net is an informative, educational, resourceful, online community and is research, quality, and community oriented.

African-American Women in Technology
619 E. College Avenue, # C3
Decatur, GA 30030
Website: www.aawit.net

The National African-American Women's Leadership Institute, Inc. recognizes the supportive role African American women have traditionally assumed in every aspect of American life. Black women have been the mainstay of volunteer support in local churches, in neighborhood schools, and in civic and social services organizations. Building on these existing strengths, NAAWLI seeks emerging women leaders who will commit themselves and their leadership talents to constructive change in the black community.

Believing that the most meaningful leadership development combines opportunities for personal growth and professional development, NAAWLI weaves together a holistic leadership model that stimulates the mind, challenges the body, and renews the spirit. The program brings together women from diverse backgrounds and varied careers and enhances their leadership potential.

In return, NAAWLI helps participants shape a vision of how they can improve their local communities and implement that vision in a project that will stimulate youth development, foster health and wellness, promote civic engagement, and encourage community involvement.

The NAAWLI office is located in Dallas, Texas. A generous grant from State Farm Insurance Companies launched the program and continues to provide support.

National African-American Women's Leadership Institute, Inc.
P.O. Box 802927
Dallas, TX 75380
Website: www.naawli.org

SELF-ESTEEM

The Dove Self-Esteem Fund (DSEF) was established as an agent of change to inspire and educate girls and young woman about a wider definition of beauty. The DSEF is committed to helping girls build positive self-esteem and a healthy body image, with a goal of reaching five million girls globally by 2010. The DSEF has already reached two million young women. The DSEF's definition of "reaching" a girl is when she has gone through an educational program that lasts at least an hour of her life.

Dove Consumer Services
920 Sylvan Avenue
Englewood Cliffs, NJ 07632
Phone: 1 (800) 761-DOVE
Website: www.dove.us

The National Association for Self-Esteem (NASE). The purpose of the organization is to fully integrate self-esteem into the fabric of American society so that every individual, no matter what their age or background, experiences personal worth and happiness. NASE believes self-esteem is "the experience of being capable of meeting life's challenges and being worthy of happiness." They also believe in personal responsibility and accountability.

Email: members@self-esteem-nase.org
Website: www.self-esteem-nase.org

I AM B.E.A.U.T.I.F.U.L. is an award-winning educational enrichment nonprofit organization dedicated to building self-esteem and leadership capability in girls and women of all ages and stages. The programs support the achievement of physical, mental, social, emotional, spiritual, and economic success.

I AM, INC.
4850 Golden Pkwy, Suite B-230
Buford, Georgia 30518
Georgia Office: (404) 545-9051
South Carolina Office: (843) 616-4415
Fax: (770) 831-0813
Email: info@iambeautiful.org
Website: www.iambeautiful.org

Sororities

Alpha Kappa Alpha Sorority
5656 South Stony Island Avenue
Chicago, IL 60637
Phone: (773) 684-1282
Website: www.aka1908.com

Delta Sigma Theta Sorority, Inc.
1707 New Hampshire Avenue, NW
Washington, DC 20009
Phone: (202) 986-2400
Website: www.deltasigmatheta.org

Zeta Phi Beta Sorority, Inc.
1734 New Hampshire Avenue, NW
Washington, DC 20009
Phone: (202) 387- 3103
Website: www.zphib1920.org

Sigma Gamma Rho Sorority, Inc.
1000 Southhill Drive, Suite 200
Cary, NC 27513
Phone: (888) SGR-1922
Local phone: (919) 678-9720
Website: www.sgrho1922.org